XML

Emerging Business Technology Series

XML

Solomon H. Simon, Ph.D.

McGraw-Hill
New York Chicago San Francisco Lisbon London
Madrid Mexico City Milan New Delhi San Juan
Seoul Singapore Sydney Toronto

McGraw-Hill
A Division of The McGraw-Hill Companies

1 2 3 4 5 6 7 8 9 0 AGM/AGM 0 9 8 7 6 5 4 3 2 1

ISBN 0-07-137188-5

Printed and bound by Quebecor World/Martinsburg.

This book is printed on recycled, acid-free paper containing a minimum of 50% recycled, de-inked fiber.

For Gus and Naomi Simon,
Thanks for your patience with my Chemistry,
Quanta, and other things Relative.

Contents

Foreword

XML is rapidly becoming an integral part of standard IT infrastructure. Most of us agree that no IT executive or IT-focused business executive can afford to ignore this fact. Even so, too few of them take the time to understand XML's business value; instead, they perceive XML as another technology solution to a technology problem. Nothing could be less true: As Solomon Simon intones in these pages, "Business on the Internet is not about a technology model; business on the Internet, as with business anywhere, is about a business model." And few technologies give rise to more interesting e-business models than XML.

Taking a historical view can be instructive. Manuel Castells, a scholar at the University of California at Berkeley, has argued that the new information economy is largely a product of two historic trends: (1) the recently emergent "post-Fordism" model of supply chain execution—one that rests on the principles of flexible and just-in-time manufacturing, *a la* Dell Computer—and (2) the development of IT networks. The intersection of these trends is giving rise, according to Castells, to a new organizational form called the "network enterprise," whose sole purpose is to process information more efficiently than the competition.

In 2001, evidence of these trends abounds. Many companies are building (or have already built) messaging transport pathways among their previously monolithic enterprise applications to enable a unified view of corporate information. The most enterprising ones are also building new pathways among each other, pathways that obsolete rigid, old-style EDI connections by enabling open, dynamic exchange of business information. Furthermore, B2B trading exchanges, which exploded in number in 2000 (although most will surely fail for business execution, not technology, reasons), are enabling market transparency that elevates in importance information about goods over that of the goods themselves—more grist for the network enterprise's mill.

These developments have a common enabler: the presence of an eXtensible Markup Language (XML) layer. As Solomon Simon writes in these pages, "XML serves as a catalyst for the integration of data from legacy systems, current systems, and future sources by creating a universal data transfer format."

XML developers can now integrate data and structure in an extremely simple way; the original XML spec, published by the World Wide Web Consortium in 1996, is fewer than 40 pages long. But perhaps more important, because XML is, as Simon describes it, an "omnimorphic" markup language—it provides a syntax for creating an infinite number of data tags, not a limited number of tags themselves—developers can add context to business information exchange. For example, the Covisint B2B collaboration hub, which Ford, GM, DaimlerChrysler, and Renault/Nissan established last year to consolidate worldwide automotive industry procurement, development, and supply chain processes (more than 30,000 participants), will be held together by a membrane of agreed-upon XML tags that describe parts, transactions, and services. No supplier need build brittle, ad hoc EDI pathways to multiple partners again: one data set will fit all.

The Covisint example is a useful one because it brings several interesting issues to light. First of all, as Simon describes, it underscores how "trading partners must come to some consensus about what XML standards to use." Indeed, as VerticalNet CTO David Ritter wrote in *Intelligent Enterprise* in 1999 ("XML: The Missing Link for B2B E-Commerce," May 11), "Even with all [its] advantages, basic XML isn't enough . . . . XML immediately begs for the next layer of standards." Scores of horizontal and vertical syntax standards are already in development by various vendors, standards bodies, and consortia; thus, independent efforts to deploy XML "microschemas" are likely to be fruitless. As Simon explains, "If a corporation embraces XML technology, but does so blindly, it may discover less functionality, not more." Thus, it's extremely important to understand business requirements—particularly those involving extraenterprise collaboration—well ahead of time.

Second, as I touched on previously, the market transparency facilitated by XML-based data exchange is already making transaction information a commodity. In the future, many successful trading exchanges may well attribute their survival to the ability to provide value-added services, such as selling market information and analytic reports to "premium" participants.

In this book, Solomon Simon carefully explains the technical subtleties of XML in a clear business context, providing a valuable resource for IT specialists and business managers alike. Read on; I'm confident you'll get the synthesis of technical and business viewpoints that is so important for all of us to have these days.

Justin Kestelyn
Editor in Chief
Intelligent Enterprise

Preface

Some of the difficulties that managers and executives have with new technologies, such as XML (eXtensible Markup Language), are separating out the hype, digging through the technical terms, and pulling out the pearls of profitable wisdom. XML is the new standard for data and information transactions, it is the foundation for B2B e-commerce, and it is as pervasive as the World Wide Web.

My intention with this book is to explain the highly technical XML language in business terms, so that an information technology manager, vice president, and chief technical officer can understand and make decisions that lead to profitable use. In contrast to most XML books on the market, this book focuses on the business reasons for XML rather than the technical reasons.

Developers who have experience with XML may find that some of the discussions in this book will help them to explain its potential business advantages to their management. Compared to the amazing palette provided by XML, HTML (HyperText Markup Language) is paint-by-numbers. With a flexibility that is comparable to Post-it Notes, XML allows developers to label any data or information, providing a context that is computer-readable. In contrast, HTML-based data and its related Web page information provide no more meaning to the computer than the string "#%$^&**&$#@%" provides to the reader of this book.

In addition to discussions of many of the uses of XML, this book offers suggestions for design, development, and implementation of an XML corporate strategy. This book also serves as an executive handbook of guidelines for using XML to support the corporate business strategies and objectives.

With such powerhouses as Ford, GE, GM, IBM, and Microsoft betting billions of dollars on XML, this new standard is clearly sparking a forest fire of change, burning through the business world. While some companies will be reduced to ashes, some companies, such as Ford, expect to rise up from the ashes and ascend to new heights as e-Ford. Other companies, like Microsoft, plan for similar transformations based on XML and the Web.

The core of XML is the XML document. XML has a set of strict rules, and an XML document has a rigorous, hierarchical tree structure. These rules and structures form a solid foundation for constructing data and information structures with near limitless flexibility. This book provides just a small taste of the XML banquet.

Acknowledgments

This book was built from contributions and the support of Max Tunnicliff, Mark Beckwith, R. Anne Hendrick, JD Davidson, Sharon S. Riley, Missy Kruger, Michelle Williams, Gillian Grady, Nancy Warner, Justin Kestelyn, Janice Race, and George Magillicuty. I appreciate the efforts and encouragement that each of you provided.

Introduction

The Internet and the World Wide Web form a collection of many subcomponents that provide overlapping information and services. Increasing market demand to supply ever-increasing capabilities fuels the acceleration of technological innovation. Industry leaders are left behind as yesterday's laggards if they cannot follow Moore's Law (see Figure I.1) to adapt, innovate, and change on a rapid cycle of 18 months or faster. Due to the fierce competition, many companies market laboratory prototypes, regardless of whether they are truly marketable products, within that 18-month cycle. One of the innovations driving these business changes is XML (eXtensible Markup Language).

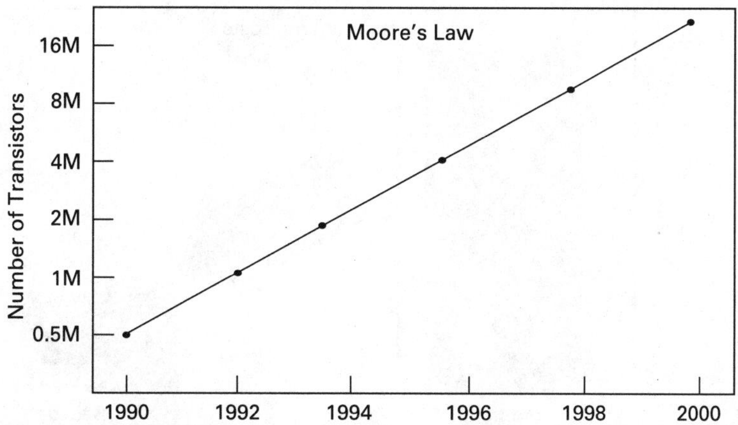

FIGURE I.1 Moore's Law states that the number of transistors on a microprocessor will double every 18 months. Another way of interpreting Moore's Law is that technology and processing power will double about every two years.

This book addresses XML from a business perspective. Although XML is a relatively new Internet technology, like many other advances on the Web, XML will soon be as commonplace as Java or HTML (HyperText Markup Language). At conferences throughout the world, one of the most sought after information and courses are about profitable applications of XML. Managers and executives recognize that XML provides a mechanism for storing and identifying information in innovative and useful ways.

B2B E-commerce

In fact, XML is the spark that lit the forest fire of business-to-business (B2B) Web exchanges. The "Big Three" automakers, Ford, General Motors, and DaimlerChrysler, announced their $250 billion Web-based supply chain collaboration in February 2000. That announcement was the catalyst for subsequent news releases describing about 20, multibillion dollar B2B collaborations in other industries, as well as nearly 1,000 smaller efforts. One detail that was missing from the announcement is that most B2B exchanges are based on and enabled by XML. The XML B2B e-commerce server is the backbone of the entire process. The companies that leverage the benefits of XML in the supply chain have the potential to win big by saving as much as 90 percent in procurement costs, as indicated in Figure I.2. A billion dollars here, a billion dollars there, with this kind of financial impact, can result in savings of hundreds of billions of dollars. So clearly XML is an important, strategic business enabler.

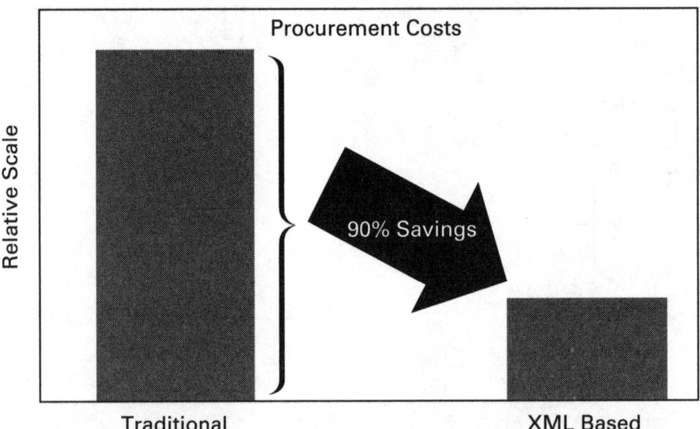

FIGURE I.2 Procurement costs will decrease by as much as 90 percent by using XML to automate the processes and paperwork that are used to transfer information among the various corporations.

According to some analysts, the B2B market may represent a market that is ten times the size of the business-to-consumer (B2C) market. The emergence of the Web as a predominant force in business results in many traditional brick and mortar Fortune 500 companies reexamining their business models. Bastions of industry, such as General Motors and IBM, are revamping their business models to enter the e-business arena. Oracle is a leader in XML development toward B2B exchanges. More than 1000 companies participate in its Oracle Exchange, which focuses on the automation of the procurement cycle and the integration of supply chain management among collaborators and vendors. The very interesting outcome is that these old dogs are showing the new pups, the dot coms, a new trick or two.

This possible reversal results from an underlying misconception. Business on the Internet is not about a technology model; business on the Internet, as with business anywhere, is about a business model. While the dot coms focus on improving their technology, the older companies merely modify their already very successful business models to include the changes needed to compete in the e-business.

From the viewpoint of these corporate behemoths, the Web is simply another opportunity to improve their value chains, increase efficiency, reduce costs, and, thereby, increase productivity and ultimately increase profits. Clearly, those companies who cannot transform themselves will be overtaken, but in the evolution of business that is always true. In the Darwinian model, the fittest survives. Those businesses who can find a niche or who can adapt and make a buck will survive. But survival is not about being the best company to work for or about producing the best product (unfortunately). Survival and growth are based on making a profit by adapting to supply what the market demands.

The new e-business entrepreneurs supply customer service and fulfillment to an ever-impatient marketplace. Traditional businesses may rest on the laurels of their past achievements, smug in the success of their business models. This is a fatal mistake. Their superior business models succeed only if they can adapt to the changing market demands. Mr. Customer says, "Yes, I want a car, but I want it in colors other than black." Or "Yes, I want an insanely great computer with a graphical interface, but I want a wider choice of software that is compatible with my computers at home and at work." Or, "I understand that your products are supposed to be better, but the other guy's products don't break, or don't crash, or don't take 6 weeks for delivery."

The ability to adapt cuts both ways. The traditional business that can adapt may eventually overtake an escalating startup that steals market share without a solid business model. Growth and flexibility need to be incorporated into the business model from the start, although it is not a necessary condition. Successful businesses can learn from their mistakes. In fact the most successful leaders are not the ones that never make mistakes; they are the ones who can quickly recover and learn from the mistakes that they do make.

Although the e-business revolution is strong in the United States, opportunities still exist in Europe and Asia, where Internet penetration is just beginning. China presents an unbelievable opportunity with 1 billion potential customers who are just now getting a taste of the Web and e-commerce.

XML Business Opportunities

In addition to igniting B2B efforts, XML also fuels other business opportunities. XML serves as the catalyst for the integration of data from legacy systems, current systems, and future sources by creating a universal data transfer format. The XML standard uses meta-data to define the content, structure, and relationships of the data within a document, regardless of whether that data is text, e-mail, images, audio, or a database. XML represents the next rung up the computer evolutionary ladder to improve interoperability, data transfer, and information communications. For example, a growing list of telecommunications companies, such as Ericsson, Nokia, and Motorola, have come together to define a common standard for wireless Web access called Wireless Application Protocol (WAP). WAP is a protocol and an open specification for requesting, transmitting, and receiving data across a wireless network in a format that can be presented on wireless devices such as cell phones, PalmPilots, handheld devices, Personal Digital Assistants (PDAs), and pagers. In contrast to desktop computers, these small-screen devices use a minibrowser to surf the Internet and to read Web pages designed especially for the smaller displays. This is where XML comes in, because WAP developers use Wireless Markup Language (WML), which is a derivative of XML, to create Web pages for these minibrowsers and wireless devices. The flexibility and extensibility of XML facilitated the creation of the WML standard, enabling many corporations to agree on the WAP features for the wireless devices that they build, sell, and support.

XML is used to create many other standard languages, such as the voice standard VoiceML, (also called VoxML) which is used to translate content and text into speech. VoiceML facilitates computer-based speech processing because the standard format permits developers to manage and predict how their information will be processed.

According to industry analysts, in June 1998 only 1 percent of surveyed Fortune 500 corporate executives were using XML in their companies. That percentage grew to 67 percent by August 1999, and to 83 percent by May 2000, as indicated in Figure I.3.

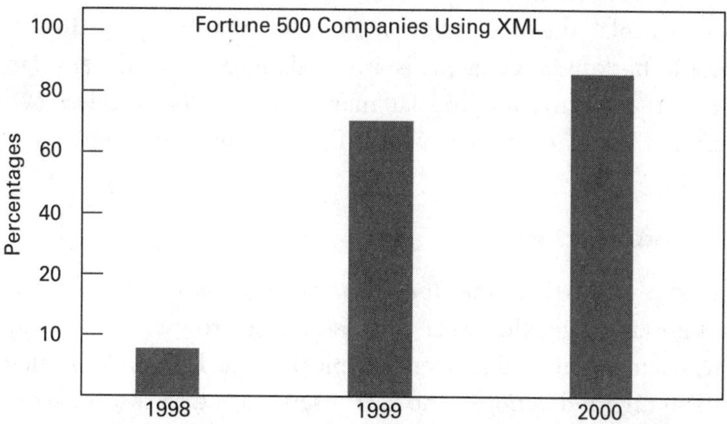

FIGURE I.3 The percentage of Fortune 500 companies using XML grew from 1 percent in 1998 to more than 80 percent in 2000.

The World Wide Web has been a catalyst for the remarkable speed of change in business and in information technology. Innovations, such as HTML and Java, are introduced to millions of users nearly overnight. This user population quickly embraces or rejects new ideas, resulting in a rapid evolution of capabilities that were previously little more than science fiction. Although the Internet has been around for more than twenty years, it took the simple elegance and flexibility of HTML to deliver the functionality to business and to the general population.

Before XML, HTML and Web browsers went through four releases since 1993, resulting in greater capabilities for the global delivery of information. However, customized applications required detailed and expensive technical knowledge of programming. XML has the potential to deliver customized applications without as much need for technical expertise.

XML Is Like a Database

According to Dr. Charles Goldfarb, one of the creators of Standardized Generalized Markup Language (SGML), ISO 8879, XML is to HTML like a database is to a word processor. A word processor can set up the appearance of a document, but a database can manage the content and the context of data. XML can manage data content, which provides information, and data context, which provides meaning. Therefore, XML supports *knowledge management* since information with context is knowledge.

The difference between XML and HTML is one of generality. HTML is the more specific markup language, providing tags that tell a Web browser how to display the text and other elements of a Web page. In contrast, XML is not a markup language; it is a meta-language: the general language used to create a specific markup language, such as the Wireless (WML), Voice (VoxML), or Mathematics (MathML) markup languages.

The DTD Foundation

The core of XML is the *document type definition* (DTD). For a specific markup language, the DTD defines how a browser should handle text or other elements in a document. Typically, the DTD relates element definitions to *tags* and *actions*. The user inserts tags into the document where the desired actions are to occur. For example, in HTML the <*B*> and </*B*> tags indicate that text between these two tags should be **boldface** type In WML, similar tags indicate menu pages. Tags can also be defined to identify elements within a document. For example, a <*date*> tag could be used to identify the date within a memo. Later, that tag can be used to sort the document by date, and other tags, such as <*price*> or <*salary*>, can be used to identify the respective price and salary data.

The XML set of tools includes a powerful XML Stylesheet Language (called XSL), an application interface called the Document Object Model (DOM), and an Extensible Linking Language (XLL or XLink).

If we look at the Internet industry as a collection of simultaneously competing and cooperating companies, then XML serves as the common basis to simplify cooperation and smooth out the cycles. In addition, the story of XML is an interesting and ongoing tale with a strong supporting cast of companies and emerging applications. XML can transform and deliver content to various devices, and XML is the key to content management. Since predicting the devices or uses for content is not feasible, XML is a good choice for providing a vanilla standard format that can be used by all foreseeable systems. As the industry and the standards mature, XML will allow a company to develop a solution once, and then implement it, reuse it, and repurpose it many times.

Chapter Summaries

Chapter 1: Executive Summary provides an overview of the trends of Web applications being driven by XML. It highlights current XML applications as well as the potential for new applications in searching the Web and in creating data warehouses. This chapter also summarizes efforts of some major corporate players in the XML game.

Chapter 2: XML Schemas and DTDs provides an overview of XML metadata: schemas and DTDs as the core to defining markup language applications.

Chapter 3: XML Documents summarizes the components needed to define an XML document. It emphasizes the hierarchical structure of an XML document.

Chapter 4: XML Style Sheets (XSLs) and Transformations (XSLTs) discusses the methods of presenting XML documents using the XML Stylesheet Language (XSL) capability. Information about transformations to other formats is included.

Chapter 5: XML Linking Language (XLink) relates some of the methods of connecting XML documents to other documents, to Web locations, and to other applications. XLink is the foundation for creating virtual documents by aggregating information from distributed sources. This chapter also discusses recent developments in peer-to-peer networking as it relates to XLink.

Chapter 6: XML Applications describes XML applications that are available for use. It also discusses methods for interpreting XML. HTML Web Browsers can be expanded to understand XML. Also, SGML parsers can interpret XML documents with only minor modifications. A summary of each application provides a URL and sufficient information for exploration, experimentation, and use.

Chapter 7: XML for Databases and EDI presents an overview of XML used to connect with legacy applications, such as relational databases and EDI transactions. One of the great strengths of XML is its ability to adapt to a wide variety of data formats, even those used by older systems and back-end data repositories.

Chapter 8: B2B Exchange applies proven business-to-business planning to address the questions to ask when exchanging data among businesses.

Chapter 9: XML Strategic Plan applies proven business strategic planning to address the questions to ask when implementing an innovation like XML.

Chapter 10: Concerns, Myths, and Hype addresses the risks and impediments within a corporate environment when implementing XML and raises questions about external issues such as evolving standards and potential pitfalls.

Chapter 11: Summary of Industry XML Projects highlights a small sample of the hundreds of XML products being developed and offered by major corporations and emerging companies.

Chapter 12: The Outlook for XML discusses emerging standards and features of XML. It also covers evolving trends in e-business, such as XHTML, B2B exchanges, and WAP.

Chapter 13: Summary and Conclusion summarizes the core business opportunities that XML provides. It discusses the trends and applications for which executives and managers should plan.

C H A P T E R 1

Executive Summary

Om ni mor phic \ ,ahm nee `mor fik \ *adj.* [L. *omnis* universal + Gr. *morphos* form] 1: ability to take on any form, structure, character, or style. 2: serving as a universal foundation on which to construct any form, structure, character, or style. <XML, just like SGML, is an~ markup language that provides the capability to tag data using a universal format so that, with no modifications, any application can use the data .> 3: having, assuming, or occurring in all forms, structures, characters, or styles. (Source: S.H. Simon, 2000.)

Introduction

XML (eXtensible Markup Language) is the spark that has set fire to a new information revolution. The level of major corporate interest and support for XML is extremely high, but there is a corresponding level of misunderstanding, confusion, and uncertainty about the basic technology. Most of the information written about XML has been technical, how-to details with little focus on high-level strategic and design information.

Briefly, XML addresses the problem of using different data formats for different applications. In analogy, consider the problem of communicating with people who speak different languages. Fortunately, for most businessmen in the United States, English is the main language of business and of the Internet. It serves as a universal language for communication. Computer programmers had the same problem, this need for a universal method of communication, until computer languages were standardized. However, computer applications still require different data formats for data exchange. For example, invoice programs, bills of materials, spreadsheets, graphics, and Web pages all use data that are in different formats. This means that data may have to be translated or exported from one application to another.

XML supplies a method for creating a single data format for many applications. English has no single word to describe what XML does, so I've coined the word, "omnimorphic." XML is an omnimorphic markup language that provides a universal data-tagging format so that applications can seamlessly transfer and exchange data. This chapter will clarify this statement and attempt to alleviate some of the misunderstanding, confusion, and uncertainty by summarizing the fundamental concepts about XML and related tools.

Overview

XML is a relatively new technology that was developed in the late 1990s to enable applications to share data and information over the Web. In addition, XML fills in the gaps to allow developers to create new features and functions in a Web page or in other XML documents.

Benefits

XML facilitates interoperability by enabling developers to extend the markup tags used in their documents and applications. They can modify existing tags, define new meanings, or create entirely new tags.

XML facilitates the use of context and meaning. An XML-enabled search engine would be smart enough to understand the term *mustang* and allow car owners and horse-lovers to retrieve two entirely different sets of documents based on the context of the query. In addition, XML will enable a new generation of Web-based data viewing and manipulation applications.

XML is the foundation for B2B e-commerce and the backbone of the emerging Wireless Application Protocol (WAP). It will simplify Electronic Data Interchange (EDI) and may level the playing field to encourage more startups to enter e-commerce. XML will continue to be the driving force behind new ways to share information, transfer data, and send communications to a wide variety of devices.

Changes

One of the first questions that a manager wants to know about any innovation is: What changes are required in order to take advantage of the idea? With XML, the changes are not drastic, but they are pervasive. Also, the changes are not about *if* you will make them, but *when*. Companies that do not follow the lead of IBM, Microsoft, GM, Ford, and others will be left behind.

Progressive companies have already implemented the biggest change—an intranet. Companies now need to form partnerships with vendors, industry colleagues, and with customers. Negotiations can then start on how to best exploit XML in order to facilitate the sharing of information and transferring of data among these partners. Finally, companies must build an implementation plan that includes a design phase for analyzing and building a corporate XML document architecture. This plan should map out how information will be reused and repurposed.

Risks

Right after the changes, the manager wants to know about risk. The risk of XML is minimal; most of the bugs have been shaken out by the mega-corporations. Assessing risks involves exploring two issues that revolve around Document Type Definitions (DTDs).

First, which DTD is best for the specific industry and the specific corporation? Many companies were concerned about making the wrong choice of DTD a few years ago, but that is no longer a threat. If the chosen DTD proves to be wrong, then developers can change the DTD by using any of the tools that are emerging from IBM, Apache, or even the XSLT (eXtensible Stylesheet Language Transformations) specification.

Second, should the company use a DTD or wait for a schema? The best business advice is "Don't wait!" A good manager is not someone who makes no mistakes. A good manager is someone who makes mistakes early and recovers quickly. Learn about XML now. When schemas emerge, the tools to convert for DTDs will quickly follow.

Companies should also consider another risk: the risk of doing nothing. XML is not a fad and it is not going away. In the auto industry alone, XML is responsible for a $300 billion supply chain. Even Microsoft cannot argue with $300 billion. So it is time to jump on the train to avoid getting left behind. In this case, the longer-term rewards for making a few minor errors up front are much greater than the immediate gratification of maintaining status quo.

Costs

The cost of entry and exploration is minimal. Many fine tools available are free. A search on the Web for some of these tools seems to result in thousands of hits. Fortunately, XML is a Web technology; so much of the infrastructure is already in place. After initial exploration, cost is proportionate to project size. However, tool quality is not necessarily related to price tag, so explore carefully.

What Is a Markup Language?

Markup languages describe how the text within a file or a document is structured according to tags. Tags are used to mark words or sections to indicate actions or identifications. For example, in HyperText Markup Language (HTML), text is bolded by surrounding text with two "BOLD" tags that are the word "BOLD" enclosed between two angle brackets "<" and ">". For example: <BOLD> important </BOLD> = **important**.

In Web pages on the World Wide Web, the tags in this example are, in fact, simplified to <B> important </B>. There are about ten categories of almost one hundred HTML commands or tags that are used on the World Wide Web to make Web pages. HTML is limited to the presentation of how information looks on the computer screen. For the most part, HTML tags do not provide any information or context about the words or text enclosed within the tags. These tags only provide formatting information that instructs the browser how to display the text on the various output devices. A drawback of HTML-based Web pages is that information and data cannot be easily manipulated by other applications. Although a table of data can be copied from a Web page into a spreadsheet, the user still must go through tedious, time-consuming manipulations to complete the transfer. XML addresses this drawback, providing additional programming functionality without the need for detailed programming knowledge.

Rationale for XML

XML was created to improve Web page functionality beyond HTML and to simplify Standardized General Markup Language (SGML). Few technologies have the breadth of industry support in the way that XML does. For example, IBM and Oracle have incorporated XML into much of their software. The "Big Three" automobile manufacturers—Ford, General Motors, and

DaimlerChrysler—have entrusted XML with their $300 billion per year parts and services procurement supply network. And Sun Microsystems, Netscape, and Microsoft have been involved with XML from the very beginning. The co-editors—Jon Bosak (Sun Microsystems), Tim Bray (representing Netscape), Jean Paoli (Microsoft), and Michael Sperberg-McQueen (University of Chicago)—carefully designed XML to be simpler and more portable than SGML, and more powerful and flexible than HTML.

XML has considerably more flexibility and power than HTML for manipulating documents, information, text, and data. While HTML was designed mainly for the display of text and information, XML was designed to facilitate the manipulation of text, information, and data. XML is a subset of SGML, and both languages are really meta-languages. A meta-language, in this context, is a general standard used to define more specialized markup languages such as the Wireless Markup Language (WML) for transmitting information and data to wireless devices, and the Music Markup Language (MusicML) for manipulating music notes. Both WML and MusicML were created using XML. A developer can use XML to create a set of structures (for example, menus for wireless devices) and a grammar (actions based on menu selection) to manipulate those structures.

The exciting aspect of XML is the flexibility and robustness that it brings to the Web. Just as HTML provides the method for presenting documents, XML provides the method for defining the meaning or semantics of the document. More important is the promise behind the hype. Many large corporations, such as IBM, Microsoft, Sun Microsystems, Oracle, are putting significant efforts into XML support. The number of XML-based applications—Biosequence ML, Chemical ML, Financial ML, Java XML, MathML, MusicML, Pattern ML, Pixel Graphics ML, Real Estate ML, TextML, Vector ML, VoiceML, Wireless ML, etc.—is growing daily. With the interest and support from the B2B activities, XML development tools have begun to mature. As a result of all the money being pumped to support B2B and XML development, the number of XML applications has exploded.

Contrasts—XML, SGML, HTML

SGML is a large complex set of rules for defining document structure. It has been evolving for almost 30 years and has been used mainly by defense contractors, government agencies, semiconductor manufacturers, publishing companies, and large data-processing users as a tool for document management systems. Toward the end of the 1980s and into the early 1990s, Tim Berners-Lee, creator of the World Wide Web, designed a simple SGML-based formatting language called HTML.

HTML is relatively small and easy to implement, but it is difficult to extend because it uses a predefined set of formatting identifiers, known as tags. XML augments HTML's static set of tags with the dynamic and extensible ability to define new, customized tags and document structures. With XML, the structure of the document is described in a DTD, which contains rules that describe how XML tags are defined and related within the document. XML also permits new tags to be created on the fly.

DTDs

The DTD is a construct that was inherited from the original SGML functionality. The effectiveness of the DTD concept is that it allows a document to be self-describing. This idea is similar to a glossary that describes the words used in a book, but it is also much more comprehensive and pervasive. A much better analogy is that of a foreign language interpreter.

An XML document is used to communicate data between two applications, in the same way that a diplomat might communicate between two countries. To avoid difficulties due to differences in the languages, a diplomat may use an interpreter who can explain the meaning of the diplomat's words to the new country. A DTD serves a similar function by defining the meaning of the data and tags within the XML document to any XML-enabled application that uses that document.

The use of the DTD was crucial to the rapid acceptance of XML. One of the advantages of XML is that most of the infrastructure to support it is already in place. The methods for transferring XML documents already exist on the Internet and on the Web. The methods for displaying XML documents exist in many of the browsers, such as Internet Explorer 5, Netscape 6, and Opera. But the most important aspect is that all XML documents that use a DTD can be read, parsed, and manipulated by existing legacy SGML applications. One reason for the wide acceptance of XML was that this expertise already existed. Now that the base of XML expertise has grown, independent of the SGML users, XML development will diverge somewhat from the SGML development path. Plans are underway to replace XML DTDs with schemas.

Schemas

The XML DTD is really an SGML construct held over from the early days of the XML specification. But a DTD is not a part of the XML simplicity. It is like a changeling that is different from its siblings. While XML has a hierarchical structure that is easy to read, a DTD has an arcane programming definition that requires special expertise to decipher and invoke. Although an XML DTD is much easier to use than its SGML counterparts, a schema provides an approach that is more consistent with the philosophy of XML.

Where a DTD uses a special format, a schema uses the XML format and structure to provide document definitions. The reason for acceptance of the DTD was one of practicality. Many people were already knowledgeable about SGML and DTDs, and these people embraced XML. As the foundation of XML developers has grown, the drawbacks of DTDs are being left behind, replaced by the simpler and more progressive schema specifications.

The schema specification is still being worked on so that it will remain backward, compatible with existing XML documents that use DTDs. Like a DTD, a schema is a meta-data construct, and it follows a simpler XML format than DTDs. Both DTDs and schemas are discussed further in Chapter 2. In addition, a significant advantage exists to maintaining compatibility with legacy SGML documents. The final XML schema specification will address many of these issues.

XML Does Not Replace SGML or HTML

Some confusion exists about XML replacing SGML and HTML. XML will not replace SGML or HTML because these languages have different purposes. For example, SGML uses special capabilities to handle very large document databases. And HTML is used mainly to present Web page information on the Internet or a corporate intranet. If a corporation attempts to apply XML in a function where SGML or HTML would be better, it will be like trying to use a hammer like a screwdriver. The incorrect application of XML will result in poorly defined DTDs and XML documents. The multiple usage would pull XML apart into many nonstandard and incompatible dialects within the corporation. In addition, XML could also split due to different DTDs based on poor document design and analysis. Finally, poor design could result in more difficult access to corporate data rather than facilitated access, as is the intent of XML.

Although XML will not replace HTML and SGML, the XML-based language, XHTML, has supplanted HTML 4.0 as the *lingua franca* of the Web. XML separates the content of a document from the display of a document. XML tags information so that computers can more easily manipulate it. HTML displays content and presents a document that is more appealing to the reader's eyes. Even with XML, HTML or XHTML can be used to display an XML document. XHTML will slowly take over for HTML in the same way that the successive versions of HTML have replaced previous versions.

For the most part, XHTML is very similar to HTML. HTML is based on SGML, and XHTML is based on XML. XHTML was designed to use XML features while following the general formatting of HTML. Therefore, XHTML coding is more rigorous than HTML, but it also allows more flexibility in the design and introduction of new, customized document tags. And XHTML was designed to allow a smooth transition from legacy HTML documents, so HTML can be easily translated to XHTML format.

For separating data and documents, XML provides the ability to put the document together once and display it any number of ways with HTML. This ability to create a "virtual document" is one of the revolutionary features of the XML toolbox. The ability to put together a reusable, hypertext document is not a new concept. But providing the tools to do this to the everyday user, the nonprogrammer, and even to children will have as dramatic an impact on the Web as the Gutenberg printing press had on books and reading in the 1400s.

XML also provides the mechanism for separating the content of a document and the display of a document. The idea of separating data and presentation is a foundation concept of computer science and of database design. However, it has been difficult to implement because of proprietary data formats. The omnimorphic capability of XML facilitates the separation of data from applications that will use, manipulate, and present the XML data and information.

For example, consider an XML document that contains all of the financial data for a corporation, including the balance sheet, income statement, and cash flow. To review all of that data, the user merely opens the document with a browser, such as Internet Explorer 5.0, and a hierarchical list of data appears. To see a balance sheet of these data, the user opens an XSL style sheet that formats the data into a standard balance sheet. The same data can be used to review income and cash flow by applying the appropriate XSL style sheets.

In addition, another user might want to run some analyses on these financial data. An XSL spreadsheet can be used to format the data so the user can run through the desired analysis. A third user might want to compare these financials with those from other companies. To run this analysis, the user employs an XSL style sheet that includes XML Linking Language (XLL) information. This XLL information enables the user to open distributed XML documents of financial data from across the Web or on the company's intranet. When these data are collected from the various locations, a browser window opens to reveal a virtual document with all the data in a predefined tabular format. This window looks the same as any other browser window, and the fact that it is virtual is transparent to the user. The user has no way of distinguishing between single XML documents and aggregated virtual documents.

The point is that the data in an XML document can be reused in many different ways, including ways that were not anticipated by the original creator. In this example, the XSL documents were predefined, probably by someone in the finance department or by a programmer.

In addition, an XSL style sheet could be used to format the data for presentation on other devices. For example, an XSL style sheet might format the data for view on a cell phone by using standards that following the Wireless Application Protocol (WAP).

Some XML documents will never be displayed for people to see or use directly. An XML document may go from one company's database to another company's database and never get displayed by a Web browser. Or an XML document might be used as a behind-the-scenes intermediary to transfer information from one application to another, or from one computer to another, such as in B2B applications.

In addition, XML will not replace the terabytes of existing legacy SGML, but XML will support a subset of the legacy documents as well as new documents.

In a small number of cases involving programming details, XML fails to be a pure subset of SGML. XML introduces the concept of a document having the property of being *well-formed*. A well-formed document is one that conforms to all the constraints of being well formed, as described in Chapter 2. A well-formed document need not conform to a DTD or schema. Well-formed documents that do conform to a DTD or to a schema are said to be "valid." Validity is simply the concept of following its own rules. For example, an interpreter hired to translate French must speak French in order to be "valid." A French interpreter who cannot speak French is "invalid." Validity is a necessary requirement for an XML parser or an application to be able to read and manipulate an XML document. These features of being well formed or valid result in a clearly defined structure for XML documents. In contrast, SGML documents and HTML Web pages do not follow the same rigor as XML documents. However, the advantage of the rigor of XML documents is that the resulting structure is much easier to parse and understand, and thus requires much smaller parsers and applications than SGML.

Key XML Technologies

The ability of the XML document language to abstract meta-data about information in an open format will increase the capabilities of Web sites and intranets. A single, unifying, omnimorphic data format facilitates the reuse and repurposing of information and data across a variety of applications. Because XML documents enable easy analysis by a variety of applications, knowledge workers can spot and understand trends among collections of data, or drill down for relevant information in related documents for data sources with a greater capability than before XML.

Users and novice developers will not need to learn all the protocols and acronyms because the tools will hide the unnecessary details. The tools may even hide the concept of programming in order to make development more like word processing or graphics design; the underlying details may be transparent to all but advanced developers. Nonprogrammers will think of an XML application as browsing or searching for information. And in most applications, that's what it will be: information searching or data mining.

XML also provides a number of methods for importing other files and defining macros and shortcuts. In an XML document, namespaces are used, especially in a DTD, to assign a URL to a name. Named entities are used to assign a string or macro to a name. In an XSL document, named styles are used to assign a style to a name and inline styles are used to define brief, local styles.

The World Wide Web Consortium (W3C) defined the XML effort in three steps:

1. XML—the syntax rules
2. XLink—the linking rules
3. XSL—the presentation and transformation rules.

Some of the tools that support XML include DTDs, schemas, XSL, XSLT, DOM, XLink, XPointer, XPath, Namespace, SOAP, SAX, and XHTML. Some of these tools are shown in Figure 1.1.

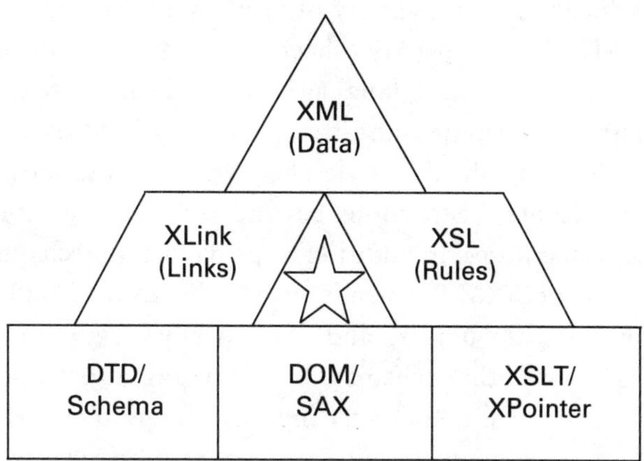

FIGURE 1.1 Some of the basic tools that support XML include XSL, XLink, XSLT, XPointer, DTDs, schemas, DOM, and SAX. Each of these technologies is described in more detail in later chapters.

DTD—The Document Type Definition defines the XML document, structures, rules, and elements. The DTD is used to define the elements and tags in a document. The tags in XML correspond to tags in HTML and they identify components in the document. Typically, the DTD is placed at the top of a document, where its tags, rules, and definitions can easily be interpreted by an XML parser or browser. The DTD is optional. It can be shared from another application or it can be used to define unique tags that are required in a specific document. Once tags are defined, they can be used anywhere and other users can copy them onto their own documents. Tags define document elements, entities, and attributes. Entities are the physical structure, and elements are the logical structure. Attributes specify qualifiers for elements.

Schemas—Schemas carry the same function as DTDs but in a different format and structure. While DTDs follow the SGML syntax, schemas follow the XML syntax. Because schemas follow the XML syntax, applications can easily manipulate schemas, extending the dynamic features, flexibility, and ability to customize an XML document. This capability is in contrast to DTDs, which have a difficult syntax to modify by computer. Therefore, schemas will add to the extensibility of XML documents over the current DTD methods.

XSL—The eXtensible Stylesheet Language refers to formatting objects that are similar to the Cascading Style Sheets (CSSs) in HTML. However, XSL provides scripting, conditional, and decision capabilities that are not available under CSS. So, XSL can be used to customize the presentation of an XML document for a variety of users and purposes.

XSLT—The eXtensible Stylesheet Language Transformations is a scripting and pattern matching language, which includes features such as templates, patterns, scripting, and tree processing. XSL is a more general language for building flexible style sheets. XSLT is a subset of XSL, which includes processing instructions beyond what is conventionally considered style sheet capabilities. In addition to providing a mechanism for presenting XML documents, XSLT instructions can be used to build scripts that can transform XML documents and data to work between other documents, other DTDs, and other schemas, by extracting information and data from the source document and converting them to another format.

DOM—The Document Object Model (DOM) is an Application Programming Interface (API) that defines the standards for developing interactions with XML tree structured elements. The DOM supplies a uniform method for external applications to interact with XML. The DOM stores the XML document information in a predictable format so that an application can easily extract pertinent information and data.

XLink—XML Linking Language (XLink or XLL) specification provides a functional approach to document linking using XML. XLink includes flexible linking capabilities such as bi-directionality and custom linking capabilities. **XPointer** is used for internal page access to specific locations or elements. **XPath** defines the pathname to the specific locations or elements.

XML Namespaces—Namespaces are used to collect data from multiple sources into one document and to tag the information with its respective source. An XML namespace is a collection of universal resource identifier (URI) names. The XML namespace specification provides the context for labeling and disambiguating tags with similar names but different intents. For example, <*Material*> could refer to *cloth*, to a type of *witness* in a legal investigation, or to the *products* in a bill of materials. In speaking, the context would be clear. Now, with XML Namespace, the context will also be clear for computers.

SOAP—The Simple Object Access Protocol (SOAP) increases the interoperability among applications and platforms by making legacy applications available through XML. As lightweight protocol for information exchange in a decentralized, distributed environment, SOAP provides intraprocess information and data transfer across computers.

SAX—The Simple Application Programming Interface (API) for XML (SAX) is a standard interface for event-based parsing of XML. In contrast to DOM, SAX is an interface for processing a stream of XML data rather than an entire XML document. It supports the use of parsers, browsers, and other applications to interface with XML documents and applications.

XHTML—XHTML is the translation of HTML 4.0 as an XML application language. XHTML provides the foundation for the extensibility and portability needed to support a wide range of new functions that are compatible with XML.

Corporate Support for XML

Fortune 500 companies across most industries are developing XML compatible applications or tools. As mentioned, the major automakers are exploiting XML for B2B opportunities. In fact, most B2B exchanges are constructed on top of an XML foundation. Microsoft, Netscape, IBM, and Oracle are all developing XML technology to enable meta-directories. A meta-directory is a directory of meta-information about files stored in a collection of directories. Just as XML can tie documents together, meta-directories link different directories to create a common index of files.

IBM has also developed an entire suite of XML-capable tools. The newest versions of WordPerfect and Lotus SmartSuite have varying levels of XML support. Microsoft has delivered MS Office 2000 with XML compatibility and has announced continuing support. Microsoft.NET is built on XML. Oracle is delivering XML tools that are compatible with its databases and legacy systems. Sun Microsystems has developed XML systems to be compatible with Java and with other applications. XML is pervasive throughout the computer industry, and it is also being widely embraced throughout most other industries.

Why Managers Are Interested in XML

XML has the potential to speed the development of e-business application and integration efforts. XML is specifically designed and optimized to run on the Web. It provides a scaffolding for creating common standards for metadata and element tags. The tags allow a developer to define a product catalog for the corporate offerings. With good planning and collaboration, these tags will transfer to other applications, other companies, and other industries. This concept is the key issue that led to the popularity of the B2B exchanges.

B2B exchanges are collaborations among many companies, as many as 30,000 different companies with diverse products and services. Exchanging information among these many companies is a nightmare if the information has to be massaged, manipulated, and translated for each new application. For example, to go from a catalog to an invoice to an inventory to a bill of materials would require at least four different steps to format the data for the specific application. XML provides the omnimorphic glue that seamlessly links these applications. All applications within a B2B exchange can use the same data. In the automotive industry alone, the savings exceed billions of dollars per year, simply by reducing the procurement steps.

Major corporations such as Microsoft and IBM have strongly embraced XML, and they are rapidly developing applications to leverage their capability for data interoperability across industries, corporations, and customers. In fact, Microsoft appears to be building a strategy that will base much of its new business on XML. Developers from one company can create an application and data that other companies will be able to use. For example, a developer could use XML to tag the genes in the Human Genome Project to build a far more intelligent and more useful database. Then other researchers and pharmaceutical companies could use the information. And size will not matter as much.

Some of the Risks of XML

The most visible drawback to XML is the wide variety of B2B exchange DTDs. Early in the game, Ford and GM created separate B2B exchanges with separate DTDs. Although this method provided savings for each company, it was a bookkeeping catastrophe for the common vendors who had to keep dual books for the two companies and their separate DTD vocabularies. After the vendors protested, the two automakers agreed to collaborate on a common B2B exchange with only one DTD. But not all industries will agree on a single DTD. The issue of converging DTDs among different industries is currently under development by companies such as IBM, OASIS, and Microsoft.

An advantage of HTML is that it is forgiving of sloppy or unplanned development. The Web caught on quickly because Web page developers did not need to be experienced programmers. XML does not forgive sloppy planning and programming. This is both an advantage and a disadvantage. A well-planned corporate data model implemented in a set of XML DTDs provides significant improvements in interoperability, communications, and data sharing. Poor planning results in miscommunications and loss of data through incompatible applications. This idea can be summed up by the anonymous statement that, "Computers are powerful tools for making more errors, more quickly, and more precisely." That statement pertains to XML.

If a corporation embraces XML technology but does so blindly, it may discover less functionality, not more. Designers and developers must carefully analyze their requirements in order to apply XML appropriately. A developer can build models of the legacy data structures and map data models to a set of XML data elements. The XML data elements are collected into a set of DTDs that can be used to build a well-defined tree structure for each document.

However, DTD development should not occur in a vacuum. As with the automaker example, collaboration is key. If a corporation tries to develop its own applications and DTDs, it may find that its development is incompatible with other companies, vendors, and partners. Developers can avoid incompatibilities and "standards wars" by learning about the various industry-standard DTDs.

Because XML's predominant advantage is for sharing data, companies will benefit by using the same standards. Compromises can be made to ensure widespread and future interoperability. These trade-offs may make XML documents larger or less focussed than other solutions, but the increase in data sharing will be more than worth the compromise.

DTD Repositories and Standards

James Watson, co-discoverer of DNA's structure, once said, "Nothing that is new comes about without collaboration." Companies and industry leaders are collaborating to develop standardized DTDs to share information and to automate business processes. For example, if Ford, GM, and DaimlerChrysler agree on a standard DTD with a set of rules for their procurement needs, then they could ensure that their partners, vendors, and customers could write compatible applications. The interoperability that

XML promises will become a reality as more and more companies develop industry-specific DTDs.

The focus across vertical industries such as the auto industry has been to define specific DTDs so businesses can exchange data. B2B e-commerce and document management are among the areas that have benefited from the use of standardized sets of XML tags. After invested parties collaborate on a set of XML tags and a corresponding DTD for a given industry and application, they can seamlessly exchange data encoded with those tags. As each company or industry decides on a level of detail for its DTD and document structure, other companies can build on top of the standards and ignore details as appropriate.

Companies should keep watch of many of the industry standards efforts to help define consistent XML DTDs and data elements. Some of these standards groups can be found at www.accord.com, www.biztalk.org, www.oasis.org, www.xmledi.com, and www.openapplicationsgroup.com. CommerceXML at www.cXML.org is a registry for order processing and catalogs, and it is growing in support.

The military is also using XML. The DII COE (Defense Information Infrastructure Common Operating Environment) is building an XML registry at diides.ncr.disa.mil/xmlreg/index.cfm used to support military operations, such as mission planning and supply chain management. DII COE promotes military-based interoperability and software reuse in a secure, reliable, and global networked environment. The DII COE data service infrastructure is implemented as shared DTDs and schema, data management services, and run-time applications, etc., for supporting military applications and operations.

CommerceXML, Oasis, and Oracle are all three working on developing a set of XML DTDs to support current industry needs, such as B2B. Microsoft, IBM, and Sun Microsystems are all working on strategies for leveraging XML to improve the portability and interoperability of data and information.

Exploiting XML

Decision makers gather information; they think about it, combine it in different ways, and finally make the decision. If information is free and easy to access, then having information is no longer a competitive advantage. Converting raw data and information into decisionable knowledge becomes the most critical competitive advantage of executives in the Information Economy.

XML provides advantages to communications, data sharing, interoperability, e-commerce, information retrieval, and data warehouses. A dramatic advantage of XML emerges when corporations within an industry standardize XML tags to automate the supply chain, communications, and business processes. B2B e-commerce ascends to a higher plane of functionality and integration with the use of omnimorphic XML formats. XML simplifies e-business by supporting Electronic Data Interchange (EDI) standards across companies, industries, and countries, providing the possibility of an international, industry-independent set of standards.

While HTML describes how a Web page *looks,* XML describes information about what the *content* of a document *means*. XML tags identify a number as a date, a price, or an invoice. So if retailers like Wal-Mart, K-Mart, and Target use the same DTD elements for *customer*, *price*, and *inventory*, they can improve information interoperability by using the same tags, as depicted in Figure 1.2. If Ford, GM, and DaimlerChrysler use the same DTD vocabulary, and enforce this vocabulary on their vendors, procurement costs drop, as in Figure 1.3. In addition, comparison shopping becomes easier, because all vendors use the same tag to identify their widgets. So, the automakers can compare widget to widget, tracking price, delivery, or other germane attributes.

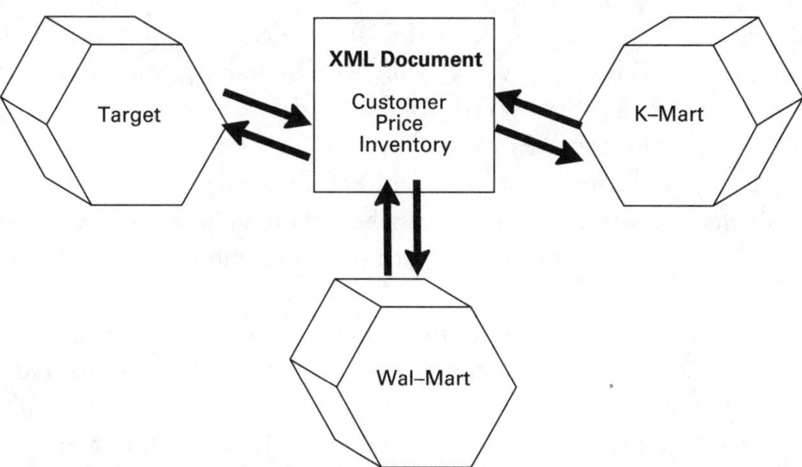

Figure 1.2 In an XML-based B2B collaboration among retailers, corporations such as Wal-Mart, K-Mart, and Target can agree to use the same DTDs or schemas to define concepts like *customer, price,* and *inventory.* Through this agreement, they can improve information interoperability and general communications by using a common set of data element tags.

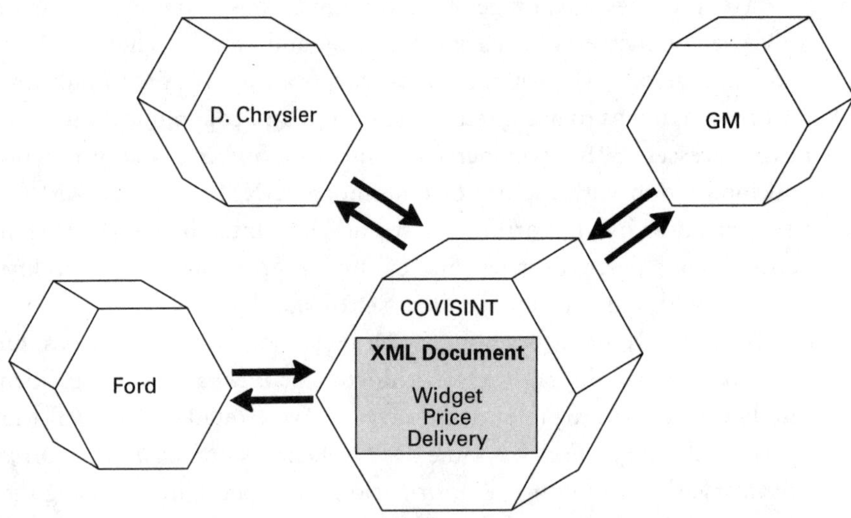

FIGURE 1.3 In the XML-based B2B Exchange, Covisint, among automobile manufacturers, such as GM, Ford, and DaimlerChrysler, these companies can gain cost advantages by using a common DTD or schema for procurement.

Similarly, interoperability is a big issue in the U.S. military. If each branch of the service conforms to a government DTD, improvements in interoperability and integration increase immensely among the military, suppliers, and coalition forces. DII COE, as already mentioned, has already initiated an XML registry that will store military, government, and contractor DTDs. As these DTDs are collected into a single repository, combining them into common vocabularies to foster interoperability will be easier. The government has a history of enforcing standards on its aerospace and defense contractors. If all branches of the military, as well as all vendors, use the same set of DTDs, then interoperability will be an achievable goal.

The commercial world and the military world may want to share some common DTDs. In anticipation of and excitement over standardized DTDs, developers have created XML registries for different industries and across industries. A registry may contain DTDs and information about tags for various industries and fields, such as automotive, chemicals, oil, retail, manufacturing, and music. A DTD registry encourages cross-communications of tags; for example, retailers might use DTDs and tags for music and for math for part of their inventory and pricing.

While developing corporate- and industry-specific DTDs from scratch is natural, the effort and the results are inefficient on two counts. First, for a given industry, a good start for a set of DTDs probably exists already. A company can use the standard DTD and modify as needed. Second, an industry-specific DTD may hinder communications across industries. For example, if a vendor trades with both the automotive industry and the aerospace industry, then two sets of DTDs may require the vendor to keep two sets of records. Having a separate DTD for each industry artificially segments products and services by industry, often requires a vendor to duplicate efforts, and then results in higher costs. However, many vendors cross industries without needing to separate and duplicate their efforts. Collaboration on DTDs across industries can result in lower costs.

None other then venerable IBM has seen the light. IBM has initiated an effort to create a common DTD that will be used across all industries and will be augmented by DTDs that are specific to a given corporation or industry. This effort, if accepted and embraced by all industries, will help the world to collaborate and share information.

Leveraging XML DTDs

At the most basic level, the context of documents can be captured manually by workers entering data into specific fields on a form or by assigning documents to various categories. But capturing meta-data and using it for searching exploits just a small fraction of its capability. The structure, composition, and use of the meta-data and its tags are valuable knowledge assets of the enterprise that are leveraged by context-mining functions. XML promises to convert the presentation-based World Wide Web into a content-based *Semantic Web*, as Tim Berners-Lee calls it. By tagging content and meaning, XML facilitates and focuses information retrieval on the Web and in intranets. One killer application for XML has been B2B e-commerce. XML is waiting for the next killer app to help drive the effort. One compelling application, possibly the next killer app, is the data warehouse.

An exciting aspect of XML tags is that they form a set of meta-data about the document. The DTD of an XML document describes the data elements and structures within a document. The data elements are represented as tags used to mark up a document. And if a common DTD with standardized tags is used for a set of documents within a repository, the result is a data warehouse with little fuss, muss, or hassle. This concept extends outward to the entire corporation, many corporations within an industry, many industries, and potentially to the entire World Wide Web and Internet. This sensational concept has broad implications that can allow a type of globally distributed data mining from the world-wide data warehouse.

A developer can design a Web page with XML tags to simplify searching. XML developers can create tags and rules that describe a document's data, information, and content. These tags provide a method for indexing the content within a document by using commonly defined elements. These common elements have specific meanings expected by a search engine or another application. Data and tables can be functional, so that their meaning can be imported into spreadsheets and databases even more easily and smoothly than Web page text is currently saved onto the local PC.

The implication of combining multiple documents is significant. In HTML, if a user wants to locate and combine information from different documents, he uses a search engine to locate the information, filters that information manually, and then combines it manually. The process can take minutes, hours, or days. With XLink, the entire process is not only automatic, but it is immediate. As quickly as the documents are accessed, their information is combined, in a way that is transparent to the user, and displayed as one document. Clearly, the process will require significant bandwidth and planning, but the payback is many-fold in terms of information access and analysis.

Peer-to-Peer Processing

One of the big developments on the horizon for XML is the idea of virtual documents. Virtual documents are collections of information that exist only for immediate use. Typically a virtual document is composed of portions of information from a variety of distributed documents across the network.

The idea of a virtual document is not new. A trivial example of a virtual document is a child's report that is glued together from information gleaned from magazines and encyclopedia articles. A more pertinent example is the results of a Web search. When someone searches for information using a search engine such as Yahoo!, then the returned collection of Web pages is a virtual document.

Unfortunately, the creation of a virtual document currently requires some programming skills. However, with XML, specifically XLink, even people with no programming skills will be able to create their own virtual documents. XLink has not yet been fully defined and implemented, but other news may support the concept. This news has to do with *Napster*.

Napster software was created to allow users to search for MP3 music files and then download them. The unique aspect of Napster is that users search through a Napster community of other users and not through the entire Web. Because of questions with MP3 files, Napster had some legal issues with copyright infringement. Those issues are not germane to this discussion. What is important is that Napster provides a method of searching and retrieving information dynamically by using peer-to-peer networking.

Peer-to-peer networking (P2P) presents the concept of sharing data among distributed systems. Data sharing is exactly what is needed to implement virtual documents. The peer content provider allows the community to access predefined information. Members of the community can then include the information as part of an XML document. In addition, the content provider can control which information is shared and under what conditions. A protocol that combines the distributed appeal of P2P with the power of XML and XLink standards will create a formidable agent for change. In fact, P2P is the potential spark of Web and Internet access that will fan the roaring flame of universal information retrieval to meet the business needs of the 21st century.

Conclusion

XML is an enabling technology. As an omnimorphic data format, it will encourage interoperability. However, as it becomes more pervasive, XML will virtually disappear from the media. If it is everywhere, it will be like an ocean to a fish, unseen. This has already begun to happen with B2B e-commerce. The first major articles in February and March 2000 about the B2B collaboration among the big automakers never even hinted at XML. The *Wall Street Journal*, the *Dallas Morning News*, and the *Washington Post* were all silent about XML. A few weeks later, though, a tidbit about XML began to surface. The enabling technology is not news. The business and the billions make the headlines. And that is the way that it should be. Business drives technology and technology enables business. But a good businessperson needs to be aware of emerging trends and how they might impact the business.

The technology that XML represents is similar to that of the transistor. Except for electronic engineers, no one cares about the lonely transistor. Just after the vacuum tube, companies used to brag about how many transistors were in their radios. Then integrated circuits were invented and microprocessors with millions of transistors. The number of transistors in a Pentium III is no longer common knowledge. Intel will be more than happy to reveal this information, but no one wants to listen, except for competitors. Consumers are now interested in processing speed. The same thing will happen to XML as happened to transistors. In fact, it is almost there.

The news about B2B greatly outweighed the underlying XML technology. More articles exist about B2B or about wireless data access than about XML. But XML is the foundation of these technologies. A general understanding about XML helps in understanding more about these technologies and what their business potential could bring. Although XML will not bring in the money, the applications that are developed using XML will. From B2B to WML to holographic processing in the more distant future; these applications are the ones that will bring in the profits.

With XML applications, the Web has the potential to become a worldwide data warehouse with connectivity to a wide variety of devices. Each application has its own separate potential to make money. A businessperson should maintain awareness of emerging technologies. To paraphrase Bill Gates, how will a user react when information is free? Each manager can answer that question in the way that is most profitable to the specific organization.

CHAPTER 2

XML Schemas and DTDs

Introduction

Schemas and Document Type Definitions (DTDs) form the meta-data that enables an XML document to be self-describing. Although they have very different constructs, schemas and DTDs serve the same general purpose: to define the rules and data elements within an XML document. They attach context to XML documents that can be read by humans and by machines. The specific flavor of XML syntax that a given DTD or schema defines is called a *vocabulary*. The vocabulary may cover a set of XML documents or only one document. Although DTDs are the more mature technology, the World Wide Web Consortium (W3C) is pushing the specification and acceptance of schemas. Each construct has advantages, but advocates believe that schemas provide the superior extensibility and compatibility with the XML format.

What Is a Schema?

Schema may be an unfortunate choice of terms because database theory also uses the term schema. In fact, the word schema is used in different modeling disciplines and means something different in each context. An XML schema has no relationship to a database schema. An XML schema is a construct used to represent the data elements, attributes, and their relationships as defined in the data model. An XML schema defines a class of XML documents by documenting the meaning, usage, and relationships of their constituent parts. The function of a schema is the same as the function of a DTD. However, a DTD does not use a hierarchical structure, while a schema does use a hierarchical structure to indicate relationships.

In other words, the XML schema serves much the same function as the DTD, but it follows the XML syntax rather than the SGML syntax that the DTD follows. Otherwise, schemas specify the meaning and rules for data elements within an XML document much the same as DTDs do.

DTDs, the only holdover from SGML, do not conform to the XML syntax. Therefore, an application that can manipulate an XML document may not be able to manipulate the DTD. In addition, a DTD does not include data typing, but a schema does. The schema will also facilitate the ability to exchange data and to transform XML documents from one vocabulary to another.

The purpose of a schema is to define a class of XML documents. A schema specifies both the structure of an XML document and the constraints on its content.

While XML is the meta-language for defining a set of data element tags, an XML schema is the specification for the syntax of one particular tag language. The tag language defined by a schema is also called the vocabulary for that schema. A schema is used to validate the XML document content. An XML parser validates an XML document by determining the vocabulary of the document and comparing the vocabulary to the schema for consistency. In addition, the XML schema describes the vocabulary for use by other applications and by other people when exchanging data.

The XML schema defines the data elements that can appear within the document and the attributes associated with a data element. It defines the structure of the document, the interrelationships of data elements, the sequence in which elements can appear, and the number of elements. The schema defines whether an element is empty, can include text, or has default attribute values. Schemas also document an external namespace vocabulary and its constraints, as described in this chapter.

Many companies, led by Microsoft, have been working with the W3C to develop the meta-data standard for XML schemas. Schemas serve the same function as DTDs in that they define XML documents and provide a mechanism for allowing an XML document to be self-describing. *Self-describing* means that an XML document uses tags to describe and mark up the data and information, and the XML document uses meta-data in the form of a DTD or schema to describe and define the meanings and actions associated with the tags.

Schemas are easier to read and to create than DTDs because they are written using a set of XML-compliant tags and following an XML compliant format. In contrast, DTDs follow the older format found in SGML; XML was piggybacked on the already existing SGML infrastructure in order to introduce XML quickly into the existing development environment.

Different file specifications are associated with schemas. Consider a file that we will call document, for lack of imagination and improvement in clarity. If it is a pure XML document containing only XML data, then the file specification used is ".xml," resulting in the file name "document.xml." If the document contains only DTD information, then the file specification used is ".dtd," resulting in the file name "document.dtd." For a schema there are two choices, not yet a single standard. The file specification can be ".xdr" (an abbreviation for XML Data Reduced), or the file specification can be ".xsd" (short for XML Schema Data). The respective file names would be "document.xdr" and "document.xsd." Notice also that all file names are in lowercase, because XML is case sensitive. This means that "document.XML" is different than "document.xml."

While we are describing file specifications, we can include three others. If the XML document is a formatting style sheet that contains XSL commands, then the file specification is ".xsl" and the file name is "document.xsl." If it is a transformation style sheet that contains XSLT commands, then the file specification is usually XSL, rather than XSLT, because XSLT is simply a different set of style sheet commands. If the XML document is used to contain linking information, then the file specification is "XLL" and the file name is "document.xll" (short for XML Linking Language). These types of files have not yet been introduced into the vernacular and may change before the XLink specification is completed.

For the most part, XML file specifications are fairly straightforward. Most of them will be simple, three-letter acronyms that represent the XML tool of interest. Now back to schemas.

Schemas make it easy to insert business rules into the core of the XML documents. The rules are usually very readable, and they have an additional benefit. As an XML document, the business rules defined by an XML schema can be manipulated by XSL and XSLT just like any other XML document. Therefore, XML-based business rules can be transformed from one set into another set (e.g., from one company's set of rules into a second company's set of rules). These transformations facilitate information exchange and data transactions among multiple companies.

Attributes

In a schema tag definition, the tag *type* is defined using either the *complexType* tag or the *simpleType* tag; then it is declared. In addition to the types, tags can also have *attributes* that are associated with them. The advantage of attributes is that they can supply a richer context to the data, providing for a much more precise meaning applied to the data element type. One disadvantage of attributes is that they cannot easily be manipulated using style sheets.

Developers building their XML document design architectures must address this question of attribute manipulation. Should developers define modifiers and create meaning by using attributes, or should they use complex tags or simple tags? With no simple answers available, the general guideline is that if the information will be variable and modified, then it should be in a tag format; however, if the modifier provides context and it will never need to be changed, then an attribute is more efficient.

Datatypes

Schemas also allow a variety of datatypes as defined in the datatype specification portion of the overall schema specification. A *datatype* is simply a kind of data. In schemas, datatypes can be simple or complex, and they include decimal, floating point, strings, and the standard datatypes used by developers in most programming tasks.

In addition, as inherent in XML, the developer can extend the datatypes to contain any information needed to do the job. For example, to build an Earned Value Management System (EVMS) that monitors cost and schedule progress on a major project, a Difference datatype could be defined to contain and monitor the difference between planned and actual costs (or any other monitored difference).

Datatypes can be defined to have default values and optional values, but they can also be defined to have a list of variables or even a set of variables that change with context. For example, in the financial field, a monetary datatype could be designed to define a variety of currency types from various countries. In addition, the definition of these currencies might be extended so that a change in the presentation display might automatically result in a correct conversion from one amount of money to the appropriate amount in the different currency.

A great advantage of schemas over DTDs is the ability to automatically import multiple definitions from different schemas, rather than having to redefine data element types each time a new schema is developed. The ability to reuse previously tested and debugged data element types or entire schemas can result in a significant savings in development efficiency. In addition, separate schemas can be created for individual departments and then combined as appropriate. Of course, what works for a few departments will also work among trading partners in a B2B exchange. This ability to combine, trade, and reuse schema information—sharing meta-data—goes a long way toward building the foundation needed for industry interoperability of information.

Although DTDs can handle many of these same functions, the DTD processing, in terms of computer cycles and people cycles, can be prohibitive. However, after the initial schema development, the schema processing is usually minor in terms of people cycles.

What Is a Namespace?

A *namespace* is a simple method of bringing multiple definitions and vocabularies into a single XML document. In addition, a namespace declaration (*xmlns:*) provides an alias that helps separate and identify data element types from different external locations. The namespace addresses many issues.

By using a namespace, a developer can reuse an existing schema in the current document. Rather than reinventing the wheel, the developer can save time and effort by building from previous work. In fact, rather than using an internal schema, the namespace can reference an external schema.

External schemas may include data element types that already exist in the current XML document. The namespace alias clearly identifies the origin of a data element type, allowing different tags to have separate but similar meanings. For example, Ford may have a *<name>* tag that means "last-name" and "first-name," while GM may simply use "name." In the schema, these differences can be represented as *Ford:name* and *GM:name,* eliminating any ambiguity.

Differences between Schemas and DTDs

DTDs have three advantages:

- SGML legacy of users
- Well-understood standard
- Mature technology with thousands of vocabularies

DTDs have four limitations:

- Not written in XML and not Document Object Model (DOM) compatible
- Minimal support to use namespaces, and only indirectly
- Minimal support for data typing
- Difficult to modify, customize, or extend

Schemas address these DTD limitations as follows:

- Written in the XML format and can support DOM
- Support of namespaces directly
- Support of data typing and element relationships
- Extensible to user-defined data elements and types

Schemas and DTDs use different content models. When a content model is open, the data elements can include elements, attributes, and mixed content not specified in the content model. When the content model is closed, the data elements can include only content and data elements specified in the content model. The DTD uses a *closed content model*, and XML schemas use an *open content model.* Therefore the data element types between DTDs and schemas may differ.

In addition, the placement of namespace (*xmlns:*) declarations is not easily modeled using a DTD. Using more than one namespace declaration with a DTD is difficult. In an XML schema, the namespace attributes (*xmlns:*)

can go anywhere. In fact, multiple *xmlns* declarations can appear in different locations because schemas follow an open content model. Therefore, the user can more easily customize definitions and declarations through the use of a schema.

Namespace placement in a DTD is not an option, but placement is a useful feature of schemas. Because of its hierarchical structure, a schema can use the same name in different places to have different meanings. For example, the term *mustang* can only be used once in a DTD. But in a schema, *mustang* could be used in an automotive context and in an equine context at different locations within the hierarchy.

Unlike DTDs, XML schemas are extensible. Developers can add their own customized elements, tags, and attributes to XML schema documents in order to extend them. In fact, a developer can create a customized schema by combining components from many external, standard schemas. With namespaces, external schemas can be used directly with a reference to the original schema rather than copying the definition. To reference an element defined in another schema, the developer must first use a namespace declaration to introduce the other schema. This declaration consists of an attribute beginning with *xmlns,* followed by a prefix name and a path to the other schema. For example, the resulting customized schema might include elements from the Ford schema and the GM schema. So elements such as *Ford:name* and *GM:name* could be sprinkled throughout the schema where the specific declarations are needed.

Why Use Schemas?

The main reason to use schemas is to improve compatibility and consistency within an XML document or application. In isolation, whether an XML document uses a DTD or a schema does not matter significantly. However, the moment that a developer or user wants to modify the document, share the document, or combine multiple documents, the differences become apparent.

Because schemas follow the XML format, developers can more easily design tools, such as XSLT scripts, that will modify them. A real concern about XML documents is that developers will use different vocabularies, which will minimize interoperability. To leverage the omnimorphic capabilities of XML, developers must be able to bend the syntax rules of a specific document without breaking the vocabulary. For example, when working both with Ford in the automotive industry and with Boeing in the aerospace industry, a vendor would like to exchange data using the most compatible format. With XSLT, the vendor may be able to build a normalized schema that enables sharing of data with Boeing or Ford without requiring any extra translation steps.

In addition, schemas are easy to create, easy to read, and easy to modify. The reason that schemas are not yet widespread is that an agreed-upon definition and specification have not yet been designed. But the use of XML technology is already beginning to push the envelope beyond the current DTD capabilities. Just as schemas permit modifications for interoperability, they also permit modifications for a changing marketplace. Currently, DTDs and schemas are fairly static, but consider an example of a very rapidly changing marketplace, such as the wireless market.

In the wireless market, the industry is changing hardware and software almost weekly as subscribers demand more and more functionality. Nokia and Motorola send specification product descriptions to their vendors every week. Imagine that these documents are in a schema format. Now, if these manufacturers design new features and capabilities, or if service providers step up the bandwidth significantly, or if the wireless application protocol (WAP) specification evolves with more capabilities, then the schema must change to reflect these improvements. A DTD might require a completely new overhaul, but schemas are more flexible, more extensible, and are omnimorphic.

To incorporate information about the improvements, Nokia and Motorola can simply add the new features to the schema. The change does not affect existing applications, because they will either use the new data or ignore it if necessary. In most cases, the new applications will be flexible enough to adapt to new information. This is what XML is all about, being able to extend smoothly to fit increasing capabilities as needed. This capability is what makes XML an omnimorphic language.

As this example implies, a foundation schema can be agreed upon and developed for the exchange of information and data. When new information is added to the schema, no modifications are needed to the applications or to the basic schema. And the information is automatically distributed to the market, to vendors, and to partners. At a later date, as the amount of new information increases beyond some threshold, the partners may come together to agree on an upgrade to the basic schema, but that may not even be necessary.

Guidelines and Best Practices

Although XML use is a new activity, the creation of meta-data, schemas, and especially DTDs is an old, well-practiced art. The design and development of an XML document and its meta-data parallels the design methodology used by data analysts to create data models and to design database architectures. DTDs have been around in SGML development activities for around thirty years. The combined experience of expert SGML developers and mature database designers has resulted in many good guidelines, rules-of-thumb, and best practices that can apply to meta-data, schemas, and DTD development activities.

First, before going through a long development on a project, carefully spec out the requirements and generate a data model. In fact, use this approach even for a small prototype to avoid those horror stories of a prototype being put into a production environment and then breaking during business critical tasks.

There is a story about an R&D engineer, who, by the gift of gab, got hold of the ear of the systems engineering vice president (VP) and explained how great XML, Java, and Web technology were for interoperability. This engineer, a very articulate incompetent, was able to con a few million dollars out of the VP to develop a prototype Web interface to a cost-and-schedule database. The prototype took 6 months to develop under the engineer's random, unwritten directions . . . and it appeared to work marvelously. The VP was overwhelmed and directed the engineer to develop an enterprise-wide multi-database production-quality Web interface.

If either the engineer or the VP had any knowledge of computers or information technology, they would have sought the experience of a data analyst. The data analyst would have purchased a $40 book (not this one) about Web-based database interfaces, popped the accompanying CD into a computer, and in less than a week, for less than $100, he would have prototyped a terrific interface. Then when the VP ordered an enterprise-wide interface in 6 months, the analyst would have laughed.

The data analyst would have laughed because you cannot scale a cobbled-together prototype into a corporate-ready interface. The engineer wasted millions of dollars and never could figure out why the resulting large interface would never work. The project was taken away from R&D and given to an Information Technology (IT) architect, who scrapped the prototype and started from scratch. In this case, the R&D engineer did not have the business sense to accept the sunken costs of the prototype and kept trying to scale it up. But trying to scale a quick and dirty prototype is like trying to use an average frying pan to make scrambled eggs for a thousand people. It simply will not scale up in the time required.

The lesson here is that if you develop a quick and dirty XML prototype, scrap it and start over when you plan for the production phase. The IT architect's side of the story is an interesting contrast.

The IT architect went through a disciplined three-phase design:

1. Gathered requirements and built a conceptual architecture, which was used to gain consensus with all the stakeholders;
2. Designed a logical architecture that depicted how all the general pieces went together, how the communications worked, what the general data element types were, and where the gaps occurred. The IT architect reviewed this logical architecture with the stake-holders, negotiated changes in the requirements, and got buy-off on this phase;
3. Filled in all the gaps, developed the DTDs, designed the interfaces, and implemented a physical architecture. While the interface had plenty of bugs, the IT architect could backtrack to the logical architecture to locate where the reasoning was incorrect. With a few changes and a few iterations, the system worked.

Even with the legacy problems inherited from the R&D engineer, the IT architect was able to put a working enterprise-wide database interface up and running in just under 6 months, and for less than one fourth the cost of the engineer's prototype fiasco.

The lesson here is that disciplined design is the key to XML implementation success. In developing a set of DTDs or XML documents, gather the requirements, build a logical model of the data element types, and then build a "prototype" of XML tags and the physical implementation. Use production-quality design and development, then iterate through the implementation to work out the bugs and get it right.

When designing schemas or DTDs, be careful of inherited changes. In good programming, developers commonly place a variable where it can be changed once and the change propagated throughout. However, with a schema, reuse makes inheritance hazardous: the ripples due to small changes may avalanche into massive modifications without the developer's knowledge. Changes in a distributed environment can have unpredictable consequences. The safe approach is to make all changes manually in the beginning of the development cycle.

Whenever a schema is developed, freeze it and put it under configuration management. Some XML document or application depends heavily on that schema. If a schema is modified, make an entirely new copy that does not depend on the original. If the new one does not work with a particular application or XML document, go back to the old one and debug the new one.

Do not simply discard the new one. Instead, try to learn from the mistakes. A few corrected mistakes result in dramatic increases in experience. These are good learning exercises.

When creating a schema, plan it like an XML document. Rather than building a collection of apparently unrelated definitions, try to build a collective whole that fits into a hierarchy. One of the advantages of using schemas over DTDs is the coherence and relationships among elements. Another advantage is the ability to build XSLT scripts that can transform the schemas as needed, automatically.

Transforming Schema Meta-Data

One of the significant issues about XML DTDs and schemas is how to convert an XML document with one vocabulary to a document with another vocabulary.

XSLT

DTDs are not easy to transform, but schemas are a different story. Because a schema is an XML document, it can be manipulated just like any other XML document. XSLT was designed to handle just these kinds of manipulations and transformations.

The XSL Transformations (XSLT) specification defines an XML-based style sheet scripting-type language for expressing transformation rules that map one XML document into another. When XML schemas become the dominant meta-data for XML documents, XSLT will be help provide the basic infrastructure for building interoperable systems. Because XSLT can transform XML documents and because schemas are XML documents, XSLT is a superb vehicle for mapping the schema of one corporation into that of another corporation.

For example, imagine that Ford wants to make fuel cells for Boeing. Ford sends its XML documents to Boeing, and Boeing's XML translation Web server compares the Ford schemas to the standard Boeing schemas. The server then runs an XSLT translation engine that maps the Ford vocabulary to the Boeing vocabulary. XSLT is a scripting or programming language, so this kind of mapping is not much more difficult than a table lookup. Then the modified Ford document is sent to the appropriate departments for review. Either Boeing or Ford may reverse the process for documents sent from Boeing to Ford. Designing the XSLT translation engine may require some clever artificial intelligence programming, but maintaining and running the engine should be straightforward. Developing this XSLT translation engine or providing this type of service is probably a window of opportunity for some clever entrepreneur.

Caveat Emptor

XSLT can address the significant challenge caused by using multiple XML schemas describing similar data within different XML documents. With XSLT, a developer can map XML documents to one another, and create a new XML document that conforms to the schema of choice. Of course, simply mapping documents and vocabularies doesn't ensure that they can work together in the way expected. Manual intervention and direct communications are still required to interpret the meaning of the data.

While the mechanics of meta-data transformation may be worked out, the logistics are a completely different story. The syntax may be portable, but corporate semantics are not. For example, if you ask for a glass of water and I bring you a glass of warm water from the tap, you may be disappointed that I did not understand you. You may have wanted: cold water, water with ice, water with a slice of lemon, or bottled water. The syntax was clear; the meaning was not. This is the same situation with data exchange between corporations.

One corporation may identify a customer by using *<name>*. However, does *<name>* refer to *last name*, or *full name?* The same dilemma occurs for *<address>*, for *<product>*, for *<inventory number>*, etc. The basic business vocabulary for a corporation varies greatly across industries and may vary within an industry. Do Sears, Wal-Mart, and Target all use the same vocabularies? They are all retailers, but they have different corporate histories to build upon.

Consider the importance of communications and vocabulary as you build a corporate XML strategy. Document all data element types from the business perspective, the user perspective, the designer perspective, and the developer perspective. And save that document as an important white paper to share with all partners when you send them your DTDs or schemas.

Why Use DTDs?

The reason to use a DTD is merely historical. DTDs are the prevalent forms of building XML document vocabularies. They exist, they work, and they are accepted. They are also obscure and arcane, requiring a little programming background to write them, and even more programming knowledge to read or modify existing DTDs.

Of course, SGML programmers are comfortable with DTDs, as are SGML applications. However, one goal of the schema definition effort is to come up with a simple way to make schemas backwards compatible with DTDs. This way, the billions of dollars that are being devoted to DTDs will not need to be redirected into manually rewriting legacy XML documents using schemas.

What Is the Function of a DTD?

DTDs are the meta-data for XML. They serve as the foundation of XML documents and applications because they define the rules for building an XML document and for instructing an XML application how to process it. The DTD indicates valid syntax, structure, and format for defining the XML markup for a document. Using different codes to identify important information, mandatory information, and optional information, the DTD instructs a parser about how to process an XML document. The DTD also identifies where elements appear and how they are related. In comparison to an SGML DTD, an XML DTD was specifically designed to be relatively easy to read by both people and computers. It presents the document outline or map for the author of the XML document, for users of the document, and for XML parsers.

The author of an XML document is like a construction worker using a blueprint. The blueprint for an XML document is the DTD. The DTD provides a list of elements, rules, and specifications that define a content model for a category of documents. These categories can be anything from catalogs, purchase orders, and inventories to data warehouses and training software.

The DTD specifies the relationships among all components of an XML document, such as item, item name, inventory number, and price. XML applications use the DTD as a guide to ascertain which structures and rules will be used in a given document type. For example, specific structures and elements can identify a catalog, a customer order, a bill of materials, or an inventory.

Defining Rules

The DTD defines rules and the elements of an XML document. The DTD is embedded within the document, or referenced from outside of the document. Because embedded DTDs are read first, they can be used to override and redefine outside definitions. This feature is useful for applying specific rules to predefined, user-customized documents. It can also be used to inherit general outside definitions.

An XML document follows two rules of syntax. First, if a document follows the general specifications of XML, then it is *well formed.* If the document has a DTD and follows the specific rules in the DTD, then it conforms to the XML specification and it is considered to be *valid.* An important characteristic of valid XML documents is that they are also compatible with SGML and can be processed by most SGML tools.

Because it conforms to the XML specification, a well-formed XML document does not require a DTD. However, the XML syntax is more rigid than the HTML syntax.

Defining Meta-Data

Meta-data describes data element tags or attributes. Many different ways of marking up an XML document exist. An XML document can be marked up to facilitate searching for information, or it may be marked up to relate information among a set of XML documents. Meta-data can tag data to help provide meaning, content, or context as germane to the requirement. Well-designed DTD meta-data will determine the success or failure of XML projects and the triumph of corporate conversion to XML documents.

The conventional definition of *meta-data* is "data about data." XML DTD meta-data is a way of documenting information about datasets. Meta-data information explains the creation of a dataset and provides an idea of what its attached document was designed to do.

When creating a new XML document, the developer, who does not know how to proceed, is like a tourist in a new city without a road map. The DTD is like a tourist information center that provides complete information on what path to follow to arrive at the desired destination. By using the DTD as a document creation roadmap, the developer is in a confident position to plan the document without wandering around aimlessly.

XML tags can be used as meta-data to enable B2B e-commerce over the Web. Existing legacy systems can exploit XML tags and Web-enabled technology for database access, migrating into a new capability without using additional software or middleware.

The Importance of Being Meta-Data

Data and information are valuable corporate assets. Unfortunately, these assets may be stored in repositories that don't support easy retrieval. One way to improve access is through the use of meta-data (information about data), which describes these intangible assets. The key is to have carefully defined meta-data.

Well-defined meta-data presents a competitive advantage because it facilitates the use of corporate information and data. In addition, providing partners, customers, and suppliers with corporate meta-data allows them to more seamlessly share and transfer information.

Meta-Data Evolves

With the advent of XML, meta-data takes on a whole new life in the form of DTDs and schemas. DTDs and schemas define the data elements and attributes of an XML document. Although simple to understand, meta-data is difficult to manage. First, meta-data is not straightforward to define at consistent levels of detail. In some cases, meta-data may describe a collection of documents. In other cases, it may describe data elements within a specific document. How to coordinate these different levels is not obvious and no clear guidelines are available. But meta-data is much too valuable not to solve this problem. In fact, XML DTDs may be worth billions of dollars.

DTDs and schemas support the ability to deliver individualized data to customers in an e-business interaction, whether e-commerce, m-commerce, or mobile Web access to data. In addition, DTDs support the reuse and repurposing of data and information. For example, the flexibility of DTDs can be used to define customizable data elements that change the look and feel of a Web page for each customer. Or a Web page can be repurposed to work with other devices such as wireless devices or text-to-speech systems. Reuse and repurposing results in lower costs for two reasons. First, information does not need to be recreated each time it is used, saving costs in redundant use. Second, by using XML to deliver customized Web pages, a corporation does not incur the costs of more detailed scripting or programming costs. Programming languages, such as Java and Perl, require higher development costs than XML and XSL. Greater use of XML and XSL results in less use of Java and Perl to define the same tasks.

XML presents a powerful paradigm for providing meta-data and data within a single document. Data element tags identify specific data elements, similar to how a Post-it Note might be used to identify an important book. The Post-it Note tags real items, and the data element tags identify electronic items, within an XML document. In the XML document, the DTD defines what the tags mean and what the data elements represent. For example, a temperature tag, *<Celsius>* or *<Fahrenheit>,* could be used to distinguish the difference between the freezing point of water, *<Celsius>0</Celsius>* and the balance in someone's bank account, *<dollars>0</dollars>*. Both values are zero, but now a computer can tell the difference and manipulate them as needed. XML provides a universal data transfer format that is independent of both platform and application.

Many computer standards are independent of platform. For example, MS Word and MS Excel can transfer data between PCs and Macintoshes. They are independent of platform. Also, ASCII is the same on all platforms. Finally, Web pages and HTML are independent of platform, working on PCs, Macintoshes, and all Unix machines. However, data from a Linux or Unix application may not work on a PC application without some intervening massaging. This extra step takes valuable machine and people cycles for the translation. XML eliminates that extra cycle because it transfers among all applications.

A significant advantage of application independence is interoperability and application integration. This means that I can take my favorite database to extract specific information, use my favorite spreadsheet to run "what-if" analyses, generate a report with my favorite word processor, generate graphs with my favorite drawing routine, and animate them with my favorite video program. Then I can deliver the entire package over the Web as a single, seamless document that anyone with an XML-enabled browser can read. Now for the caveats.

Caveats

What I have described is not here, yet, but it is not a pipe dream or an idealized vision. Mega-corporations such as IBM, Microsoft, and Oracle are all collaborating to make this vision into a reality. Oracle has already made some progress towards interoperability in the B2B e-commerce supply chain arena. Greater capability is rapidly approaching. We are currently at the same stage with XML as we were in 1995 with HTML. In fact, we are much further along because the infrastructure in already in place and many prototype tools are available.

Just as no one had heard about the Internet yesterday, but everyone uses it today, XML will silently mature and appear in just a few months. Two issues to overcome are specifications and vocabularies.

The specifications are easy. Web committees are working furiously to define all the necessary specifications for XML. Vocabularies are another thing.

A vocabulary is the set of data elements defined by a class of DTDs. For example, a chemist may define a mole as *<mole>6 10**23</mole>*, and a zoologist may use more to define *<mole>small furry animal</mole>*. But seriously, in inventory management is something called an *<item>*, a *<product>*, or an article, part, or component? This is a real issue that the automobile industry had to deal with. Should customers be identified by *<customer>* or *<name>* or *<Last_name>*? Each company uses a different method. Each method can be defined using a DTD, and each DTD defines a different vocabulary.

The issue and the question is how to correlate the various vocabularies. No one answer has surfaced yet because the field is still immature. However, two possibilities exist: XLST and Apache's Cocoon software. XSLT might be used to transform from one DTD to another. And Cocoon might also be used for transformation. This early in the game, Cocoon is a little more reliable. But the problem is well-known and many smart people are working on potential solutions.

DTD Standards Debate

DTDs are a growing subject of debate because some industries want IT vendors to provide industry-standard DTDs. But industry groups, not vendors or consultants, should define DTDs. A number of DTD standards are available. A DTD starts out as a content or data model that describes an application or a class of documents. For example, Oracle has created a DTD for B2B e-commerce, which describes the structure of that class of documents. If the developer of corporate DTDs carefully creates a well-thought out, logical model, then the defined DTD standards can be simple to understand and use. From this logical model, the developer can use existing industry standards, such as those already defined by vendors, defined in DTD repositories, or found in Microsoft's BizTalk repository.

As with any standards process, creating DTDs can become more complex as the number of people to please increases. DTD developers could learn a lot by using a bottom-up approach to solving big document problems. Creating DTDs that describe corporate applications and then standardizing the results will help cooperation. Corporate business partners can share DTDs to improve interoperability. By solving one part of the data interchange problem and doing it logically, simply, and correctly, DTD developers provide a target for others to shoot for if they want to share information and data. Going halfway and starting with any DTD is better than having no standards at all.

The auto industry presents a good example. Ford and GM had the chance to compete or cooperate in the definition of their B2B DTDs. Happily, they chose to cooperate to develop Covisint, an automotive B2B exchange. Scratch the surface a little bit and you find Oracle enabling the B2B technology. Dig a little deeper and you find the potential for a global XML vocabulary standard... backed by a $300 billion per year flow of parts and services from the auto industry. The Covisint DTD sounds like a candidate for a global de facto standard, considering that it has the backing of the "Big Three" auto makers to the tune of $300 billion-worth of business and 30,000 vendors are using it.

Although the retail industry and the food industry will not want to use the DTD from the auto industry, some concepts probably overlap. Rather than splintering the XML vocabularies created by various DTDs, industries would save money by finding a way to cooperate on the DTDs at some level. By working behind the scenes and keeping quiet about it, Oracle was part of the massive Covisint venture. If Oracle continues to build up quiet collaborations, it has the opportunity for being the XML integrator of choice. If these multi-billion dollar B2B efforts result in (XML-based information transfer) bridges among the various industries, the promise of information anywhere, anytime, to anyone, about anything, may become a reality within 18 months or faster. The company that pulls off that unification will gain more than profits, it will gain corporate and public support.

CHAPTER 3

XML Documents

Introduction

An *XML document* is an ordered, hierarchical tree structure that has elements and attributes, as shown in Figure 3.1. This is not the conventional definition of a document as words and text placed in some order for a specific purpose. But this simple definition provides significant potential. An XML document is much more than a conventional document. An XML document is a flexible and extensible collection of information that is structured for some purpose. While a database record is not a document, it can be restructured into an XML document. The important parts are the structure, elements, and attributes.

One of the useful functions of an XML document is the ability to contain information and data in a format that is independent of any platform or application. XML takes the device independence of HTML and Web clients one step further. XML wraps data into a self-describing document that can tell an application about its structure and elements instead of counting on the client for all of the processing capability.

The schema or DTD associated with a document describes the contents. XML is an object-oriented markup language and the schema or DTD defines how to use the language. The DTD defines how objects, attributes, and their values are used within an XML document. XML physical elements are defined by the DTD, and they are indicated in the document by using

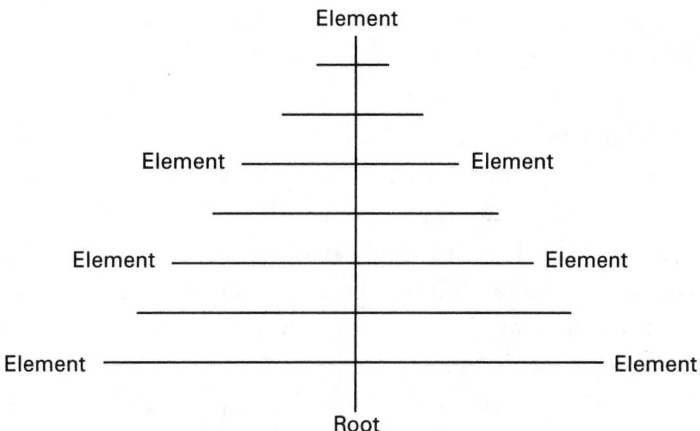

FIGURE 3.1 An XML document is a hierarchical tree-structure of elements and attributes. Some elements have been omitted for clarity in this picture. All XML documents also have one root element as a foundation.

logical tags. In the process of building an XML document, the designer keeps the logical parts and the physical parts separated, just like in the process of database design. If an application can read and parse the DTD or schema, then it can process an XML document.

The XML document designer is the architect who identifies the design, the subcomponents, the internal structure, and the relationships with other XML documents. This designer takes responsibility for mapping the business model to the XML document. An XML document architecture is not just how documents are used in the enterprise. It also touches on databases, procedures, configurations, and products. It is about which processes use the data, information, and documents, and how they will use them.

The first part of an XML document architecture is a conceptual model of all functional subcomponents. The architect will synthesize an understanding of the entire corporate XML document situation by identifying the relationships among subcomponents and sub-elements. The purpose of a given document, the current corporate standards, the industry standards, and the influencing standards will be identified. Then the architect can easily map one set of XML application tags to another as the standards mature.

XML allows the architect to create flexible XML documents that can be extended in various ways, such as including specific, one-time changes and unique requirements as needed. And the changes in the local document can be independent of the general XML document structure, so they will not affect other users. Well-designed XML documents enable communications and information transfer among computers, and between computers and people in a more natural manner.

XML document design is becoming very important to developers now that major vendors such as Microsoft, IBM, Oracle, Sun Microsystems, and others are becoming heavily involved with XML technologies. Many traditional structured techniques, such as database design and object-oriented analysis, can be integrated into a basic framework for XML document creation. XML documents constitute a uniform methodology for transferring and processing information. Well-established structured analysis and design techniques can be successfully applied to build a robust XML document architecture.

An XML document architecture that consists of many document templates is more flexible and more stable over time. When the architect and developer analyze business requirements and model the XML document templates based on business functions, the resulting capability provides a strong foundation for building XML documents and migrating existing, legacy documents to an XML document environment.

Reasons for Building XML Documents

One reason that an organization may choose to use XML documents is that data can be stored and accessed in a way that aligns with the corporate structure. Another reason is that XML documents provide robust access to data—information does not have to be stored in one location. XML documents can manage large amounts of information with minimal extra overhead. By using a standardized XML document template and by reusing document information to create new documents, a corporation can more easily manage and control its intellectual assets.

In addition, many legacy systems have been built using older technology. These legacy systems cannot simply be scrapped, but they also cannot easily be maintained. XML can facilitate the transfer and upgrade process. Some of the benefits that result from the upgrade include:

- Enhancing current systems
- Implementing changes and upgrades faster and more effectively
- Improving system quality

- Developing new systems faster
- Migrating to new architectures and tools
- Taking advantage of new technology and new capabilities

XML document design with its emphasis on extensibility, growth, and flexibility, supports more sophisticated applications than were possible with legacy systems. It makes sense to invest the dollars today to transform existing and historical corporate documents into XML documents.

Taxonomies

We need to take a further step in identifying a property that is crucial to understanding the distinctive qualities of complex XML documents. This property is the hierarchical relationship among all components within a document. This hierarchy, represented as a tree structure, enables the designer to show relationships between document components in a systematic, orderly fashion. For example, by using outer tags, such as <horse> or <car>, the XML document designer can distinguish a <mustang> data element as an equine or an automobile as needed by creating the appropriate hierarchy to establish the appropriate semantic context.

A specific hierarchy template can define an XML document type. A systematic collection of related XML document templates is called a *taxonomy*. For example, the XML document taxonomy of business cards, e-mail, memos, business letters, and white papers for an organization's R&D department might differ from the taxonomy of XML documents for the sales department. However, the defined patterns of ordered relationships within a set of XML documents provide a predictable and powerful way to represent data and information.

A process is something that someone wants to accomplish including the flow of actions from start to completion. The processes are a subset of the architecture. XML documents and processes can help integrate activities across departments and stovepipes to leverage resources and improve efficiencies.

Processing data about the environment is fundamental to understanding an environment or an enterprise. A data model embodies the rules for documenting what a company has done, is doing, and will do. It would be nice to have a modeling tool that works with both XML and databases.

XML is the foundation for Web-based application. Remember that just because XML is an open standard, documents created with XML are not necessarily open. The XML used to create the document may not be compatible with other XML applications.

Loss of integrity and performance can occur due to translation from one model to XML to another model for the sake of interoperability.

XML Document Design—Deciphered, Delineated, and Demystified

One of the issues to be aware of when designing XML documents, especially Web pages, is that the information may be used on a variety of devices. Obviously, many applications are being used to support wireless surfing by cell phone and by PalmPilot. Anticipating all the possible permutations of devices that might use an XML document is not possible. In addition, XML provides a new adventure for the user, who can experience the Web page in a way uniquely customized to personal tastes and choices. For example, a totally blind man regains partial vision through the use of implants and video cameras. If he unplugs his video camera, he can plug his implant directly into the video port of a PC. His implant works just like a monitor. But how do you anticipate a device like that? Again, you don't. You simply create a well-designed XML document architecture, and the resulting omnimorphic design will adapt to most situations.

A dramatic advantage of XML is the granularity of the definitions and logic that it supports. A Web page can be constructed from many different XML documents, from sections, or even from individual elements by using multiple, distributed XML documents. Simply by synchronizing the documents, the designer can create a myriad of Web pages using minimal bandwidth. This provides some of the best features originally described in the client/server literature of separate tier maintenance.

The XML document life cycle involves a number of steps: creation of well-formed XML documents, defining them with DTDs or schemas, and retrieving segments of XML documents using XLink and XPointers.

When books, magazines, and trade journals discuss developing XML documents, many times they describe coding the schema or DTD, but important steps must occur before developing the DTD. One critical step in developing XML documents is the process of designing the XML document architecture. Document design is a well-defined activity. Using simple commonsense, a rational design can result in a clear, logical XML document architecture.

The most efficient use of XML for document exchange and data exchange revolves around the broad adoption of a uniform, industry-strength vocabulary of tags, meta-data, schema, and DTDs.

We want to interchange documents with others and we want to use each others' documents. This involves the contention of customized languages vs. universal tags and also the support for the full document life cycle.

The Simplicity of Modular Design

For example, consider Mr. Potato Head, a Hasbro toy, made famous by Pixar's movie, *Toy Story*. This modular toy has a standard potato-shaped head and a set of eyes, ears, noses, mouths, and hats that can be mixed in almost infinite combination. The well-defined facial structures provide a solid foundation for creativity. The rules, guidelines, and tags of XML provide a similar foundation for data and information transfer.

XML will help to organize the Web and improve the quest for knowledge in the tidal wave of information. XML standards and products support a method for unlocking content from legacy and proprietary data formats to facilitate free exchange among businesses, partners, customers, and vendors.

XML offers dramatic advantages for Web publishing and document management. Once a document has been marked up with XML, its contents can be easily combined with the content from other XML documents. When the user retrieves an XML document, he can view the contents in many different ways, simply by changing the style sheet used to define the presentation tier. For example, a presentation could be built from text, and a training system or a service manual might be built from the same technical data.

Everyday massive amounts of paperwork traverse corporate boundaries, both from the outside and on the inside. Much of that paperwork is electronic, but information still needs to be converted from one format to another. XML documents help reduce that conversion by providing a universal data transfer format. However, there is still the question of creating XML documents to optimize information flow and reduce the need for conversion.

One reason that XML poses such a quandary to executives is because the standards are being stretched in opposite directions by very strong forces, as depicted in Figure 3.2. No, these forces are not Microsoft and Oracle. For the most part, major corporations (such as IBM, Microsoft, Oracle, and Sun) are all pulling in the same direction towards some standards of uniformity.

FIGURE 3.2 Bidirectional forces pulling XML document schemas and DTDs for different purposes.

The misperceived instability in XML is caused by opposing forces to create a single, universal XML standard and forces to create separate industry-specific standards. One company calls customers by one name, and another uses a different name. Or the terms profit, revenue, and income have different meanings across the different industries. There needs to be a common ground where each company can describe its terms.

An XML document can represent any relationship that can fit a tree structure. There is a question of self-reference, but hypertext is a nonlinear proposition. New datatypes and attributes can be added as needed. Data are separate from the presentation and can be separate from the document. Data can be widely distributed, aggregated only for the specific document application. Distribution, layers, and nesting are limited only by the Web, the bandwidth, and the speed of the processor hardware. Data may be used by any application—it is a universal format. Standards remain in development.

The idea of data management is well understood, with corporate departments devoted to it and an entire industry supporting it. Data management deals with managing operational data to process transactions and historical data processed by decision support systems.

As data management evolves to include information and document management, business users will require facile access to the wide varieties of corporate data, information, and documents. They want to access, manipulate, and manage this information, but it has been difficult because of differing formats.

XML documents deal with data and information, just as data management systems deal with data and information. Although data management systems use repositories and query languages, XML documents may be searched using a variety of Web-based search engines or XML applications. The documents may be stored anywhere, even distributed throughout the Web, rather than in a controlled, centralized corporate repository.

XML documents do not focus on the activities of conventional knowledge management or even information management. However, XML documents support these activities as well as data warehousing, data mining, and decision support systems. As the collection of XML documents grows, it becomes like a data warehouse, which is easily searched for useful patterns. These patterns may be used for data mining, just like current HTML-based Web pages. With the appropriate applications, the documents can be used in decision support.

Data vs. Documents

An XML document is a new creature. It is like a Web page, it is like a text document, and it is like a database. In fact, it is a hybrid with the best features of all these things. Like a database, the data are organized and accessible—unlike an HTML-based Web page, where data are not organized in a format that can be easily manipulated by computers. For example, assume a Web page includes the statement that "My inventory includes 10 widgets at $7.00 each." If this statement is written in HTML, the information is all text with no computable meaning. However, if this is an XML document, then an XML application can determine the number of widgets, how much they cost, and how much total cash is tied up in widget inventory.

HTML only presents the information. With XML, the information is presented as simple text, or it can be processed for other purposes. As a simple analogy, consider data as grapes and the XML document as the grapevine. Data mining is like picking the grapes. A data repository might be like a bushel basket or a grocery shelf. A document repository is like a vineyard. There are many ways to get at the grapes or the data, as well as many ways to process the product after retrieval.

It is possible to cut a section of the vine that has the grapes. This is analogous to the document with its data. An alternative is to use some expert grape pickers, data mining tools, to select only the best fruit. Developers can design applications that separate the various types of (data) grapes, green vs. ripe vs. finest, (inventory and cost of inventory). And it is possible to calculate how much the grapes are worth, or to develop XML applications to perform similar manipulations with the data in the documents.

XML enables a company to repackage and reformat information so that it can be resold over and over again to different marketing segments. Data and information—in the form of intellectual capital—do not rot, rust, or spoil, so they can be resold over and over again, as proven billions of times by Microsoft. This concept of repurposing XML document data will be a killer app for the next generation of the Web.

Customer Example

Suppose a company wanted to collect all information for a customer from across the Web into one local report. In fact, let's go one better to a more realistic example. Suppose the company wanted to collect all information for one customer about specific preferences and demographics into one report: all documented preferences and trends, such as buying patterns, buying trends, interest in sales, and whatever else the customer provides as potentially useful information. Some companies already have partial information about their customers, but the information is clearly not complete and may not be up to date. And some information was entered manually, not automatically.

But the information is available. This sounds like an excellent opportunity for a startup service—to provide collective public information for informed customers by using XML. For the sake of privacy, customers would have to explicitly agree to allow this collected information. But most people will not mind if a major business (such as Ford, Burger King, or Wal-Mart) were to collect information that could not be shared and could only be used for targeted marketing purposes. Although the privacy laws may not be sufficiently strong in these cases, if the industries are prudent, then many customers—a profitable group—might be willing to provide the information. Once the information is collected, it can be placed into an XML document format and shared internally for various marketing purposes.

For example, when a young mother gives birth to a child, she will receive various offers related to diapers and newborns. If she provided information about her family status to Ford, Burger King, or Wal-Mart, these corporations might develop a marketing strategy to follow the growth of the child and of the family. With permission from the family, Ford might send offers for new, larger cars or for a child's seat. Wal-Mart might send coupons for baby food and clothing. In fact, it might create a long-term marketing campaign that notifies the mother about toddler's clothing, children's toys and clothing, and teenager needs. A long-term plan of this type would need to include an option for the mother to opt out. But if the sales and ads are for items that have to be purchased, why not consider Wal-Mart, or Ford, or Burger King?

XML supports this type of data exchange, and Financial XML standards called FinXML and OFX (Open Financial Exchange) already exist for exchanging personal finance information between financial business and products. Similar automotive, food, and retail XML standards would support the previous example.

If an organization keeps its customer data in the standard XML format, then data exchange and collection are a piece of cake. And if a company requests data for a specific customer, it only has to use the agreed upon tags in order to retrieve the data.

So a customer requesting a mortgage loan can use the same application information for other credit applications without rekeying the information. The real estate broker, the title company, and the county title office can all use that original loan information.

XML will have a profound effect on all data exchange industries—financial services, e-commerce, supply chain, etc. All businesses today are information corporations and depend on information exchange to further their revenues. Future success will hinge on interoperability and the ability to share information seamlessly. Leveraging information effectively requires the ability to understand its context and to resolve conflicts in meaning. XML provides the foundation to launch the information industry rocket.

Dual Functions

Two different types of XML documents are available. One type of document is used for presentation similar to a Web page but with a little more potential for self-description. The other type, used for data exchange, is more like a database with better labels and communication skills, rather than tables. These two types issued from the standard model of data processing, where data, processing, and presentation are separate. As the number of XML applications grew and developers grew more sophisticated, the two types of XML documents are understood to be different sides of the same coin. Because of the existing Web infrastructure, XML functionality has caught on quickly.

The result of using one type of document, or two, should not be a significant issue, because the reality of an XML document, as a collection of text, does not change in either case. The importance of the document does not come from what it looks like. The usefulness of an XML document comes from how it is packaged, parsed, and processed.

Hierarchical Structure

As illustrated in Figure 3.3, an XML document uses a hierarchical tree structure that is reminiscent of hierarchical database technology in the 1960s. The artifacts of the 60s, hierarchical databases and sequential processing, were left behind when relational databases were built. However, an XML document is not a step backward: it is a dramatic leap forward. Even though an XML document hierarchy will initially be processed sequentially, what happens next will be revolutionary. The revolution comes in the form of schemas, DTDs, data element tags, faster computers, and associative processing.

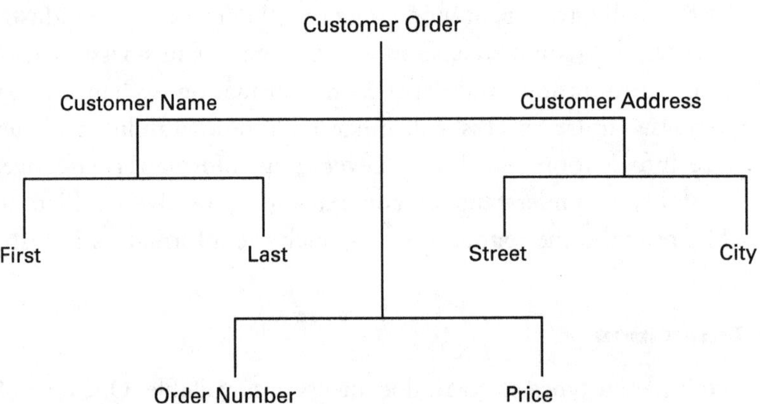

FIGURE 3.3 An XML document is a hierarchical tree structure. This organization is very easy to parse and manipulate.

The exciting contrast between a hierarchical database and an XML hierarchy comes from the DTD and tags. The database used the hierarchy in order to identify data elements. XML uses the hierarchy to identify associations during the initial processing by an XML application. Because the hierarchy introduces a neutral structure, different applications can use the XML document for completely different purposes, resulting in the foundation for omnimorphism. The initial processing of the XML document does not result in the poor response that was typical of hierarchical databases; computers in the 21st century are much faster than computers were in the 1960s. Moreover, the simple hierarchical organization of an XML document can provide a new capability called associative processing.

The specifications for associative processing are still emerging, but XML will support the ability to search a corporate document management system and aggregate the retrieved information into virtual documents that are related through the query. Extending this concept to the Internet and the Web, XML documents will be able to use multidirectional linking to build connections with associated Web sites. Associative processing, as a reality, is a new concept and the details are still being defined.

Made for Man and Machine

XML documents use data element tags to facilitate computer processing, but the tags also facilitate human processing. XML documents were defined to be marked-up text files that can be read and understood by both man and machine.

All three markup languages, XML, SGML, and HTML, employ a hierarchical relation of data element tags to designate where a section of text belongs in the tree structure of the XML document. From the tree structure perspective indicated in Figure 3.4, the XML tags identify branches, nodes, and leaves. These text-based tags are indicated by left-angle and right-angle brackets, "<" and ">" respectively. For example, *<price>45</price>*, indicates a price of 45.

Although the concept of machine- or man-readable formats is not new, the ability to view data elements by man or any application is new. People can read and understand a text document, like a manual or a Web page. However, the binary data used for data interchange formats and database update commands could only be read by specialized programs. With XML, both man and machine can read data formats.

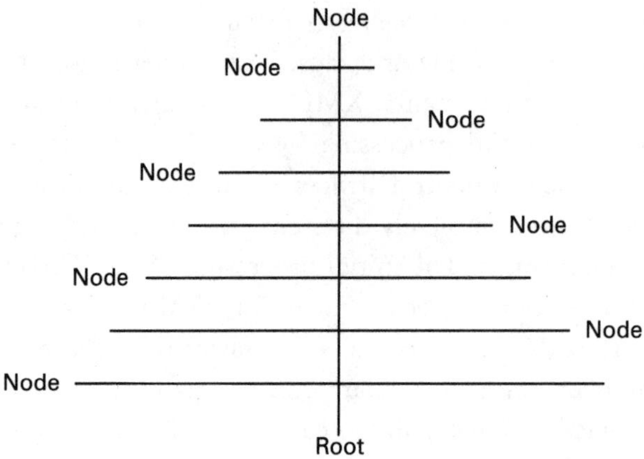

FIGURE 3.4 An XML document is a tree of data element nodes.

Users can use their browsers to display XML data structures and commands. Initially, they may even modify them with an editor. However, developers will design intelligent interfaces to protect users from themselves and allow them to modify XML data safely.

XML will drive new methods of computing because it separates the data from the application. The XML document is emerging as a universal data exchange format, and browsers are becoming universal interfaces for a wide variety of applications. The boundaries between data, databases, and documents grow less important as XML grows more pervasive.

The text in an XML document is built of character strings that represent the markup tags and data content. The markup tags describe the document's logical structure. For the most part, XML documents and HTML-based Web pages look similar because the data element tags are similar.

Security

There is no single correct answer for security with XML. A full range of security capabilities is desired from the document level all the way down to the detailed tag level. An XML document may contain both secure and unsecured information. Having the server determine which components are restricted and which are open may not be the most efficient form of security. Although not part of the XML specification, the security concern is an active effort among the development community.

Although XML has no specific security features per se, XML can be used with other systems to secure data. For example, according to the Aberdeen Group, XML can be combined with LDAP (Lightweight Directory Access Protocol) and PKI (Public Key Infrastructure) to provide data and document access control. LDAP is a method for providing access to a directory of all corporate information. PKI is a security system using encryption and digital certificates that maintain both information integrity and information transmission security to the sender and the receiver.

One way to provide security capabilities to XML is to have the LDAP catalog cross-reference XML documents and tags, and then provide a deeper level of directory intelligence down to the tag level if desired. Security access information can be tagged and LDAP can record that parameter also. LDAP can use PKI verification to automatically ensure access control.

How Does XML Provide More Meaningful Markup?

Most managers have never thought deeply about the kinds of information contained on their Web site or perhaps even their document repositories, much less about the relationships that occur between these kinds of data. Nevertheless, in order to devise meaningful element names, a developer needs to analyze the best way to group together, label, and classify the different kinds of corporate data.

The next step is to determine which of those corporate data classifications will be defined independently and which are more generic for the industry, in which case simply building upon the experience of others might be more efficient.

For example, BEA Systems in San Jose, California, offers the E-Collaborate transformation engine, which maps between different XML schemas.

As discussed in Chapter 2, a schema is the method of building the meta-data that defines and describes the content, meaning, and structure of XML document's data elements. Two extremes exist with regards to XML meta-data standards for document type descriptions, whether DTDs or schemas. On one hand, there is the concern that XML will splinter into many, different, incompatible corporate standards. On the other hand, there is a wish to have a single, universal standard that covers all document examples, serving as a panacea that cures all document ills for all people.

In fact, the best solution is a negotiation of the best of both worlds. IBM, OASIS, and the United Nations are separately working on tpaML and ebXML as methods to provide a common foundation of standard XML tags and definitions across all users worldwide. These vocabularies are not designed to cover all requirements. They were designed to provide a set of common, overlapping tags that are used across most applications and business needs. Creating a single common format for all XML data transfer and exchanges is not feasible. However, a common foundation on which to build customized DTDs, schemas, and XML documents should fulfill the needs of the individual industries and businesses and also serve as a guide for achieving greater communications and information exchange interoperability among all users. And that is what the ultimate goal is. Not a set of rigid standards, but an omnimorphic vehicle for wider, seamless communications.

Content

The idea of document management (archiving, maintaining, protecting) will soon be automated by XML and will evolve into the notion of content management, which focuses on reuse and repurposing information. XML provides the backbone needed to add value to documents and to the information that they contain. The value added is the ability to link and manipulate information and knowledge, wherever it may exist, in the same way that you can currently manipulate data using a spreadsheet or a database.

To make this happen, information and content have to reside in a single, common format so that they can be used by a variety of applications. The format must be standardized so that information can be used with legacy, current, or future data.

At the heart of this capability is XML, which pumps new energy into the lifeblood of business—its information—by giving it meaning. By identifying the meaning of data and information, XML tags enable this information to flow across business arteries from one application to another with no slowdowns or impediments due to translation from one format to another. The fast flow of information can quickly turn from a trickle into a tidal wave, so it is important to have useful content with the appropriate level of detail for the task at hand. To address that concern, XML permits the concept of content tuning, customizing the information for the specific user, as well as for the method of access, such as desktop or wireless.

XML Structure and Grammar

Like any other language, XML has a structure and a grammar that are composed of a syntax, a vocabulary, and semantics. The syntax is clearly defined by the XML specification, which provides the rules for creating an omnimorphic framework. Although these rules of syntax are quite rigid, their crispness and clarity support a very malleable XML structure within a set of simple guidelines.

The vocabulary is defined by the DTD, schema, and meta-data. Each XML document may conform to a separate vocabulary, or a class of XML documents may all follow a single standard vocabulary. Each XML language, such as XHTML and WML, is made up of its own individual vocabulary. Each industry is also customizing its own specialized XML vocabulary. Just for B2B e-commerce, more than one thousand different XML vocabularies may be needed. With some corporations also defining their own unique vocabularies, clearly the resilience of XML can lead to more XML languages than existing natural languages.

However, just like the natural languages of the world, most of the XML vocabularies overlap, with many similarities. For example, only a few ways exist to define customer information, inventory data, or financial facts. As discussed previously, efforts are underway to collect the common subset of vocabularies into an agreed-upon standard across multiple industries and corporations. A common standard will help smooth communications and data exchange.

The semantics are defined by the data element tags and how they create the context and meaning in the XML document. Just like the traceability matrix defined in a business-based Information Technology (IT) architecture, the semantics of an XML document link a business function to a data element tag. The tag is more than just an identifier; it also provides perspective and context, showing the relationships among the data within an XML document. For example, consider the word, *balance.* To a creditor, *balance* relates to accounts receivable. To a financial analyst, *balance* may refer to the record of profit and loss. To a chemist, a *balance* relates to weights and measures. The combination of XML tags and the document tree structure form the semantic relationships that define the most pertinent context.

Typically, the business functions that are defined to support a corporate strategy follow some general trends for consistency within a corporation.

The data element tags that describe these business functions follow the same consistency trends. A common semantics and understanding emerges from the consistent mapping of function to tag. When creating a DTD or schema to define this mapping, the XML document designer is, in effect, creating a traceability matrix. This mapping results in an XML document architecture that defines uniform semantic meanings for the data element tags. Uniformity in XML semantics encourages a common pattern of XML usage and results in better transfer of data and information at both corporate and industry levels.

One of the important issues worth reemphasizing is that even when two companies agree on a DTD or schema, differences can still exist in the semantics. For example, when Ford uses tags such as <products> and <services>, these will have different meanings from when Wal-Mart uses them. In addition, the options and attributes under <customer> and <services> have very different semantics when comparing Ford and Wal-Mart. So, even though the vocabularies may be the same across companies or industries, the meanings may have subtle differences to the corporate business or culture. When drawing up a carefully crafted XML document architecture, a designer will take these variances into account to disambiguate conflicts in meaning and to normalize tags when possible.

When the differences between two DTDs or schemas are too great to combine them, the designer may use another approach to unify the exchange of information. The XML Stylesheet Language for Transformations (XSLT) was specified to help the transfer of XML data and documents among different users. Developers can use XSLT to transform an XML document that has one DTD or schema into a new document that uses a second, predefined DTD or schema. The concept is similar to the fairly straightforward translation from one language or dictionary to another. For example, imagine that Ford and Wal-Mart want to exchange XML documents. The receiving company programs an intermediate XSLT transformation style sheet that translates one set of tags to the corresponding set of tags. This style sheet is another XML document that serves as a look-up table, dictionary, or translator between two predefined DTDs or schemas. XSLT can even convert between DTDs and schemas.

However, XSLT is limited to simple transformations. For example, a transformation from Wal-Mart schemas to Target schemas may be straightforward. However, a transformation from Wal-Mart schemas to Eli Lilly schemas may not be feasible because of the diversity of the vocabularies. The business processes may be similar enough to convert, but other translation may require a more hands-on touch until more intelligent, automated tools are developed. Moreover, because schemas follow the XML syntax and DTDs follow the legacy SGML syntax, converting between two schemas is much easier than converting from or to a DTD.

These translation limitations are well understood, and new tools and methods are under development to address them. As mentioned earlier, the Apache Cocoon and the IBM transcoder are a first attempt. As the technology matures, which it does very rapidly in Internet time, these issues will be addressed, resolved, and codified.

However, the current methods using XSLT are completely adequate to allow the early majority of users to apply XML documents to core business functions, such as data exchange and B2B procurement activities. Some companies have hesitated in their experimentation with XML because they are waiting for a final standard to be defined. That final standard was released in the late 1990s, and its evolution has involved only minor tweaks and refinements that have not hindered IBM, Microsoft, or Oracle from embracing the language and building a corporate strategy to exploit it. Now is the time to explore the use of XML and to create XML documents in order to avoid losing a competitive position.

The explosion of B2B activities has resulted in a growing number of XML meta-data repositories. Since many of the schemas and DTDs in these repositories can be transformed using XSLT, a new XML specification will *not* obviate all the old XML work. XML is forward compatible to new and improved standards. So if a company, such as Microsoft, creates early XML tools and XML documents that do not conform to a new standard, then a simple XSLT style sheet can be used to update the changes. Incompatibility and technological dead ends will be minimized.

XML Document Size

One important trade-off with XML is file size. The omnimorphic capability and the uniformity come at a price. An XML file is large. An XML document is larger than most corresponding files because of all of the text tags. First, it is larger than a text file because it includes many tags. Second, it is much larger than the corresponding binary file because it contains Unicode text.

When efficient binary files are converted to XML, they grow tremendously. An XML document may be ten times larger than the corresponding binary file. Compression can partially counteract this size because the redundant text tags tend to compress very efficiently. However, for the sake of significantly improved interoperability, businesses and vendors will have to consider the trade-offs of converting all or part of their systems to XML.

In the 21st century document size should be less of a problem than it was in the 1960s. Compression ratios are very good for XML documents, but, in today's environment and with the immaturity of the tools, short-term, internal document transfer may be more efficient in existing formats. There is a significant caveat. Be very clear that non-XML documents are truly short-term and truly internal. Misconceptions about the concept of short term led to the Y2K problem.

In addition, gigabit (10^9 or 2^{30}) transfer rates are common. Terabit (10^{12} or 2^{40}) storage capacity is a standard corporate requirement, with some corporations already eyeing terabit transfer rates and petabit (10^{15} or 2^{50}) storage capacities. Even home Internet connections using cable modems and DSL can achieve megabit (10^6 or 2^{20}) transfer rates.

So the problem of manipulating and e-mailing multi-megabit XML documents across the 'Net and the Web will not be a major problem over the next few years. But initially, as with any emerging technology, the trade-offs must be considered.

According to Chris Lovett, who writes for Microsoft, a rough rule of thumb of the computer memory requirements for processing an XML document is on the order of four times the disk storage needed for the XML document. This means that a 100 MB XML document file stored on disk will require 400 MB of RAM to process and manipulate the XML data using an application. These estimates depend on the number of tags used in the document and whether or not the document is in a Unicode format. Lovett's formula for estimating XML document size is given by

```
WS = 32 * (N+T) + 12*T + 50*U + 2*W
```

where **WS** is the working set in bytes;

N is the number of element and attribute nodes in the XML tree structure;

T is the number of text nodes;

U is the number of unique elements and attribute names;

and W is the number of Unicode characters used in the text.

Note: Single-byte ANSI characters translate into double-byte Unicode characters.

Lovett describes his formula in detail, with examples, in his article, *Inside MSXML Performance*, which can be found at (http://msdn.microsoft.com/xml/articles/xml02212000.asp).

Saving Some Work

Whenever possible, a corporate document developer should use an existing DTD or schema. Using a standard schema or DTD makes data interchange easier and may make it possible to use data-aware tools developed by others. If an industry standard exists, consider referencing that DTD with an external parameter entity or a namespace. Two common repositories for industry-standard DTDs reside at the Organization for the Advancement of Structured Information Standards (OASIS) at www.XML.org and CommerceOne's XML Exchange at www.xmlx.com.

XML Tools

Many companies have documents written in different formats. Historically, it has been easier to transfer and translate raw text to different formats and across platforms. One vendor advantage and user disadvantage was the switching cost that related to the transfer and translation. For example, some corporations simply did not want to deal with the trouble of switching between Macintoshes and PCs, or WordPerfect and MS Word. This avoidance helped Microsoft capture the PC software market. However, XML opens information transfer, leading to reduced switching costs. Aware of this, Microsoft has put an XML strategy in place to guarantee customers that they will be able to exchange information with other customers, corporations, and entities.

One thing to consider about an XML parser when creating a document concerns validating the document. An incomplete XML document may be neither well formed nor valid. Although the developer may be aware of this fact about works in-progress, some XML tools may not make this distinction. So, during the development process, the author of the XML document must be aware that some tools and parsers will simply fail to work adequately with an incomplete XML document. The stubbornness on the part of the tool may result in frustration on the part of the developer. This is a function to keep in mind during tool selection.

XML Trees

by S.H. Simon

[With a nod to Joyce Kilmer]

I think that I shall only see
That XML is like a tree.

A tree that's built from documents
To show the data elements;

A tree whose structured elements
Show logic from the concept, thence;

A tree that represents what's meant,
To disambiguate intent;

Upon the schema, it is shown;
The meaning that each tag will own.

Data are made by fools like me,
But XML can make a tree.

CHAPTER 4

XML Style Sheets (XSLs) and Transformations (XSLTs)

Introduction

XML documents contain data and text with little regard for the ultimate display, presentation, or device. In this way, XML serves to separate data from presentation, fulfilling the standard client/server model of computer processing. To support the other part of this equation, XML also provides methods for extensible presentation and for processing. These methods are special XML documents and are part of the XML style sheets specifications for XSL (eXtensible Stylesheet Language) and XSLT (XML Stylesheet Language—Transformations).

XSL includes a formatting capability and a transformation capability (XSLT). Both capabilities are XML applications and they are represented as XML documents. The two different capabilities are represented separately as two different specifications, XSL and XSLT. The formatting capability functions like a style sheet language to process a document for presentation.

The transformation capability provides elements that define rules for transforming an XML document into another format, such as HTML, WML, TeX, or even another XML document. The transformed XML document may use the tags and schema from the original document, or it may use a completely different set of tags. XSLT can transfer data between two XML documents, between applications, or between computer systems. Its ability to move data from one XML document to another is a critical component of e-commerce, XML-based Electronic Data Interchange (EDI), schema transformations, and other conversions between different XML representations.

Formatting Capability

XSL is similar to the Cascading Style Sheet (CSS) in HTML. However, just like the extensibility and flexibility of XML over HTML, XSL provides greater fine-tuning and flexibility over document scripting and display than CSS does. And just as XML evolved from SGML, XSL is related to DSSSL (Document Style Semantics and Specification Language), which is the powerful formatting and scripting language for SGML documents.

A style sheet can be used to fine tune text placement and overall appearance of a Web page. Just as CSS serves as the predominant style sheet language for HTML-based Web pages, XSL defines the programming, presentation, and appearance for XML documents. In general, style sheets furnish a method for designing Web pages that can conform to a variety of different displays and devices. However, CSS can only be used for presentation, while XSL can also be used for *conditional processing*.

For example, HTML is a presentation language itself. Therefore, it does not absolutely require a CSS. The "data" and the display are one and the same. However, CSS gives the developer much more control over the appearance of the resulting Web page. In contrast, XML is a data description language, with no predefined formatting tags for presentation. The data, the processing, and the presentation are all separate. Therefore, to display the XML data, a developer has to create a corresponding XSL document, which will present the XML document in the desired way.

XSL functions at both the detailed and the coarse levels as it provides presentation instructions for both XML elements and documents. Just as with a programming language, developers can use XSL to script instructions that can manipulate the XML document at the element level to carry out actions and make decisions based on conditional statements.

XSL can be used to build an XML document's tree structure, which characterizes the relationships among the element nodes. For example, think of an XML document as the main root of a tree. Document components branch off from the root. Element nodes form the branches of the tree, and each branch may have many twigs and leaves that stem from the branch.

XSL uses the tree structure to define the relationships among the elements within the XML document. The relationships of one element to another will drive the style sheet actions that are performed.

In general, XSL rules are elements, or, more precisely, meta-elements, that contain information about formatting other elements. XSL rules and condition statements match predetermined patterns to decide which style sheet rules to apply to which element nodes within the source XML document. A developer can effectively provide access control by creating a separate style sheet for a variety of views of the XML document. For example, one style sheet can show a summary of the document for executive presentations, and another style sheet can show successive levels of detail. Or in the case of financials, one style sheet could present details to the executive committee yet provide only high level views to other readers.

A developer can design a set of XML tags and then write a style sheet that will interpret the tags similar to the way that a browser interprets conventional HTML. Condition statements and decision trees in XSL depend on patterns found in the XML document; these patterns determine which presentation or processing instructions to apply. In many ways, XSL is just like any other programming language with conditions and actions. The difference is that XSL has much of the power of Java for high level functions, yet it is less complex than Java Script. This means that most HTML coders can learn to write XSL in a few weeks by simply copying some existing XSL examples from the Web—in the same way that they learned HTML.

In contrast to most conventional programming languages, XSL is a declarative programming language. Typically, a declarative language is used to build statements that describe the desired end result, rather than defining the details and steps required to achieve this result. Using a declarative programming language can be easier because the developer is not concerned with the process details. The details and the steps are left up to the processor, application, or browser.

Repurposing XML Documents

XML does not describe the appearance or layout of a document. The original designers did this on purpose. By separating the structure of a document and its appearance, the designer can quickly and easily modify the presentation of the document or the device used to display the document (for example, monitor, voice, Braille, handheld, or wireless telephone) without a significant amount of reprogramming. The document can easily be formatted in different ways for different audiences and for different platforms, as indicated in Figure 4.1. Also, readers of the document may be able to reformat the presentation in real time using customized styles as desired.

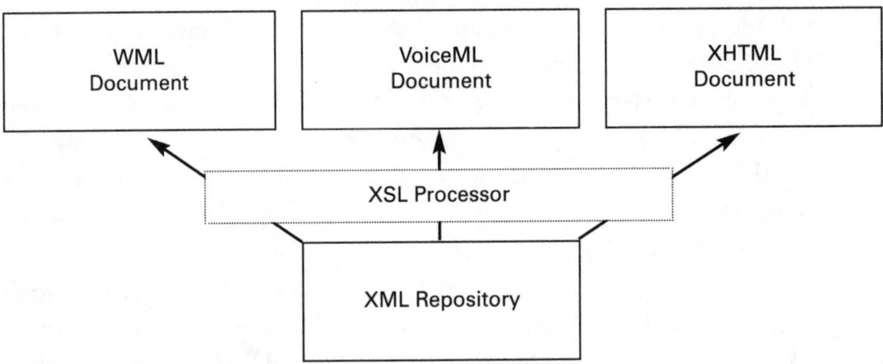

FIGURE 4.1 XSL can repurpose an XML document for presentation over wireless devices, voice, XHTML, etc.

The different style sheets that process XML documents may have different purposes. The term *style sheet* is very broad. It may have nothing to do with the presentation style. It may have to do with the math calculated on a price data element. Any script that can be referenced from a dynamic HTML page can also be referenced from an XSL style sheet to process an XML document. XSL provides the mechanism for keeping these three things separate: the data, the markup tags that provide the meta-data information, and the XSL-scripted processing procedures. This separation follows the standard computing paradigm of separating data, processing, and presentation into three conceptual layers, so that items in any layer can be modified without affecting the other two layers, similar to the way a database is constructed.

With XML, this computing paradigm is realized. The XML document designer can use markup tags any way desired and can create more when needed. This freedom is allowed because XML tags do not come with predefined meanings as HTML tags do. The developer can also change the data as needed. Then the XSL style sheets can be separately created to control processing or presentation. An XSL style sheet is an XML document that tells an XML application, such as a parser or browser, how to process or translate the logical structure of the source XML document into a new format or a new presentation structure. XSL can also specify what an element is, how it should be presented, and what the semantics of the source document are.

What all of this means is that XSL can use the data from an XML document to create a variety of outputs. Where financial data in an XML document might have been created for an annual report, an XSL style sheet might repurpose the data for a balance sheet, for a stock performance report, or for a portfolio comparison, when combined with the financial from other companies. An XML document may be used for many different purposes than it was originally intended and XSL can enable this repurposing.

XSLT

XSLT has a complete expression programming language with a very powerful pattern matching syntax. XSLT is not a pure programming language, but it can access other languages to import other applications and increase capabilities. XSLT provides the capability for selecting one or more elements, specifying the conditions for modifying these elements, and generating new elements for the result tree.

Rather than doing all data processing on the server, a developer or user can use XSL and XSLT to off-load processing to the local client. Style sheets facilitate the capability of modifying an XML document offline, then sending the processed document back to the server. XSLT provides the power of an entire programming language in a comparatively easy-to-use package. XSL is infinitely more flexible than HTML.

XSLT excels at mapping one XML-based representation onto another. The XSLT specification defines an XML-based language for expressing transformation rules that the developer can use for transforming one class of XML documents and vocabularies to another or one schema definition to another. XSLT is similar to a traditional, but simplified programming language. So, the developer can also use XSLT documents as a general-purpose programming language for manipulating XML documents by applying some simple processing instructions.

As described before, different industries will use a different vocabulary of schemas and DTDs for their XML documents. When corporations want to exchange XML documents, they need a common schema. It is difficult to correlate schemas unless a person manually reads and understands both schemas to determine the relationships among the data element types and attributes. After those relationships are determined, recorded, and tabulated, mostly by hand, XSLT provides the transformation instructions for converting XML schemas and documents from one definition to another.

Example: Building XSLT Conversions

For example, when Ford and Wal-Mart share their XML documents, a developer from Ford will have to sit down with a developer from Wal-Mart to compare their respective schemas and data element types, as well as the meanings of these data element types. They can perform these comparisons by e-mail, telephone, and telecommunications, rather than having to take the time to meet face to face.

After they build a table that maps the Ford vocabularies, schemas, and elements to the Wal-Mart vocabularies, schemas, and elements, the developers can codify the table into an XSLT document. Then when XML documents are exchanged, the XSLT document will convert them from one corporate format to the other. If one corporation modifies its underlying schemas, these changes can be easily incorporating into the XSLT document with minimal effort. Once the original manual collaboration is completed, the resulting XSLT document should serve as a continuing and dynamic Rosetta Stone between the two companies.

Why Not Use Java

Possibly a transformation table could be built in a traditional programming language such as Java, C++, Perl, or LISP. These languages could easily handle the pattern matching and the translations from one schema to another and from one XML document to another. However, using one of these languages requires a higher level of programming skills. Also, modifying the resulting program to make additions and changes would require the same level of programming skills. In addition, these programming languages require a server or a special environment to execute their code. Typically, the source code can only be read and understood by an experienced programmer.

But XSLT simplifies all of these tasks to free up the programmer to concentrate on tasks that are more difficult or challenging than the simple table transformations that are typical of XML document translations. XSLT requires logical thinking, but not detailed programming expertise. It is an XML document, so it does not require a special programming environment. All that is needed is a simple text editor to create the XSLT documents and an XML-enabled browser to run them.

Example: Using XSLT Conversions

Running an XSLT document is fairly straightforward, but understanding the process requires a little rehashing of the basics of XML documents. An XML document is a text file that contains tags and data. Typically, no formatting or presentation instructions exist within the XML document itself; however, the XML document may refer to an external file, such as an XSL or XSLT file, for the formatting commands. For example, a Ford XML document about car data might be presented as directions to the salesman, as a price comparison to the show floor manager, as marketing collateral for the general public, or as a focus video commercial for an interested customer. Each of these applications uses the same XML document, but the individual presentations use separate XSL documents for the display. In addition, all the presentations are run through a standard XML-enabled browser as the interface. In a thumbnail, this is the basic theory of operation of an XML document.

XSLT follows the same general format. Ford sends the XML document to Wal-Mart. Someone in the Information Technology (IT) department uses a browser and the XSLT document to convert the Ford document to a Wal-Mart format. The source Ford document is placed into an archive, and the target Wal-Mart document is distributed to the various departments. If the Ford XSL documents used for the presentations accompany the XML document, then the XSLT document might also convert them into Wal-Mart formats. This would enable Wal-Mart associates to review the presentations, which would also be compatible with other Wal-Mart XML documents.

XSLT Foundations

As described in the previous paragraphs, XSLT is an XML-based style sheet and scripting language that describes transformations from XML documents into other text-based formats. These formats are not exclusively XML. For example, they can also be HTML, WML, XSL, XSLT, TeX, or

PDF. XSLT depends on the use of three text documents: source, XSLT, and target. The source document is the initial well-formed XML document, which requires transformation. The basic reason for the transformation is to convert from one vocabulary to another. The XSLT document is a text document in an XML format that uses the style sheet transformation vocabulary of rules to convert from the source document vocabulary to the target document vocabulary. The target document vocabulary does not have to be based on an XML schema. It could also be a completely different format, such as a TeX file or a PDF file. The only requirement is that the target document is a text file. The XSLT generates the target document by applying the transformation rules to the source XML document.

The target document can be any of a variety of text formats. Although XML, TeX, PDF, and Postscript are common formats, there are many other types of text formats, such as WML for wireless, VoiceML for voice, and even more formats for graphics and for Braille. In addition, text is not limited to English or even to the Latin alphabet. A discussion of alternate character and symbol transformations using Unicode follows.

Conditionals

An XSLT document is composed of XSLT templates. A *template* is a conditional statement made of a pattern to match and a set of actions to follow, depending on the pattern match. The set of commands and actions available in XSLT is as rich as those in most other programming languages. The most common action is to write a text string into the target document. The text string can be a direct copy of text or tags from the source document, it can be a copy from text in the XSLT document, or it can be some modification of these elements based on XSLT actions.

The conditional statements used in XSLT, such as *xsl:if* and *xsl:when*, are similar to those found in Java and in C++. Although these statements have sufficient flexibility to generate most of the required test situations, the underlying functionality remains the same. XSLT runs a specific test, pattern, or condition. If the terms of the test are met, then the subsequent action is carried out. The actions are also sufficiently flexible to generate most of the required results needed to build the target text document, either one tag at a time, one line at a time, or even the entire target document.

Pattern Matching

XSLT processing is based on pattern matching. Because pattern matching is at the core of this language, XSLT has a complex hierarchy of how templates and patterns are matched. For example, imagine that an XSLT document is searching through the telephone book and looking for names. It might contain a rule that looks for names that begin with the letter *J*. It might also have a rule that looks for names that start with *John*. These two rules may result in a double result, because both will match the word *John*. In XSLT, template rules are independent of each other, so the duplicated match would result in an incorrect target document. To prevent these conflicts, the XSLT pattern matching hierarchy permits only the most important rule with the highest priority to achieve the match. So in case of a tie, the most important rule is invoked. In case of equal importance, the first rule wins. In this example, the *J* rule always wins over the *John* rule because it is first. Therefore, a careful developer would give the *John* rule a higher priority than the *J* rule, or make it come first.

Style Sheets

XSLT template rules are used for simple pattern matching. For more complex patterns, template rules can be collected into style sheets. The *xsl:stylesheet* format is used to define the collection of template rules for pattern matching. The output from a style sheet match can range from a simple action to a partial document tree to a full document. The output can also be to multiple documents. For example, XSLT might use a source XML document to generate an HTML document, a WML document, and a VoiceML document. The simultaneous creation of multiple target documents that use the same content, but in different predefined formats, saves time and maximizes one of the foundations of XML—the ability to reuse and repurpose XML document data.

Iterations

As with any other programming language, XSLT has a mechanism for repeating actions. These looping instructions are similar in syntax to those found in C++, Java, Perl, and LISP. The developer can use the looping instructions to traverse the XML tree structure, locate element nodes, and perform the required transformation actions.

XSLT loops permit linear iteration, nonlinear iteration, and recursion. Thus, looping can be programmed to be efficient and to work with parallel processing if the capability becomes available. Also, a very complex XSLT document might be designed to run over multiple Web sites simultaneously, enabling the Web as a parallel processor. Although this capability was not the intent of the designers, parallel processing using XSLT via the Web may open opportunities for language transformations that were previously too computer intensive to be practicable.

Parameters and Variables

The XSLT specification includes the use of parameters and variables, named respectively *xsl:param* and *xsl:variable*. The terms are used to define general variables or specific parameters for use in the XSLT document or to be passed on to the target document or style sheet. The main difference between *xsl:param* and *xsl:variable* is that parameters can have their initial values changed at run time. Also, *xsl:param* occurs only at the beginning of a template, while *xsl:variable* can occur throughout the document. Both instructions are global, as opposed to lexical, in scope.

Once the value of a parameter or variable has been defined in XSLT, it cannot be changed. In this way, XSLT differs from Java, C++, and Perl. This difference is due to the way that XSLT functions. The execution of the XSLT processing model was designed as simply as possible to support the independence of template rules, allowing for enhanced and distributed processing capabilities. If a template changed the value of a parameter or a variable, then subsequent templates would be affected. The results of the subsequent template rules would depend on the first template, and this would complicate the XSLT processing model, requiring dramatically more overhead.

Although XSLT can be used for other purposes, the main goal of XSLT is to transform a source XML document into a target text document using the simplest path.

Specific Output Formats

The XSLT specification includes four commands that produce specific outputs. These commands are *xsl:comment*, *xsl:element*, *xsl:attribute*, and *xsl:processing* instruction. From a high-level perspective, these commands simplify the developer's life. To include comments or instructions in the target document, a developer would have to write a long, complex string in order to prevent the XSLT document from processing the string. The developer may want to use the results of a namespace or XPath (which defines the pathname to the specific locations or elements) in the target document. Rather than constructing these four items in a convoluted manner designed to circumvent the XSLT processor, the developer can apply these commands to produce specific results. These four commands may not be used with high frequency, but when they are used, they will greatly simplify the programming and the readability of the XSLT document.

In addition, the target document of a transformation is not necessarily another XML document. The default output is an XML document, but that can easily be changed to an HTML format or to a text document. HTML format is the familiar Web page. But a text output format has an under estimated value with many broad implications.

As long as the source document follows the rules of being well formed, XSLT can create any document format that uses a text format. Of course, this includes XML and HTML, but those formats are already defined. But XSLT can also generate other markup language formats, such as WML and VoiceML, as well as any B2B e-commerce format. Also, the possibilities do not stop with markup languages. As mentioned before, XSLT can transform XML documents into TeX, PDF, and Postscript formats. In addition, an XSLT document can be developed to convert an XML document into Rich Text Format (RTF), which is a standard used by Microsoft Word. Finally, XSLT may be used as an intermediary to transform among any of these text formats. Just as XML will become the universal data transfer format, XSLT may approach the concept of a universal transformation format.

Transforming the Tower of Babel

XSLT transforms an XML document into another text format. This text format does not need to be an XML document, and it also does not even need to be in the same language or character set. One very important clarification is that XSLT will not translate the contents of a document; it will only translate the tags or the format of the information. However, format translation is still very useful. For example, XSLT can translate the vocabulary, schema, and tags for the format of one company, such as Ford, to that of another company, such as Wal-Mart. This transformation could also occur among countries rather than companies.

Ford has subsidiaries in the United Kingdom. Rather than enforcing U.S.-centric tagging conventions, an XSLT document could transform from U.S. terms to U.K. terms. For example, in the United States, customers are interested in trunk capacity. In the United Kingdom, that transforms into boot capacity. XSLT can easily transform <trunk> into <boot>. There are a number of simple translations of that type. In addition, XSLT can convert measurements and capacities from English to metric.

For subsidiaries in France or other non-English speaking countries, Ford can produce an XSLT to translate the tags to the language of choice. Although Ford could build a monolithic XSLT document for all Ford dealers, having one document for each language is more prudent and efficient. The XSLT to convert numbers from English to metric can be reused by simply importing it using a namespace.

One issue to consider about non-English language is the use of accent marks and special characters in the tags. This simple matter is addressed by using Unicode. XSLT has no trouble transforming an English tag into a non-English Unicode equivalent. To map one representation to another simply requires a table lookup. From this point, the potential for XSLT grows more interesting and very exciting.

If Ford can use XSLT to translate XML document vocabularies to non-English, can it develop an XSLT document to translate to a new alphabet, such as Greek, Russian, Hebrew, or Arabic? Sure! Again, we have the caveat that XSLT is transforming one XML tag and vocabulary to a corresponding XML tag and vocabulary. A real translation of meaning is not occurring. It is simply a mindless table lookup.

In addition to transforming alphabetic tags, XSLT can exploit Unicode to transform between alphabetic tags and symbolic (ideograph), character-based tags. So if Ford wants to transform its XML documents into Chinese, then it can build an XSLT document to make the appropriate transforms. Again, these transforms are dictionary lookups, not language translations.

However, we can stick our toe into the translation ocean. We can take a sip of a few words, but XSLT will drown if it is used to translate free text. In the specific case of cars, the text information is fairly well bounded with terms such as color, speed, and distance. These simple terms and their translations can be stored as a table or a dictionary in an XSLT document, and then transformed. The glorious marketing analogies that magnify car ownership with terms like *joie de vivre* or *liefs lieben* are much more difficult to transform using XSLT.

Conclusion

XML style sheets, in the form of XSL and XSLT, enhance XML's ability to separate data from presentation. XSL provides a flexible and extensible way to allow the developer to control the display format of an XML document. By creating a range of style sheets, the developer provides the user with a choice of different displays. Different style sheets allow the user to view the data according to individual tastes. By supporting the creation of different style sheets, XSL enables the reuse of XML documents.

XSLT provides a flexible and extensible way to allow developers to change the data format of the XML document. By using the content in the source XML document, the developer can transform the information into other documents. The transformation may be as simple as a change of schema and tags or as complex as a change of underlying natural language. The transformation can even result in a target document in a new format, such as HTML or TeX, or in a new markup language, such as WML, VoiceML, or Braille devices.

XSL and XSLT cannot yet transform meaning and intention. People are still required for that type of translation. XML style sheets and transformations, however, provide a good start. And someone may yet build an XML-based translation markup language. Many of the tools are already here.

Although XML DTDs and schemas provide the methods for representing data type definitions, their extensibility could be a bottleneck to communications as each company tends to roll its own schemas. Therefore, without a single, unifying DTD or schema, people are still needed as boundary spanners between organizations, industries, corporations, and even departments to establish tables to map among different vocabularies. But once the map is built and the communications links are forged, XSLT is an XML-centric method to strengthen the chain of interoperability.

CHAPTER 5

XML Linking Language (XLink)

Introduction

The terrific expansion of the World Wide Web is due to the hyperlinking capability of HTML beyond other functions, even its simplicity. The concepts of hyperlinking and hypertext have been written about and applied for decades. Millions of Web pages are linked worldwide using HTML, and developers are always looking for more capability. The World Wide Web Consortium (W3C) XML committee leveraged the infrastructure of the Web and extracted linking features from SGML to extend to XML the power and the popularity of hyperlinking.

The goal of the W3C XML committee was to use XML to bring the flexibility of SGML to the Web and to include a new kind of linking. Developers use linking to connect documents, pages, and sites so that users can gain access to information distributed throughout the Internet, the Web, and the corporate intranet.

The XML committee designed XML to fulfill some of the limitations of SGML for use on the Web. XML applications are smaller than SGML, so they use less bandwidth, and XML documents transfer faster. Also, each SGML application requires separate linking features to be defined for each instance.

In addition to the limitations of SGML, the XML committee wanted to overcome the limitations of HTML links. HTML links are the best thing to hit the Internet. They are clean, simple, and easy to navigate, and that is where they are also limited. HTML links have three basic drawbacks: location, states, and relations. It almost sounds like a real estate ad.

The standard URL takes the user from one Web page to another—not from paragraph to paragraph, not from title to contents, and not from table of contents to pages. If the developer carefully inserts anchors within the Web page, then the user can make these navigations, but these anchors have to be explicitly designed into the Web page before use. In addition, the user cannot go just anywhere within a Web page. The user can only go to a specific anchor, not to the next paragraph and not to three or four different anchors without a few extra clicks.

The HTML Web page is a stateless system. A browser does not remember the state of the Web pages or the history of navigation. The existing record of previous Web sites is a static list with no interactive capability; therefore, the Web page visitor cannot skip around in his or her search history unless it is done manually. Also, the standard browser does not keep a memory of user-entered information. Again, there are ways around these limitations, but they exist outside the HTML specification.

Things are relative, but not within HTML Web pages. The standard browser maintains no connection among the various Web pages that a user might visit. For example, if a user visits three Web pages on the Yahoo site, five pages on Ford, and two pages on the Wal-Mart site, the browser has no mechanism for making the connection. As far as its records go, the user visited ten unrelated Web pages with nothing to link them together.

The W3C XML committee wanted to address these limitations and to design a permanent, extensible linking language to complement XML's other extensible capabilities. To satisfy this requirement, they built the specification for *XLink*, the XML Linking Language. Throughout the various W3C steps leading to specification, XLink has also been called names such as XLL, XML Linking Language, and Extensible Linking Language. All of these names refer to the same functionality.

XLink Linking Classifications

XLink specifies the methods used to travel from one document to another, and to link information among many XML documents. The XLink specification defines two methods of linking using either simple links or extended links. XLink *simple links* provide the same general functions as HTML hyperlinks. XLink *extended links* provide new features that usually require a conventional programming language.

Simple Links

A simple link is similar to an HTML link in that it can link to XML documents, HTML Web pages, the corporate intranet, and other information on the Internet or the Web. In addition, the similarity with HTML continues in how an XLink is used in an XML document because simple links include other standard features, such as event handlers, that previously required Java, Perl, or Java Script in order to implement the same features in HTML.

An XML document has a well-defined tree structure. Therefore, it is relatively easy for an XLink simple link to access a specific point in a Web page or a specific XML document element. One way to achieve this treasure hunt is to access and follow a map, the schema of the XML document, to the treasured element. In addition, a simple XLink extends beyond the capabilities of HTML by linking structures because it includes qualifiers such as link labels, opened link information, and link activation options that allow the developer greater linking freedom than possible with standard HTML links.

Extended Links

While simple links correspond to HTML hyperlinks, extended links provide a new set of advanced linking features. Some of these features include multidirectional links, two-way links, out-of-line links, and menu capabilities. Multidirectional links allow the user to circumnavigate a selected collection of documents. The documents usually have some relationship, such as a collection of restaurants or a list of semiconductor companies. Two-way links are a limited multidirectional capability between only two documents. Out-of-line links are external links that are collected in a separate file. Menu links give the user options from which to choose, just like a customer in a restaurant who can choose one entrée or select different items from a buffet. The extended links menu function in XML allows the user to sample from the larger buffet of many choices, rather than the single entrée provided by HTML. The out-of-line and multidirectional attributes allow XML to create a network of documents for the user to traverse.

XPointers

HTML has internal pointers, indicated by a pound sign (#) in the anchor link and used to link to a specific location within an HTML Web page. Through clever coding, a Web page developer can guide a user from a location in one Web page to locations in other Web pages. However, just like HTML links, HTML pointers have some limitations. First, the specific target anchor point within the Web page must be explicitly coded in the correct location. This involves an extra step in the Web design process, and, if a Web page belongs to someone else or it is read only, then a new pointer cannot be inserted. Second, an HTML pointer refers to a location within a Web page, not to a section of the Web page. Thus, an entire Web page must be downloaded in order to access only a portion of it. If the Web page is huge, there is no way to reduce the resource requirements. XML eliminates these limitations through the XPointer Specification.

The XPointer specification defines the syntax for stating the location information within an XML Document. XML Stylesheet Language Transformation (XSLT) also uses XPointers to process transformations. *XPointers* are indicated by a pound sign (#) and are similar to HTML pointers that specify a location within an XML document. They can also be indicated with a bar (|) to specify a fragment within the document, discarding the remainder of the document. This feature is far more efficient than the HTML pointer.

XPointer is used to link from the current location in the document to another location within the document or to a specific location within another document. It does not point to another location in general; it points to a specific location within a document. Unlike HTML pointers, XPointers can reference existing nodes and tags within an XML document. This means that an XPointer reference can point to information in any XML document without having to insert a target location.

One feature of XPointers is the ability to define a number of ranges within the same XML document, so that a long file can be decomposed into manageable components. This feature is important in repurposing XML document information. For example, imagine that an XML document contains quarterly financial data. Developers can use XPointers to extract only the information needed for a balance sheet or to show cash flow. Developers for a financial analyst might use XPointers to combine selected information from the original XML document with similar information from other corporations to provide an overview of the industry. XPointers are an important contribution to the idea of reusing and repurposing data.

XPath

The XPath specification outlines the syntax for defining an XML document's precise location information down to the tag level or even down to individual characters in a text element. Both XSLT and XPointer use XPath to access nodes within an XML document. XPath operates on the details of the logical structure of an XML document, and it supports basic string manipulation. Traversing the internal hierarchy of an XML document, it uses the logical tree structure to locate pertinent tags or predefined text elements. XPath operates on the internal structures of XML documents and provides detailed references to data elements, attributes, text strings, as well as other document nodes within a specific XML document.

A simple functional hierarchy describes the relationships among XLink, XPointer, and XPath. XLink manages external links and interdocument connections. Control is passed to XPointer to manage access to information components within an XML document or resource. XPath manages the specific address for locating information components within an XML document.

For example, to connect two or more XML documents, a developer uses XLink. To obtain specific information with an XML document, the developer also uses XPointer and XPath. To access specific tags or text elements within a single XML document, then the developer uses XPath. To collect components and fragments from multiple documents in order to create a virtual document, then the developer uses all three specifications.

XPath uses a path-based syntax that is reminiscent of URLs and paths in Unix. It defines the navigation process through an XML document using a specific set of nodes. The XPath specification defines node types such as root, element, attribute, text, comment, processing instruction, and namespace nodes. It provides an efficient syntax for specifying a location within an XML document. Developers can use XPath rather than programming instructions to climb the XML document tree structure. In addition, the XPath syntax supports other XML technologies such as XSLT, XPointer, and XLink. Finally as the specifications for XML grow and mature, the specifications for XPath will also change

XML Infoset

The XML Information Set (Infoset) specification standardizes the abstract data model defined by the XML specification. A standard data model facilitates the design of an XML document architecture. Designers can use the higher level abstractions without having to know the details of XML.

The Infoset data model is a hierarchical tree structure in terms of general, logical data elements, such as parent and child. It is independent of the physical data. As the Infoset specification is better defined, tools will emerge to help designers to create robust, corporatewide XML document architectures.

Implementing XLink: Speculation

The XLink information specification defines what XLink can do, but not how to implement it. For example, one big question is how to implement out-of-line links. XPath has no mechanism with which to peer into any XML document available on the Internet, the Web, or a corporate intranet. The logistics and the infrastructure simply do not yet exist. However, XLink, which is a foundation-enabling technology for XML, provides the powerful ability to collect remote information into a virtual document. One approach for implementing XLink might be using the current rage: peer-to-peer networking. But first a little background.

Napster and MP3 were in court and in the news because of copyright issues, which are just a diversion from the real issue of a grass roots effort to build peer-to-peer networking over the Internet. While these networking efforts are effectively open, they are nonmainstream, network communities within the Web that do not use centralized servers. These distributed network communities will have a significant impact on traditional content providers. First we will look at these peer-to-peer applications, then further explore their implications.

MP3 is a music standard that was released a few years ago. Although not its intent, MP3 can be used to record music from existing music CDs and then to upload these music files to the Web. The words *piracy*, *copyright infringement*, and *violation* easily come to mind and are reminiscent of the old Internet cry that "Information wants to be free."

Napster software indexes MP3 music files on the user's PC and displays this index to other Napster users over the Internet. A simple search locates the music of interest, which can then be downloaded through the free Napster network. Napster, as well as other network software, enables peer-to-peer networking (P2P). This means that I can connect directly to your computer, and you to mine, without the intervention of an external server.

If Napster were an isolated instance of P2P, it might not be so interesting. But there are five or more different P2P offerings. One of the more flexible P2P systems is Gnutella, which works with more than just MP3. It will also work with corporate data!

Gnutella Network

Gnutella is a protocol for connecting computers on a peer-to-peer basis across the Internet, in contrast to Napster, which is more like a centralized index of file servers. Gnutella client software on the local computer allows users to select what they want to share, to index that information, and to search for shared files and information across a distributed Gnutella network. Gnutella provides more than simply a search engine and file server. It also provides the protocol for a distributed capability that is similar to the founding concept and protocol behind the Internet itself.

In fact, Gnutella is like a mini-Internet within the Internet. While the Internet uses large servers and Cisco switches, Gnutella leverages the resulting bandwidth capabilities to permit local computers to function as nodes and servers for the Gnutella network.

Software and protocols such as Napster and Gnutella provide the pipe, the pathway, the journey, and the network rolled all in one. The network of a million nodes starts with but a single user. It is how to get to where you want to go as well as how to find out where you want to go. One user can connect successively through other users to gain access to the entire network of content providers. The destination is the millions of distributed PCs or other content providers. And the content can be music, multimedia, or corporate data. This is where P2P gets tremendously interesting.

The P2P protocols, architecture, and approach that enable content to flow directly from client to client, without the intervention of a middleman, middleware, or central server, present both a threat and an opportunity to traditional content providers. Indeed, this kind of P2P across the Web has two interrelated implications. First, P2P changes the nature of search engines and content providers because it enables direct and fresh access to the content without time delays from centralized indexing. Second, P2P may be the method of implementing some of the advanced, complex linking features of the XML Linking Language.

Content Is King

Currently, the Web and the Internet are massive sources of content for the user. This content is stored on millions of servers throughout the world. Companies such as Intel may spend as much as $80 million to support the servers and network infrastructure that supplies the Internet content to the world. If bandwidth requirements shift from a server model to a P2P model, then that $80 million budget will have to be reconsidered.

Rather than building up bandwidth resources for centralized access to the content server, corporations will have to redirect these resources to satisfy P2P software requests from individual computers. This is not a bad thing, just another decentralized thing, and that can be significantly leveraged into a good thing.

Today, standard search engines catalog server-based, centralized Web-based content and store the indexed information in a centralized database for retrieval. As they have demonstrated a few times, hackers can attack and shut down a centralized content server. However, a distributed content network, just like the Internet itself, is much more difficult to attack successfully. Sure, hackers can shut down one segment of a network, denying access to its information. But for the most part, traffic will be diverted to other segments.

Another limitation of conventional search engines is that they retrieve Web page information by using intelligent agents or automated Web crawlers to index Web sites. However, search engine technology has not been able to keep up with the increasing number of Web pages, estimated at more than one billion and growing. In fact, according to George Cybenko, a Dartmouth computer scientist, the Web is growing so fast that a search engine needs a 50 Mbps (T3) network line just to keep up with its automated Web crawlers and spiders as they index new Web sites. The unverified extrapolation is that the number of Web pages doubles every 60 days. This is not unreasonable when you recall that a Web site will have many Web pages and that corporations can publish or update hundreds or thousands of Web pages per day.

So, much of the Web site information is static, out of date, and incorrect, pointing the user at broken links and nonexistent Web pages. Even Yahoo!, which screens its information manually, has the problem of too much information to keep it all up to date. Moreover, centralized search engines cannot retrieve dynamic content from pages that are built on the fly from e-commerce sites, database searches, or user interactions. Users have been screaming for better search engine technology since the start of the Web popularity in 1994.

The next step up the Web evolutionary, information-sharing ladder is a P2P parallel search and file-sharing community, distributed throughout the regions of the Web and the Internet. P2Ps decentralize information as well as the search capability. They also provide access to dynamic content, rather than the static information provided by traditional search engines.

Content providers can define which files and content are sharable. This is a departure from today's search paradigm in which search engines merely point users to the correct Web site, and then the user has to navigate to the information of interest. With P2P capability, the journey is also the destination because users can search for and go directly to the information of interest, *as defined by the content providers*.

The potential behind this is remarkable. Simply select content and share it. It's really that easy, and the power of sharing content is limitless. The file and information formats are not important. Any media can be shared—and pushed. Because the user has control over what is shareable, the user can also "push" information as responses. This capability provides a significant opportunity for portals, traditional search engines, and other commercial content providers.

Just as search engines such as Yahoo! and Altavista make money by selling keywords and advertising, any commercial content provider can create interesting content-rich advertisements that are pushed in response to search queries. However, these ads will present a double-edged sword because they cannot be purely self-serving.

In a competitive information space like the Web, where time and attention are golden, users resent content-free ads that waste time by providing no information or entertainment. P2P software works both ways. Users can boycott a blatant ad and filter out an entire Web site. Just as SPAM refers to unwanted junk e-mail, the P2P user community will coin a term to describe content-free ads to be ostracized.

But the financial opportunities are too great, so commercial content providers will learn quickly what works and what does not. This has been a part of the Web browsing experience that companies have not been able to manage previously. Now companies will be able to control how search queries are answered more intelligently. They will be able to take charge and drive the flow of information traffic. P2P-based content will do for searching what the Web did for information, and it will do for the Web what advertising did for radio and TV. The die is cast and the map is in hand; the only question now is how long the journey will take. Like everything else that is Web based, probably not very long.

Leveraging P2P for B2B

Intel has started a P2P working group accessible at http://www.peer-to-peer-wg.com/ to explore the various technical and business implications of P2P. This working group, which includes IBM, Hewlett Packard, and numerous dot coms, will ultimately agree on standards that will have an impact on the Internet and on B2B. Rather than storing all information on servers and letting search engines index this information, corporations will be able to leverage P2P to provide focused and up-to-date information, services, and products to the interested customer.

Clearly, P2P will be linked with m-commerce, so that some peers will be interconnected by wireless LANs and by Bluetooth applications. In addition, one XML technology, the XML Linking Language, will also be an important P2P business enabler.

Implementing the XML Linking Language

The second implication deals with the XML Linking Language (XLink). XLink is a very powerful language that dramatically extends the capabilities of linking documents much beyond the abilities of mere HTML Web pages. XLink enables bidirectional linking, multiway linking, and out-of-line linking. Bidirectional linking implies the idea of visiting a Web page and returning to the starting point by clicking on the same link again. Multiway linking is the implementation of Web rings by using XLink. Rather than using the navigational buttons, a user can traverse back and forth and all around within a predefined set of Web pages. Out-of-line linking is the concept of hyperlinking between two or more pages that were not originally linked; a separate file is used for the links that connect the Web pages. Menu links provide the user with a selection of pathways from which to choose. The concept is similar to the results page generated by a search engine. If a user wants to learn more about the specific companies in an industry, a menu link would provide a selection of company links to explore. These and a few others are the specifications for XLink.

These extended linking capabilities support the virtual XML document feature because these links will allow a developer to access specific content within a variety of distributed documents and then to display the results to a user. The user will not be aware of the fact that the "current" document exists only while it is being looked at. Another type of individualized, virtual document already exists. When a user interacts with a database-generated or script-based Web page, the resulting Web page of dynamic content exists only in response to the user's unique parameters. Although traditional search engines cannot index dynamic content from other Web sites, these same search engines create dynamic content, themselves, in the form of retrieval results. Dynamic content was once the realm of the Perl or Java programmer. XLink provides this ability to the nonprogrammer.

The issue with XLink is that implementing the solution to these specifications is not clear. One possibility may be a relative of Napster or Gnutella that will define a robust P2P protocol for developing the XLink capabilities. A protocol that combines the distributed appeal of P2P with the power of XML and XLink standards would be a formidable agent for change. In fact, P2P is the potential spark of Web and Internet access that will fan the roaring flame of universal information retrieval to meet the business needs of the 21st century.

P2P Acronym

The acronym for peer-to-peer networking is still up in the air at the time of this writing. Although this author uses P2P, both PtP and PPN have been used. Each one has pluses and minuses. P2P can also refer to person to person. P2P is limiting, because peer-to-peer networking may quickly evolve into peer-to-peer computing. Both PtP and P2P capture both ideas, and P2P has the visual appeal to ride the popularity of B2B. Nevertheless, the final acronym is up for grabs.

CHAPTER 6

XML Applications

General Trends

XML has enabled many different business applications. Business-to-business (B2B) e-commerce is quickly becoming a business competency, because XML facilitates a simpler way to transfer data. Some of the features of e-commerce include electronic methods for on-line catalogs and order fulfillment because the information that supports these features is easier to control and maintain by using XML.

In addition, XML supports document and information handling, control, and management. An XML document is easy to put under document configuration control by careful definition of its components. The hierarchical nature of an XML document is a natural match to the drill-down capabilities found in product data managers and in data warehouses. All of these capabilities help to create the general foundation needed for intellectual capital. These trends are described in more detail below.

E-Commerce

XML lit the B2B e-commerce rocket by fueling a new choice to Electronic Data Interchange (EDI) systems. XML supports the ability to transfer data and to modify electronic business forms as simply and rapidly as needed. Developers can create new XML vocabularies to provide individualization. For example, an invoice from Ford can be modified to include new options, price changes, and data exchange activities with Wal-Mart or other corporations. Then any XML-enabled application can read the documents and register the changes.

XML empowers both people and companies to exchange information clearly and simply. While this is useful in the creation of both Web pages and XML documents, XML's greatest return on investment exists in B2B e-commerce. XML expands upon three concepts in e-commerce: the exploding use of electronic ordering, the accelerating application of Web sites for product catalogs, and the transition from traditional commerce to Web-based storefronts.

B2B E-Commerce

B2B e-commerce includes sales of products and services between different companies rather than from company to customer. B2B also covers partnering information, vendors, subcontractor support, etc. For example, the auto companies provide parts and service requirements information to vendors and to subcontractors. This information is transmitted by using the Internet, Web, intranet, extranet, or direct connection using the same general protocols established using agreed upon XML formats.

Legacy EDI systems use relational database structures because that was the simplest method for implementation. XML fuels the wildfire growth of B2B exchanges by supplying an omnimorphic standard for data generation, collection, processing, and transfer. Chapter 7 discusses EDI in more detail.

On-Line Business

The homepage of an on-line business helps to establish the brand and entices customers to enter the Web site. Books on marketing communications and on Web site design are useful resources for developing a compelling on-line business. The main idea is to bring a visitor into the Web site and then to transform that visitor into a paying customer. To sell the merchandise, the vendor has to display it. XML supports the activities needed to build an appealing and easy to find Web site, because the data element tags can serve as meta-data information to guide search engines directly to the products and services. The layout and information still require the human touch, but XML provides the capability to develop a Web business that can automatically customize to meet the requirements of each customer.

On-Line Catalogs

A mix of HTML, databases, and a programming language is the conventional way to build on-line catalogs. However, XML provides a simpler mechanism for developing on-line catalogs that are easier to search. One advantage of XML is that the schemas, DTDs, and data element tags can be developed and supported by using emerging applications and automated tools. Many levels of applications are available and being developed for handling XML. Developers use XML editors to build the DTDs, XML systems, and catalogs. Developers also use presentation to simplify posting the catalog to the Web site. Customers use browsers to look at the catalog items, and they also use search engines to locate products, services, and information. Finally, site maintenance tools and applications help the developer to update the catalog, build the inventory, send the bills, etc. Catalog software is being developed rapidly to meet demand.

Order Fulfillment

The process of taking catalog orders can be represented in five steps: receive the order, accept the credit card, generate packing instructions, fetch the order, and mail the order. XML simplifies these steps by providing a common presentation language that transitions each application transparently. With the use of XML, the customer's client-side computer supports many of the computing activities that recently required a large server for processing.

A developer can easily create an XML system that sends payment, shipping, and other order information to the order-entry computers. At the same time, the application provides the customer with billing, shipping, and tracking data. The system might also handle procurement and reordering of out-of-stock items.

XML Document Configuration Control

XML provides the capability to build structured, omnimorphic documents that separate data from presentation. By isolating the data in the document from the method of presentation in the browser, the XML document can be applied to many different, and perhaps, unrelated applications. Also, because the documents contain a schema or DTD that self-describes the document data, information within the document tends to be easier to locate because it has useful tags. Therefore, when the document is being searched, it actively helps the search function, because the tags serve as red flags to focus the attention of the search engine. The use of similar tags allows similar XML documents to be collected into a combined configuration of information. Then all similar information can be more easily controlled. This type of function is the core of a document management system.

XML facilitates the storage and retrieval of information from a document management system. First, XML makes the storage of documents easier, because they are in a uniform format and they are independent of application. In addition, they can be stored electronically without the need for special document management software. A simple computer-based file system found on standard platforms can work as an XML document repository.

Second, XML makes retrieval of the information easier because documents with similar tags are stored together. However, this implies that the information within the documents is tagged in a uniform format, so that tags and meta-data have been normalized. Again, because XML document data is independent of application or presentation, keeping the data synchronized is easier. In the past, a secretary or filing clerk would keep all the documents coordinated in her mind. So she would know that location in one document meant the same as address in another document. XML will help to automate and standardize these activities.

Efforts are already underway to build the XML tools needed to support document management and configuration control. Search engines are also being developed to exploit the capabilities of XML. As B2B expands, and as other XML applications become business critical, the applications will become more commonplace. However, growth in the field makes any attempt to produce an exhaustive or up-to-date list of XML applications futile.

Product Data Manager

A Product Data Manager (PDM) is used to store data about the products offered by a corporation. This data is usually stored in a relational and hierarchical format, resembling a well-structured tree. The PDM application allows the user to traverse the tree and to drill down for increasingly detailed levels of information about the product. In addition, the PDM allows the user to extract portions of the data and to combine different data to produce a variety of customized views. XML is a natural for this process. In fact, replace the term PDM with the term XML, and the paragraph reads the same. However, a PDM also offers workflow management and automated reporting and notification functions.

The marriage of a PDM with XML applications is a natural combination of structure and automation. PDM vendors are beginning to provide XML capabilities to PDM users. Automated tools and interfaces can be developed to improve the data entry process to support XML or PDM. XML will drive the development of these kinds of tools and applications, while PDM workflow will support the general program management needs of the corporation.

Intellectual Capital

Intellectual capital is a growing concern in most corporations: how to capture it, store it, retrieve it, and protect it. With the dramatic mobility of today's knowledge workers, intellectual capital collected over years or decades can easily walk out the door. Although XML cannot help with the retention of this intangible good, it can be used for collecting and storing this valuable information in the forms of documented processes, customer information, and other valuable lessons learned. By storing documents in an XML format, memos, meeting minutes, and e-mail can be easily combined and searched to glean the results for valuable tidbits of knowledge. In addition, an exit interview form can be designed to help automate the collection of intellectual capital. As the collection grows, more and more valuable lessons learned and best practices will emerge from this knowledge.

Data Warehousing

Data warehousing systems are developed using well-structured information that is similar to the foundation of XML documents. Also, XML provides meta-data that enables the user to search for exactly the term, in context, germane to his requirements. For example, a user wanting information on currency can specify the type and country, while excluding terms that are of no interest. The XML-based search engine will locate the correct information and exclude other information based on the data element tags and document hierarchy.

A seductive power of XML is the ability to search distributed XML documents, then create virtual documents that satisfy the query. This function is vaguely similar to how a conventional search engine works with HTML-based Web pages. However, the conventional search engine function relies on powerful programming languages, and it returns only a list of interesting URLs. An XML-based data warehouse would return the actual information gathered from the separate documents and collected into a single document that intends to satisfy the query. The implication is that the million dollar data warehouse development project will one day be replaced with a much cheaper XML-based data warehouse project that is also part of the corporate XML document design architecture.

General Markup Language Applications

XML has spawned a number of general markup languages. Extensible HTML (XHTML) is the XML replacement for HTML, which is based on SGML. Scalable Vector Graphics (SVG) provides a flexible method for using markup languages to create two-dimensional graphics. Synchronized Multimedia Integration Language (SMIL) makes it easier to work with data from various media types. Electronic Data Interchange (EDI)-XML and Open Financial Exchange (OFX) are transaction and financial standards that XML improves by providing a uniform base. The Channel Definition Format provides a standardized way for pushing information to the user.

XML also facilitates a set of standards for the wireless industry. The Wireless Application Protocol, Wireless Markup Language, and Bluetooth protocols are built on top of XML or are compatible with XML. All of these applications will expand e-commerce to a more mobile m-commerce and into an even more global endeavor. This section discusses these applications in more detail.

EXtensible HyperText Markup Language (XHTML)

Although XML does not replace HTML, EXtensible HyperText Markup Language (XHTML) is an XML-based markup language that does replace HTML 4.0. In fact, HTML 5.0 will never truly exist because whatever the next generation is, it will be a variation of XHTML, not HTML. However, XHTML will replace HTML for Web page development only gradually, because people like HTML and know how to use it. Also, HTML is adequate for many Web developers and is compatible with all browsers.

For the most part, XHTML is exactly like HTML, with the programming rigor and rules of XML. Most Web developers can read and understand XHTML Web pages immediately with only minor guidance. For example, an HTML-based Web page uses relaxed programming because the browser is big and smart enough to handle minor tagging errors. By definition, an XHTML Web is well formed, following the stricter XML standards for document design. So, XHTML may be the initial XML application released for prime time on the Web.

XHTML inherits all the tags from HTML, in addition to a few from XML. XHTML also inherits the rules for well formedness from XML. This means that each tag has a corresponding close tag or a termination tag. So commands such as list tags <li> and paragraph tags <p> have corresponding close tags </li> and </p>. Unlike HTML, XHTML is case sensitive, so <LI> is different than <li> in XHTML. HTML is forgiving about nesting tags, but a browser cannot read an XHTML Web page if the tags are not correctly nested. Also, HTML is forgiving about attributes, so <FONT Color=Red> is allowable. With XHTML, the same tag must use quotes for the attributes, <font color="red"> and have a corresponding </font> somewhere in the document.

In reality, the changes from HTML to XHTML are minor and should be used as a matter of good programming to produce clean, crisp Web page programming. Mainly, Web developers need to embrace better coding habits. Tools are under development to convert HTML to XHTML. And as more Web pages conform to XML standards, developers will apply companion technologies, such as XML Stylesheet Language (XSL), XML Stylesheet Language Transformations (XSLT), and XLink to well-formed Web pages.

Scalable Vector Graphics (SVG)

Scalable Vector Graphics (SVG) is the technology that will simplify two-dimensional graphics on the Web. SVG is an XML technology that developers can use to create graphics that work equally well on high resolution and low-resolution devices, small screens and large screens, digital and paper. An SVG picture is smaller than a corresponding GIF or JPG format. It can be scaled up or down smoothly to meet the needs of the device or presentation.

Just as XML allows the developer to reuse text and data, SVG will allow the developer to reuse graphics. It already has the support of IBM, Adobe, and Corel, among others. The next step in the process will be for Netscape and IE to include SVG as a native graphics format.

Synchronized Multimedia Integration Language (SMIL)

As bandwidth rates across the Web exceed megabit per second speeds, multimedia presentations become more feasible and more available. The standard combination is movies with audio and video. A variety of multimedia tools are currently available for creating these kinds of information. Quicktime, developed by Apple Computers, is one of the oldest multimedia applications. Macromedia and Flash provide other formats. All of these multimedia formats are proprietary, requiring special tools, plug-ins, or extensions to develop and view.

RealNetworks, famous for streaming audio (RealAudio) and streaming video (RealVideo) lead the development of Synchronized Multimedia Integration Language (SMIL) as a generic multimedia language. SMIL is an XML-based language that describes media type, intermedia synchronization, and external media location links. SMIL is not a method for creating the multimedia files; it is instead a language for integrating and coordinating multimedia into a coherent presentation. It describes the media data and relationships. In addition, as an XML vocabulary, SMIL can take advantage of XSL, XSLT, XLink, and other XML technologies.

XML and EDI

During the Information Age, the exchange of data and information has accelerated to a frenetic pace. As corporations attempt to exchange megabytes and gigabytes, they fly into the format barrier. The format barrier has to do with the problem of agreeing on standard data formats needed to exchange data between companies. XML transcends that barrier by providing a universal data transfer format that collaborating companies can concur upon. However, before the advent of XML, companies depended on Electronic Data Interchange (EDI) as the uniform method for sharing data, such as bills of material, invoices, personnel information, and schedules. EDI provided a common data structure encoded in data dictionaries at both the sender's and receiver's sites. Because of the similarity between EDI and XML, EDI-XML combination is a natural evolution.

XML can describe the EDI data, the EDI structure, the EDI exchange, and the EDI messages, so that existing software can be updated to read and process the EDI-XML data streams. The advantage of this approach is that the existing investment in EDI does not need to be written off. The existing

EDI can be leveraged to support the XML modifications. This allows a migration from proprietary EDI tools to more general XML applications. The EDI-XML information can take advantage of XSL, XSLT, XLink, and other XML technologies, promising forward compatibility with future technologies. This example demonstrates how XML can be used to provide backward compatibility to leverage an existing legacy system. For more information about XML and EDI, see Chapter 7.

Open Financial Exchange (OFX)

Microsoft, Intuit, and CheckFree used XML to create a financial markup language called Open Financial Exchange (OFX). OFX is an XML vocabulary developed to coordinate and simplify the transfer of financial data among financial institutions, customers, and applications. A single, universal financial data format facilitates electronic checking and on-line banking.

The OFX example demonstrates how business competitors can benefit by agreeing on an open standard for representing, exchanging, and sharing business data and information. Providing superior services, products, or proprietary data to manipulate and leverage the data and information creates the individual competitive advantage. The proprietary format is no longer the discriminator.

Channel Definition Format (CDF)

Channel Definition Format (CDF) is an XML vocabulary for defining and describing methods for pushing Web information to the browser or desktop client. These methods are called channels. Channels are simply pathways for information and are analogous to marketing channels, TV channels, or channels of waters. When setting up a Web channel, a user requests an open line of communication that the Web server will use to push information onto the user's screen without having to ask for the information explicitly after the initial link is established.

After the user subscribes to the channel and gives the server permission to send information, the CDF document can be used to define the channel, the format, and the presentation layout. Typically, a browser reads the CDF, accepts the information push to the client desktop, and configures the information layout based on the CDF document.

Wireless Application Protocol (WAP)

Wireless Application Protocol (WAP) is one of the emerging XML applications and it is smoking. With more than 100 million users worldwide, wireless access to data is the wave of the future. In fact, it is already huge in Japan and in Europe. The United States is only just beginning to catch up.

Only a few years ago, the World Wide Web was the next big thing for global information transfer. Today, the Web is an accepted part of our culture—the cost of doing business—just like a telephone and fax. Tomorrow offers a new promise: wireless Web access, anytime and especially anywhere, by using wireless devices such as a laptop computer, cell phone, handheld computer, or even pager. This new freedom from wires and cables is the purpose of WAP.

WAP is a fresh new innovation with much potential. It's a protocol for requesting, transmitting, and receiving data across a wireless network in a format that a mobile platform can present on a small screen through a minibrowser. It is based on an open specification distributed by the WAP Forum, which Ericsson Inc., Nokia Corp., Motorola, and Phone.com Inc. (formerly Unwired Planet) founded in 1997 to create an Internet standard for wireless phones. Phone.com also makes the standard WAP minibrowser that it licenses to wireless phone manufacturers. WAP Forum has grown to include most of the wireless industry, including hardware, software, and service providers. In fact, most new cell phones are manufactured with WAP capability already built in.

WAP requires minimal resources on the wireless end, making it useful for small devices like cell phones and palmtops. The real work happens at the server end, just as in many browser-based applications on PCs. WAP devices, both server and minibrowser, communicate using Wireless Markup Language (WML), an XML derivative that is based on the earlier Handheld Device Markup Language (HDML) developed by Phone.com.

The WAP standard works with Cellular Digital Packet Data (CDPD), Code Division Multiple Access (CDMA), Time Division Multiple Access (TDMA), Global Systems for Mobile Communications (GSM), and other wireless standards. Wireless devices communicate through the wireless network to a WAP server. A WAP server converts data or Web pages between WAP and TCP/IP. This conversion lets conventional Web servers send WML pages to wireless devices, which use minibrowsers that let users surf the Web.

The conventional Web protocol, HTTP (HyperText Transport Protocol), is mainly text-based and works poorly over a wireless network. In addition, browsing an 8-by-11-inch page represented by an 800x600 screen would be difficult on a 3-inch cell phone screen. WAP and WML are optimized for small screens, two-line text displays, and the graphics on smart phones, handheld devices, and palmtops.

WAP capability is different from conventional desktop browsing. A WAP-enabled device can browse only WML sites. If the Web site doesn't have WML access, then a WAP device can't get to it. Wireless technology must both support and enhance productivity of the enterprise, or it's not worthwhile.

WAP supports business by improving productivity with its other capabilities. For example, Web-based calendars and messaging services are useful business applications for personnel on the road. WAP can send data from a Web page to any WAP-enabled wireless device. Other productivity-enhancing applications include address books, email, and Web-based database access. Users on the road can access their email, and salespeople can access customer and catalog data. For example, they can check inventory, place orders, and confirm order status, providing on-demand information to the customer as needed. Real-time data goes a long way toward closing the deal and satisfying the customer. For those who can accept the size vs. data-access trade-off, the cost, productivity, and convenience can be very appealing.

Most commercial wireless networks support only about 9,600 bps data-transmission rates. (Remember V.32 modems in 1994?) More important, what kind of surfing can the user do on a three-inch screen? At those transmission rates, graphics are minimal or nonexistent at best. Although the user cannot use complex graphics, he can browse simple things such as email, messaging, customer information, and catalog data, as well as access weather, stocks, airplane reservations, and so forth. The disadvantage of simpler presentation may be balanced by the advantage that business travelers can access information on the fly.

Wireless Markup Language (WML)

Wireless Markup Language (WML) is the wireless markup language that sits on top of WAP. WML is to WAP what HTML is to the conventional Web. WML is similar to HTML, but it is derived from XML (eXtensible Markup Language) to specifically support the delivery of Web pages on the limited real estate available on most wireless devices. WML lets Web page developers create information that handheld computers, palmtops, smart cell phones, pagers, and other wireless devices can read.

Because of the unique nature of WML, simply porting HTML pages to WML is not straightforward. Although XSLT can be used for transformations, a separate site may be necessary. WML sites are mostly text and maybe a few simple graphics. However, most phones do not even display graphics yet. WML has tags, just like HTML, with some modifications to adapt to the needs of the small screen. Wireless Web sites are mostly a set of menus through which to navigate. Due to the screen size constraints and difficulty of text entry on today's devices, simplicity of use is key to design.

Other than developing the content, which is mainly text, the wireless-enabled Web server must be configured to distinguish WML devices from the traditional desktop browsers and serve up different content. Then, the information available on the HTML Web page is reformatted in WML for wireless devices. Or completely new information and services is presented to the wireless devices.

Although WML sites are much simpler than HTML sites, they are inherently more personal and must be more customizable. Personalized services and Internet-based services specified to the user's needs are easier to deploy with a personal item such as the mobile phone. In practice, the wireless-enabled Web server can gather more information about the user to provide a more individual experience. WAP and WML simply extend the Web and its information sources for the wireless arena. The applications are limitless, and the possibilities for profit are plentiful.

Bluetooth

Bluetooth technology was named for the ancient Viking Warrior, Harold Bluetooth. The technology involves a small, single chip, short range (30 feet) radio transmitter that allows a wireless device to transmit short-range signals. These can be Local Area Network (LAN) type signals or financial transactions (like electronic credit cards).

Bluetooth is completely WAP compatible and totally complementary with WAP functions. There are two major differences between WAP and Bluetooth. First, the ranges are different. WAP is LAN to Wide Area Network (WAN) distances, covering whatever access is available to a cell phone call. In contrast, Bluetooth is short range, on the order of 30 feet, although it may expand up to 30 meters.

The second major difference between the two technologies relates to the recipient of a WAP or Bluetooth message. WAP is intended to connect to the Internet or to the Web via a cell phone relay to a Web server, allowing the user to surf the Web or to get access to data via wireless. In contrast, Bluetooth is a device-to-device protocol that provides the user with a service, not necessarily information or data. For example, a Bluetooth interaction may involve credit cardlike access to buy a soft drink. Or a Bluetooth dongle on back of a desktop PC may, with the appropriate authorizations, allow it to connect to any wireless LAN within a 30-foot radius. Or a Bluetooth-enabled PalmPilot may move in and out of different corporate LANs, as the user walks from one department to another. What this means is that the Information Technology (IT) department can set up a corporatewide LAN environment without the need for cables. Simply establish the wireless servers, then provide all computers with a Bluetooth LAN card. No more spaghetti cables to connect all the desktops.

Bluetooth technology is simply a short-range radio on a single chip that can translate digital data from computers. For explanation purposes, another way of thinking about Bluetooth is to consider it to be like a radio-based modem rather than a telephone-based modem. The radio sends and receives voice and data signals generated by other Bluetooth radios that come within the broadcast range of 30 feet. Because radio waves pass through walls and other barriers, Bluetooth devices can communicate in situations that stop competing technologies such as infrared.

A Bluetooth-enabled cell phone becomes a portable phone as soon as you walk into your home, or functions as a walkie-talkie when communicating with another Bluetooth cell phone. A Bluetooth headset leaves your hands free to talk on the phone while you wash the dishes or drive to work. In fact, your cell phone can automatically unlock your car and set up your seat and stereo preferences as you are walking in the parking lot. In short, you do the walking. Your devices do the talking.

Mobile Commerce (M-Commerce)

Mobile commerce (m-commerce) is not a new technology; it is simply the natural convergence of wireless data access and Web-based electronic commerce. M-commerce elevates e-commerce to a new level of mobile freedom for Web commerce. E-commerce provides access to anyone at anytime. M-commerce provides the next dimension in access to anyone anytime, to include *anywhere*, not just from a fixed desktop, but also from the highway, the restaurant, and eventually from the beach.

M-commerce is accelerating faster than Internet time. In the next few years, the majority of devices accessing the Web will be wireless, and most e-commerce will be wireless m-commerce. It took nearly four years for the Web to develop a base of 50 million users. However, the infrastructure was not really in place. Now, more people buy wireless devices than PCs and all the technologies are in place. In Europe, Japan, and Finland—as shown by *60 Minutes*—people are using their wireless devices to access information and to conduct financial transactions. In fact, the United States is behind the learning curve in m-commerce. We are like a Third World country compared to Finland, Japan, and some parts of Europe, and we are just now catching up.

In Asia and Europe, wireless phones are everywhere, used for communications, financial transactions, and information. The typical Asian or European businessman travels frequently and depends on the wireless phone as a portal to the world. This portal allows easy checks of calendars, stock portfolios, bank balances, and airline reservations. As Web access evolves from wired to wireless, e-business evolves into m-commerce. And, as U.S. companies embrace the wireless world, they will indeed tap into a wireless world! This is because there are more Web-ready wireless phones than wired Internet connections from a global perspective. So, U.S. companies that embrace the wireless Web will tap into a surprisingly large wireless market, which is not easily accessible from the desktop.

One aspect of m-commerce development is designing for multiple devices, which include both wireless and conventional Web pages, and anticipating emerging platforms, such as voice, TV, and Nippon Telegraph & Telephone (NTT) i-mode.

Each type of information has to be tagged and repurposed differently for each platform, but with XSL and XSLT, data can be automatically transformed from one device format to another. That is the core foundation of XML: to provide an omnimorphic format that is independent of platform, device, medium, and application.

Overall, Europe is far ahead of the United States in its adoption of wireless data. Since cell phones are usually charged on a per-minute price basis in the United States, the consumer incurs a significant cost when using a cell phone to browse the Web. However, the m-commerce business model can replace this pricing scheme by free unlimited access, with m-commerce service fees and advertising used to offset the costs.

A variety of services are feasible. For example, a sports trivia team may compete together against other teams using their cell phones at the local pub. Or a bicyclist can be notified when the latest carbon fiber Trek road bike is delivered to his local bike shop. Your phone can notify you if a movie starring Sandra Bullock is out, where and when it will be playing, how to get there, and how much it will cost. Your cell phone can even buy the movie tickets for you! Or you could walk up to a soft drink machine and then order and pay for a soda via your cell phone. The cost is part of the resulting phone bill.

Advertising is a major revenue source. Advertising is what transformed radio from an interesting technology into a viable business. However, m-commerce-based advertising will be much smarter than the conventional Web advertising. For example, your phone may display an advertisement for Burger King at lunchtime. When you select this item using your mini-browser, directions to the nearest Burger King will be displayed, perhaps also reserving and prepaying for a burger.

The main appeal to mobile devices is giving people on the go easy access to products and services without being tied down to their desktops. People will want to access services when mobile and away from their desks. This customer need will drive businesses to deliver mobile services. As a result in customer growth, there will be a corresponding growth in customer demands and services. All companies in all industries will need to adapt to maintain a competitive advantage. The cost of doing business will quickly become business as usual, just as telephone, FAX, and Internet have become.

The following is an interesting and compelling scenario resulting from m-commerce: Mark walks into Wal-Mart and finds a PlayStation 2 he wants to buy. He takes out his cell phone and finds on the Internet that he can buy the same model for $50 dollars less. So Mark shows the salesperson the competitor's price and tells the salesperson that he will leave unless Wal-Mart matches the price. If the price is not matched, Wal-Mart becomes just a really nice show room. In addition, after seeing how the wireless Web is hurting business, Wal-Mart automatically lowers its prices when the on-line catalog is accessed from a wireless device within a competitor's store!

The two technologies at the core of m-commerce are WAP and Bluetooth. According to Gartner Group, technologies such as WAP will create the foundation of the new m-commerce capabilities for wireless devices over the next three years.

The emerging way for a corporation to implement m-commerce is to focus on WAP and then explore Bluetooth after gaining a little experience. The WAP Forum is the organization that sets the protocols and standards for m-commerce. The organization, working with a collection of nearly 400 member companies, developed WAP as the standard for wireless Internet applications. The WAP forum includes large companies, such as Motorola, Nokia, and Ericsson, as well as an increasing number of smaller dot coms. The WAP standard has been adopted by 95 percent of all handset manufacturers. WAP-enabled phones are already the rage in Europe and will proliferate in the United States over the course of 2001 and 2002.

Businesses of all sizes are discovering remarkable opportunities as they use m-commerce to tap into the global marketplace, providing both B2B and business-to-consumer (B2C) services. For example, NTT's i-mode provides a wide variety of services like news, stock prices, on-line banking, and even car navigation. I-mode has a user base that exceeds 4 million subscribers and a mission statement called Vision 2010, which used to sound like magic or at least science fiction. But now it merely sounds like advanced technology: "A world in which mobile communications are limited only by imagination and actions speak louder than words." The future will be mobile. Perhaps the most important event in this decade will be the convergence of the Internet and the mobile phone.

In Scandinavia, cell phone penetration is very high and m-commerce is a way of life. In Finland, as described on *60 Minutes* in 1999, mobile users can buy CDs, bid in auctions, pay for car washes, or get a drink from a vending machine using their cell phones. The wide range of WAP shopping services is not far off in the United States either. However, true m-commerce requires fast connection speeds and reliable coverage so that consumers feel secure about their connections.

China has a population of 1.25 billion, and each of these people is a potential candidate for m-commerce. Siemens and Deutsche Telecom are working in a joint venture called Xin De Telecom to build thousands of miles of fiber optic cable infrastructure that follows the country's railroad and will potentially set up train stations as centers for e-commerce. In addition, the Chinese wireless market includes more than 40 million WAP-enabled cell phone users. To fulfill exploding market demand, wireless Web access and m-commerce will probably grow at triple-digit rates for the next decade.

As a major city, Shanghai also affects Chinese Internet and wireless activity. Because of city competition with Beijing, Shanghai is sometimes more friendly with foreign technology companies. Chengdu is a large southwestern city off the beaten path that also treats foreign companies well. In fact, to take advantage of the competition and the regional government agencies, interested companies and Internet entrepreneurs might set up a main shop in Shanghai with representative offices in Beijing and in Chengdu.

XML Browsers

The primary application for using XML documents is the browser. An XML browser consists of a parser and a display or processing application. The XML parser interprets the tag information and extracts it from the XML document. After the parser extracts the data, it then passes it to the application, such as the browser. The XML parser reads the schema or DTD of an XML document and then verifies that the document is valid or well formed. Most XML applications include a built-in parser to verify XML documents. Many XML parsers are available for free throughout the Web. An XML parser is simpler than an SGML parser because the XML specification requires that all elements have complete start and end tags. The parser also validates the XML document by comparing elements with the schemas or DTDs. Because of these more rigorous requirements, an XML parser can be simpler and smaller since it does not need as much built-in intelligence as the corresponding SGML parser.

Just like an XML parser, an XML processor also checks whether an XML document is well formed and whether it conforms to all the rules. However, a processor does not check an XML document against the DTD for validity. A processor may apply XML data in a variety of ways, such as editing, printing, or transmitting.

Although a well-formed document uses correct structures and syntax, it may not conform to its schema or DTD. However, a valid document is a well-formed document that also conforms strictly to its DTD, schema, or meta-data. Also, an HTML can be well-formed, if it follows the syntax rules of XML. If a document is not well-formed, then an XML parser and some applications will signal a fatal error. For this reason, some XML applications, such as editors, do not include a validating parser.

Processing an XML Document

A developer can use two different ways to process an XML document. SAX will process the document incrementally into its elements and subcomponents parts, and DOM will process the document as a single hierarchical structure. The advantage of SAX-based incremental processing is that data is accessed piece-by-piece and processing is faster. The disadvantage of this approach is that data must be accessed sequentially. The advantage of the DOM-based hierarchical structure processing is that data can be accessed directly, in any order, and less systematically than in SAX processing. The disadvantage of hierarchical structure processing is that it is slower, because the entire structure is read into memory before processing can occur.

Both SAX and DOM are interfaces for accessing XML document information without the need for writing a new parser. The XML format facilitates the use of SAX or DOM Application Programming Interfaces (APIs) to retrieve document information because the XML standard specifies that parsers must implement SAX and DOM for uniform information access. So both SAX and DOM were created to serve the same purpose, which is providing access to the information stored in XML documents using any programming language and parser of choice. However, SAX and DOM take very different approaches to information retrieval.

XML and HTML Data Contrasts

XML is a method for defining markup languages such as HTML. Its predecessor, SGML, requires detailed technical knowledge to use. However, just as HTML made the Internet available to the masses, XML makes mark-up languages available to nontechnical users. In addition, tools and browsers are under development to automate the use of XML and make implementations transparent to the end-user.

HTML data is primarily free text. XML data is text-based information that has context. The text basis allows XML data to be read by any application. The context adds meaning and usability to the text. In contrast, HTML text is used only for display purposes, not processing.

With XML, the designer creates a DTD that defines the document structure, as well as logical elements, tags, and attributes that are fine-tuned to the needs fulfilled by the document. The DTD provides instructions for parsing the document accurately. After the document is parsed, an XML application can use the data for display, transformation, manipulation, database processing, spreadsheet calculations, graphics, and many other capabilities that depend on the data.

This is the core concept behind omnimorphism. With no modifications, any application can use the XML data for the need at hand. In addition to being independent of platform, device, and operating system like HTML, XML is also application independent.

The well-defined tree structure of an XML document allows the data to be individually updated. By making only the necessary modifications, XML processing is more efficient than requiring a full document reload. In addition, an XML browser or any XML application can display only the changes, resulting in more efficient user interactions. In contrast, an HTML Web page must be totally refreshed every time there is any change, no matter how minute.

Developers can easily add new data element types and tags, such as <item_color>, <wholesale_price>, and <whitewall_tires> to an XML document. This expandability is a natural outcome of the tree structure. These additions can be displayed on the client browser, or they can remain unseen, depending on the application.

Tags are repeated throughout the XML document. The tags compress well, resulting in efficient data transfer requirements. Data compression and data transfer are important issues in Web-based systems because one major purpose of the XML specification is to enable information to be transferred across the Web from a source to a requestor.

XML allows the ability to embed database-type information in a document without limiting names or specifying order. The data element tags, as defined by the DTD, serve a similar purpose as the tables in a database. When each company or industry uses an XML document, it can decide on a level of detail for its DTD and document structure. And other companies can build on top of the standards and ignore details as appropriate. Therefore, if Ford creates a DTD for a B2B document that only uses <customer_name>, GM can use the same document and add tags for <first_name> and <middle_initial>. Ford can use the new document and include the new capability in its applications. Or it can continue to use its existing applications, which will ignore the new GM tags with no significant loss in processing.

Universal Data Exchange Format

The omnimorphic use of XML as a universal data format improves corporate interoperability and data transfer. One advantage of XML is that the DTDs will be downloaded into the browser along with the document. It is like having a translator interpret automatically during all international telephone calls. XML enhances an application's ability to work with systems from yesterday, today, and tomorrow. A universal data format alone does not guarantee interoperable access of information to everyone, everywhere, every time. Data exchange applications require uniform standards for communications. These standards include the data element types, a common definition of the types, and uniform methods for data transfer. Meta-data, in the form of XML schemas and DTDs, address the requirements for inter-application standards and data transfer.

XML tools and applications can process, share, and modify XML documents very simply. XML's database flavor integrates well with many existing database applications, such as Oracle. An XML document can be easily represented in a database format. If the components of an XML document are stored in a database, the results of a query can be presented as an XML document.

The most exciting development in data-integration, middle-tier, and application-server tools are the B2B applications that facilitate different companies, partners, and vendors talking to one another. These applications, which enable one Web site to use data from another Web site, ultimately allow the user to compare information from many different vendor Web sites. That is what's new about XML in terms of browsing.

Another area of new development is XML-based vertical applications such as integrated browsers, editors, and tools for a specific XML vocabulary. One of the fast moving companies involved in XML development is Intrig (www.intrig.com), based near Dallas, Texas. Intrig is a forward-thinking company that is providing visions, strategies, and implementations that are needed in today's XML environment. In addition to significant WAP and WML development, Intrig has developed an XML-based vertical application suite. This next generation software suite is used to develop advanced Internet and wireless protocol software.

The specific application is dependent on the needs of the user. It is comparable to how different people might process information as they walk down the street. One person might notice the people, another person might see the cars, and a third person might focus on the noise. The information obtained from an experience or from a document is based on the needs germane to the requirements. XML provides a method for tagging information for easy filtering.

CHAPTER 7

XML for Databases and EDI

Introduction

XML is really all about data and databases. XML can be used to tag data and information that are stored in a set of files. For example, the information for invoices, billing information, and inventory data can be stored in a single file that each application accesses and formats as needed. In addition, the components of correspondence (such as addresses, dates, data, and even text) can be stored in a set of files using an XML format and then reused as appropriate. However, file systems are not always the best repositories. So, XML formatted information can also be stored in databases.

XML is like a database technology in that each XML document is a table within a database. This analogy, however, stretches thin fairly quickly because a relational database is a relational, random-access beast, and an XML document is a hierarchical, sequential-access animal. The underlying assumption is that today's and tomorrow's faster processors and networks will enable the hierarchical and associative aspects of XML to function adequately, even in a sequential mode. And that's a good assumption that already has multibillion dollar backing and proof.

However, can we have the best of both world's—a multifunctional, relational XML database? The answer is a resounding "Yes! Of course!" Without the need for genetic engineering, we can design a new animal, called an XML database, by taking components of XML documents and storing them, like any other data, within a relational database.

Retrieving a complete XML document from one database or many is no more complicated than creating an XML document from any set of distributed sources, such as Web sites. With data retrieval out of the way, this leaves two topics: data storage and data transfer. The topics that we will explore are how to store the XML data in a database and how to exchange XML data among different database sources to build dynamic XML documents. During these explorations, we will also see how XML helps to bridge data from legacy systems, current systems, and future systems.

Storing XML in Databases

Typically, a user stores XML documents in a file system so that they can be reused. Remember, XML data are independent of applications. A specific XML document may have to be saved to a file system or to a database in order to be reused in the same format. An XML document is a text file, so after it is saved in a file system, it can be manipulated by a text editor, a word processor, a spreadsheet, or a database.

Storing XML documents in a file system is adequate for many purposes. However, a file system is too limited for mission critical information that will be widely shared or reused. For example, a simple file system is not adequate for very large documents, which are more easily broken into segments for simpler use. Just as with Web pages, a set of smaller pieces is much easier to navigate and manipulate than one very large document.

If these segments will change frequently and independently, then separating them is superior to maintaining a single monolithic document. With different segments, each section can be worked on separately and in parallel with other sections, resulting in faster changes, and more current, up-to-date documents.

In fact, each segment may be a different format, so that different tools are used for different sections. A simple example is a compound document under Microsoft Windows. If a spreadsheet and a graphic are embedded within an MS Word document, then MS Excel and MS PowerPoint are used for those sections. However, XML enables the next level of functionality.

Rather than a lower level application, a higher level system might be used to manipulate the various sections. For example, an inventory system might combine data from a few different sections and then automatically make changes throughout the document as needed. Then a billing system might make different calculations and propagate them throughout the document without modifying any changes due to the inventory. Finally, a labor reporting system could go through other modifications by using only the data that it needs and then making changes only where pertinent. With conventional applications, people guide the machine to the data. With XML documents, the tags filter the information automatically and save some people cycles in the process.

Even though a user can apply different programs to modify different sections of an XML document, it is still difficult to let many users safely and simultaneously make different modifications to one document. However, rather than using a standard file system, developers can use a database to overcome this difficulty.

Document Decomposition

XML facilitates the creation of a reusable document, and a database facilitates the storage of an XML document. But a database does not store an XML document as a flat file or as a text document. If that were how a database functioned, it would provide no advantage over a file system. No, a database stores an XML document as a collection of document nodes.

An XML document is a tree structure that is composed of a hierarchical grouping of nodes, as shown in Figure 7.1. The node structure of the XML document is based on the XML tag syntax, as in Figure 7.2, for example. The structure and the syntax enhance the ability to assign meaning and context to the data. They are also the basis for efficiently storing an XML document in a database. A database can handle large amounts of data and can allow multiple users to access and manipulate different sections of the same document.

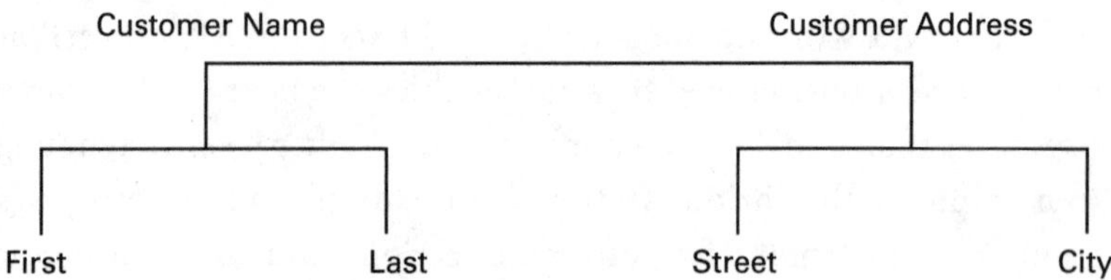

FIGURE 7.1 An XML document has a hierarchical tree structure dictated by the relationships among the data element tags.

```
<customer>
  <customer_name>
        <first>Harris</first>
        <last>Blatt</last>
    </customer_name>
  <customer_address>
        <street>56 Clemson</street>
        <city>Brooklyn</city>
  </customer_address>
</customer>
```

FIGURE 7.2 The data element tags in the XML document provide the scaffolding for building the tree structure.

The XML document is decomposed into its nodes, and the nodes are stored in a database. Two common types of database systems can store XML documents: a Relational Database (RDB) and an Object-Oriented Database (OODB).

An RDB can store an XML document in the same way that it might store any other files, such as image, audio, or video files. The XML document is stored as strings of text in the familiar row and column approach. The row represents an element, and the column represents the attributes. For example, in Figure 7.3, a Name table can be designed to hold *<first_name>* and *<last_name>* elements, and an Address table can be designed to hold *<Address>* elements. In addition, text attributes, such as *Street*, *Drive*, or *Boulevard*, can be represented in a column called PCDATA in order to parse these specific attributes as text elements. In addition to storing elements in the rows of a table, node relationships must also be defined.

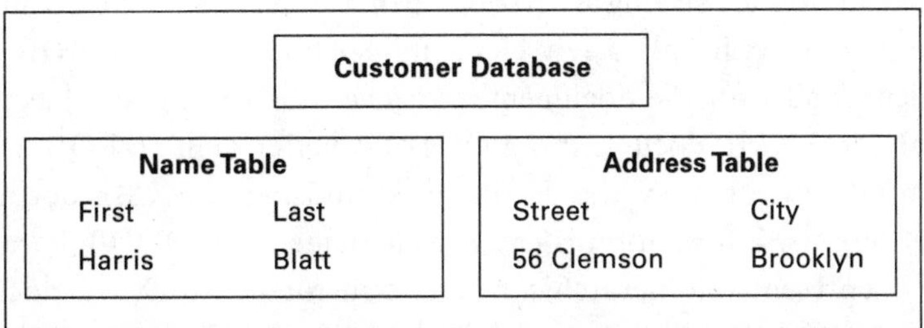

FIGURE 7.3 A relational database can be designed with tables that hold XML data elements. For example, the Name table holds first and last names, while the Address table holds address information.

Defining tables to represent XML elements is easy, but the power of an XML tree is the structured relationships among its nodes and elements. Relationships in a relational database are defined by creating a separate table called a *join*, which links two or more tables based on their keys. For example, an Address table can be linked to a Customer table by using a Customer Address table to join them, as seen in Figure 7.4.

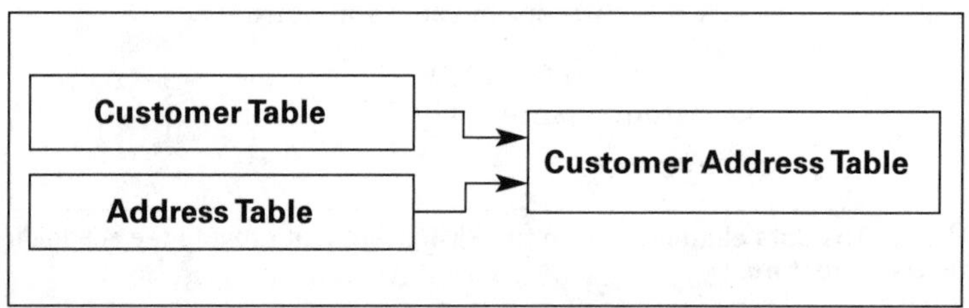

FIGURE 7.4 A Customer Address table can join a Customer table and an Address table.

Using an RDB to represent XML documents presents two limitations. First, representing a hierarchical XML data model in a relational format is inefficient. And second, although a RDB can represent a simple, fixed XML tree structure, it cannot represent the more advanced structures that include optional or variable relationships. For example, a special row is needed to account for an optional middle initial. In another example, an RDB may not be able to represent two different relationships for an element, such as a CD that belongs to a Music class or a Data class. A similar example is a cell phone that is a voice telephone or is an Internet data device.

For the most part, an RDB can represent many XML elements and XML documents. There are many cases where these exceptions do not appear. As long as node relationships are well structured and fixed, an RDB is an adequate solution for storing XML documents. When the XML document hierarchy is flat, with only a few elements per node, then the RDB can be an efficient model for the document. However, for storing an object-oriented, hierarchical XML document, an OODB is better than an RDB.

An OODB can store the decomposed nodes of an XML document as a set of objects. Information is easier to manage in an OODB, because it can easily represent the hierarchical node structure of an XML document. In addition, multiple users can manipulate information from a single XML document by using an OODB.

The object approach is a natural complement to the XML representation. An OODB allows analysts to build a faithful model of the XML document, nodes, and data. In additional, an object tree is easy to represent within an OODB. So, the basic foundation of an OODB does not have the limitations that an RDB has with respect to advanced relationships. It provides a powerful structure for a wide variety of XML documents and data.

A relational database RDBMS is not good with complex relationships. A many-to-many relationship requires a Join table. If new unforeseen data types or attributes are needed, then the tables must be rewritten to accommodate. Also, putting tables within tables is considered to be an advanced skill. Typically data are in a DBMS-specific format.

An object-oriented database ODMS is good with complex relationships. Each object holds data and relationships within it. If new datatypes are needed, inheritance can help, but if new attributes are needed, work arounds and wrappers can greatly complicate things. Data are usually integral to the object, so sharing data can result in redundancy. Objects can regularly hold other objects; however, from a practical standpoint, the number of layers is limited. Typically data are in an ODMS-specific format.

One of the great advantages of XML over a conventional database is that data can occur anywhere. For example, on one form *last_name* can come before *first_name*, and on another form the reverse. Data can come in any order because the tag—not the location, the table, the column, or the key—determines the meaning of the data. An XML application or parser can select the data needed, ignoring the rest, and then use and present the data in any way desired.

Because of the complexity of the document object model of XML, as well as its hierarchical components, relational databases aren't practical for storing XML documents. In a relational database you have to be concerned about foreign keys and model depth. However, mapping an XML component model to an object database results in a simple object structure. The object approach provides advantages in performance and simplicity.

Being able to combine information from large databases and repositories is a significant competitive edge. Providing users with the right data at the right time on an ad hoc, as-needed basis is a killer app.

An XML document is naturally subdivided into nodes and data elements. This natural subdivision makes it easier to store XML in a database. XML can be stored in the more widespread relational database or in the more functional object-oriented database. In an RDB, tables of XML data elements can be joined in order to establish the relationships among the nodes. In an OODB, the relationships are a convenient outcome of the structure of the database. The bottom line is that, regardless of the specific type, a database is a convenient place to store XML data, facilitating the user's ability to modify and reuse the data.

Exchanging XML Data

With any new technology, there is always a risk related to change. One way to mitigate the risk of changing to a new technology is to ensure that it is backwards compatible and that it will work with legacy data. Working with legacy data helps to reduce the risks of incurring additional costs through loss of historical data or from translating all of the old data to the new system. XML supports these factors in three ways. First, XML creates a standard format for transferring data among different systems, whether legacy, current, or future. Second, it provides a standard format for retrieving data from these different systems. Third, XML renders a more robust embodiment of the client/server model.

Data Transfer Format

XML provides a universal format for data transfer between applications and systems. In addition, it provides a strong foundation for implementing a client/server data model. By exploiting the standards that XML enables, a developer can create a method for transferring data among different applications, easily, seamlessly, and smoothly.

Using Legacy Data

Although converting legacy data to an XML format is possible, it is not necessarily a good idea. Because of the investment and overhead, a strong business case for converting the data should be present. Once the business case is justified, a phased approach to XML conversion may be the most cost-effective method. In any case, after the business needs and financial cases have been made, converting legacy data to XML should enable maximum reuse, compatibility, and interoperability with other corporate data, applications, and systems.

Data Warehouse

XML allows a company to create a set of standards for an XML document architecture that facilitates data and information exchange. Definition of the full range of XML documents is a well-defined process. A well-defined XML document architecture can help to automate the supply chain process; the order fulfillment process; the blueprint, bill of materials and assembly process; and the creation of a data warehouse from letters, memos, and e-mail.

XML data elements and formats can link databases so that data and information can easily be cross-referenced and retrieved, creating the virtual data warehouse capability.

By analyzing the information in a corporate relational database, you can determine trends about sales, inventory, and customers, etc. Documents, e-mail, help desk logs, memos, letters, and white papers are examples of unstructured sources of valuable corporate information.

XML documents support access to all of this valuable information through data, text, and information mining activities. Data mining typically dealt with information stored in a relational database. Before XML, mining collections of documents was not easy. A user could use full-text searching on single documents but could not easily link the information. With XML documents, the information can be linked through data element tags. The user can mine the text of a document collection by using the tags as search terms.

XML is also great for knowledge discovery. The user can automatically discover nonobvious trends in the document that lead to new knowledge, decisions, and opportunities.

Implementing an XML document system increases reusability and interoperability, and, therefore, also increases the value of existing intellectual assets. Productivity increases because information is reused rather than reinvented. Also, users can draw new associations because they have seamless access to a wider collection of information from a diverse document set. A competitive advantage emerges from the new associations and integrated information that can be extracted from XML documents.

One way that XML can integrate data from legacy systems with data in relational databases is to leverage the meta-data, DTD, and tags. The DTD and tags supply XML with an open architecture that can be more easily integrated with older systems without having to expend the resources to totally redevelop them. For this reason, many database vendors are including some form of XML functionality in their databases.

In fact, Oracle has developed completely new products that leverage the capabilities of XML. These products embody Oracle's experience developing B2B e-commerce projects for the Covisint automotive exchange and the Sears B2B retail exchange.

In addition, IBM has developed software that will transform an XML document into the rows and columns in a database. The software uses Java and SAX to interactively drill down the XML document and successively transform the elements to the appropriate rows and columns.

The data in a data warehouse comes from the operational environment in almost every case. The data warehouse is a physically separate store of data transformed from the application data found in the operational environment. Data warehouses support information processing by providing a solid platform of integrated, historical data for analysis. They are constructed in an evolutionary, step-at-a-time fashion to provide a facility for data integration in a world of nonintegrated application systems. Data warehouses organize and store the data needed for analytical processing and trend analysis over a long historical time perspective.

One of the goals for XML is to collect various forms of information and data into a common format to facilitate access, evaluation, and analysis. XML supports the extraction, transformation, and loading of the data into a fused perspective, where applicable, with the intent of creating decision support, trend analysis, and knowledge discovery capabilities within a data warehouse environment.

XML provides the capability to transform all corporate documents into very flexible data warehouse entities that permit near infinite variety in the information search possibilities and that can be searched using a Web browser. This is in dramatic contrast to today's reality for data warehouses.

A *data warehouse*, according to its inventor Bill Inmon, is a collection of integrated, subject-oriented databases designed to supply the information required for decision making.

Integrated

The most important aspect of the data warehouse environment is the fact that the data is integrated. Integration appears in various ways, such as meta-data, naming conventions, variables, and data formats. Compare the level of integration with that of the applications environment, and the differences are startling.

Applications designers have made many separate choices in building applications. The style and choice of design appear in myriad ways. These differences have resulted in the lack of integration in the applications environment. However, in a data warehouse environment, the data are integrated regardless of their original sources. Because of its need for consistency and integration, XML is a promising enabler for data warehouse development.

Subject Oriented

The real world revolves around the flow of data and information such as competitive information, inventory, financials, and medical information. Corporate warehouses focus on subjects such as customer activity, vendor information, and product data. The organization in subject areas influences the design, development, and implementation of the data in the data warehouse.

Application developers are involved with database design and process design. Data warehouse developers concentrate mainly on data modeling and database design. Data warehouse developers have little functional interest in process design.

The difference between a data warehouse and an operational database is that a data warehouse uses only decisional data that is germane to the decision support systems. Operational applications and databases are more transaction oriented, focusing on the immediate requirements. In addition, operational data is interrelated only in the current contexts, while data warehouse data may be related over a long span of time. Except for these functional differences, operational systems and data warehouse systems are similar. Indeed, both types of systems can be represented by a set of XML documents with equal ease.

Time Variant

The data warehouse contains data from a range of times. As mentioned above, this is a difference between operational and data warehouse systems. Operational systems have current data, and data warehouse systems have time-spanned data. Thus, data warehouses are called *time variant*. In addition, because of this time variance, data warehouse data are not updated but collected continually. XML supports time variance in data warehouses because it can be used as a common format for representing legacy, current, and future data.

Nonvolatile

Because data are never updated, they do not change or expire. Therefore, the data in the data warehouse tend to be fairly stable and nonvolatile.

The characteristics of a data warehouse—subject orientation of design, integration of data within the data warehouse, time variance, and simplicity of data management—all lead to an environment that is very different from the classical operational environment.

The source of nearly all data warehouse data is the operational environment. It is a temptation to think that there is massive redundancy of data between the two environments. Indeed, the first impression many people draw is that of great data redundancy between the operational environment and the data warehouse environment. Such an understanding is superficial and demonstrates a lack of understanding as to what is occurring in the data warehouse. In fact redundancy of data between the operational environment and the data warehouse environment is minimal.

XML Advantages

Conventional data warehouses are expensive and complex client/server applications that require technical expertise to maintain and special training to query. The Web and XML can unlock the treasures buried deep in the warehouses to provide access to corporate intellectual capital in ways never before possible. XML can also help to recover lost nuggets of knowledge buried within the mountains of corporate documents, paperwork, and manuals. And, considering the rate of accelerating change inherent with any Internet-related technology, XML-based data warehouses and knowledge management will quickly become the standard across most industries and will be considered the cost of doing business, just like having a Web site or a FAX.

With XML, a corporation can define one access point for all enterprise information sources, including databases, documents, reports, manuals, applications, and query tools. Broad intranet access to corporate data and information resources is just the beginning. Extended access to industry partners, suppliers, and customers (with reciprocal agreements) will trigger an explosion in the creation of distributed data warehouses. As access to useful information increases, the focus will shift dramatically from tools to data. Top level executives will ask their staff for different ways to use, analyze, and leverage this newfound wealth of data.

Another advantage of XML and a distributed data warehouse is the ability to get information into the hands of the workers and salespeople who need it. People will be taught how to think about their jobs, not how to use complicated tools. Rather than training everyone on the use of difficult data mining tools, training efforts will shift to knowledge management and business intelligence concepts.

With the advent of accessibility, people will always want more. We have insatiable appetites for information, intelligence, and insight. Instead of the simple queries using SQL, there will be a new paradigm for searching information. Data mining and data visualization tools will be simpler with XML documents. XML has the potential to balance the user's need for information power and ease of use.

Data, Information, Knowledge

Data are the facts and the noise. *Information* is the patterns in the data. *Knowledge* is validated information within a certain context. For the mathematically minded, think of data as being a scalar, a single point or fact. Information is a vector, a fact with some direction or meaning. Knowledge is a tensor, information with a specific orientation, context, or perspective. Wisdom is knowledge coupled with history and experience.

Data are simple facts, such as 100 degrees Centigrade. Data can be stored in a spreadsheet or in a database. Information is the combination of two or more facts, such as water boils at 100 degrees Centigrade. A database query that joins different data into new facts is creating information. Because of the current flood of data and information, executives value people and tools that can filter out irrelevant information and focus on useful information.

Knowledge is aggregated information within a specific context, such as the knowledge that water boils at different temperatures as the elevation changes. One reason that knowledge management is so hard to define compared to data is because of this difference. Data is fairly simple and fixed, so it is easy to characterize with simple logic. However, knowledge changes with context or use, so it has to be characterized with a very flexible format, such as XML, to anticipate unspecified usage. It is difficult to build a logical, open-ended structure to store knowledge.

Wisdom consists of ideas or actions that are flexible and are based on experience, such as the wisdom that says that a watched pot doesn't boil. In business, wisdom is revealed by the ability to put knowledge into useful action.

Data Mining

Data mining refers to using tools to find trends in the data automatically, or to identify hypotheses that may yield valuable information upon exploration. While standard SQL database queries can filter data into a specific answer, a useful query depends on a good hypothesis. Data mining uses algorithms or statistical models to locate less intuitive trends in the data in order to provide new insights that a business executive can use.

Data mining is typically a complex activity that used to require the Information Technology (IT) department to handle and then load the results into the data warehouse for the business users. It is not considered to be a desktop application. XML has the potential to completely revamp the data mining landscape. XML tags may serve as a type of meta-data. *Meta-data* is information about data, and XML provides content information about data in a document—not too far apart. Meta-data solutions such as XML can be incorporated as an important enabler in the strategic enterprise IT plans and architectures.

XML supports the data warehouse, and XSL supports the data mining. A little Java may help but is not necessary. A data analyst, preferably with some artificial intelligence experience, can help generate the knowledge elements and structures. XML will provide dramatic functionality to data warehouse and data mining applications. Not only does it allow for modeling, XML also uses built-in meta-data in identifying data content, context, and meaning. Taken the next step, an XML document repository can serve double duty as a data warehouse with no additional development. This capability can easily be extended to the Web. More and more documents will be published in XML format, and these documents can be used as part of a worldwide distributed data warehouse for intelligent data mining using XML-enabled search engines and tools.

EDI

Before B2B there was Electronic Data Interchange (EDI). EDI was where e-commerce truly began. By using EDI, a company could build electronic communication and business transaction systems that processed orders and transferred invoices between organizations. The pure EDI architecture is too cumbersome for the Web because transactions were direct computer-to-computer links from a database on one mainframe to another database on a mainframe in a different organization. The interactions were transacted over privately leased lines as opposed to the open Web networking.

EDI was an important method of communicating data transactions between companies. Before the Web, this was the main digital form of B2B. However, B2B is real time, in contrast to EDI's batch processing. In addition, EDI communications were fixed to specified partners connected across a Value Added Network (VAN), not a World Wide Web that enables B2B communications with any corporation across the globe. To summarize, in comparison to EDI, B2B communications are real time, automated, and open to the world.

An EDI implementation was based on an explicit two-step agreement between two companies. First, a specific industry or a group of cooperating companies negotiated on the data element types and formats used for the transactions. Second, the transactions and data formats were implemented in the EDI systems. Because of the complexity of the EDI implementations, each trading and transaction agreement was specific to a set of partners. With each new set of trade agreements and business partners came a new EDI application.

Corporate activities in conventional EDI are being replaced by B2B e-commerce activities based on XML and Java. EDI was developed for proprietary, leased VAN connections, not for the Internet. Industry analysts predict that, over the next few years, EDI will grow in the billions of dollars, while XML-based B2B e-commerce will grow into the *trillions* of dollars. Therefore, the smart bet for EDI-based companies is to explore XML solutions and technologies for data transactions.

EDI structures can be used as a basis for XML communications, allowing both EDI and XML users to share the system. Corporations do not have to write off all of their EDI investments and make a complete switch to XML. After a few test cases are developed for selected departments, an

EDI/XML system can propagate throughout the corporation addressing yesterday's systems, today's problems, and tomorrow's opportunities.

Although EDI is typically a limited transaction between two companies, the EDI structures are applicable to B2B efforts. B2B is typically an open and unlimited trading agreement that can change fluidly and dynamically. EDI was also based on building a consensus among trading partners. On the Internet, this is a near impossibility, given the global nature and culture differences among partners.

B2B e-commerce is based on an ephemeral community of trading partners, vendors, and suppliers, who join and leave the community as needed. This fluctuating environment requires a robust foundation, such as XML, to maintain the dynamic stability required for today's interactions.

Because of the cost and complexity of EDI systems, companies are looking to XML as a method for cheaper and simpler data transfer. The companies that use XML will have an uphill battle trying to persuade companies entrenched in EDI to try something new like XML. The popularity of B2B has helped to drive the XML market. The growing market means a growing demand for conversion services, which include XML and EDI. To address this potential crossover, a growing number of companies are developing EDI/XML tools that work with both systems. In addition, many EDI vendors see the handwriting on the walls and are beginning to offer translation applications that convert EDI transactions into XML documents.

Even though an XML document is a data file, it was not originally developed as a replacement for EDI or as an enabler of B2B e-commerce. It was designed to provide developers with extensible markup, so that they could build interoperable systems, seamless data exchanges, and application-independent information that could be displayed on any device. These noble design goals barely hint at the transactions typical of EDI, and they are silent on e-commerce. However, developers can exploit XML to define business meta-data, vocabularies, rules, and transactions.

An XML text file plus an XML DTD or schema equal a very structured XML document. If all companies agree on the DTD vocabulary, then you can zap your XML catalog document to another business who can then apply an XSL style sheet to represent the data as a purchase order, an inventory, or a mailing label. If the vocabularies are different, that's OK too, because an XSLT script can transform between the different vocabularies.

One useful function of XML schemas and DTDs is that they convey meaning to applications, so that the applications can accurately distinguish between useful and extraneous information. By using a simple XML document, corporations can distribute information and data transactions across a variety of business systems. In addition, XML documents can be transferred across the open Web at virtually no cost and can also cross the firewall to enable data transfer in ways that are much more efficient and cost effective than EDI.

XML and B2B efforts do not abruptly eliminate EDI. They gradually incorporate lessons and best practices from EDI experiences and make adjustments in the B2B e-commerce model to accommodate these experiences and practices.

XML/EDI Foundation

The XML/EDI combination provides a new way to create documents and to handle data transactions. The use of XML to handle EDI capabilities provides an additional layer of processing intelligence to the transaction equation. The XML standard provides a solid foundation for e-commerce and e-business by enabling documents to be shared, searched, catalogued, and inventoried. All of the basic building blocks for B2B e-commerce are contained in the XML specifications. As more and more companies jump on the B2B bandwagon, XML is the catalyst that will effect rapid business change in managing and controlling critical transaction information.

XML provides a simple way for handling electronic business transactions while also maintaining all the functionality of the legacy EDI systems that were so complex and cumbersome. XML can adapt to existing technologies, link with past databases, and be extended to include future business requirements and technologies. With all of that, XML is also an open standard, unlike the various incarnations of EDI; therefore, it is being broadly embraced by many industries. However, passing the baton from EDI applications to XML applications is much more involved than simply waving a magical mark-up wand.

An EDI to XML transformation requires a solid XML/EDI foundation. The first requirement is that all EDI functions can be mapped to corresponding XML capabilities. This should not be a difficult task because XML is a more encompassing technology. However, it is an important exercise for the XML developer to insure that all the EDI bases are covered and that nothing sneaks in out of left field to shut down the operation.

EDI used leased networks, batch processing, and fixed format. In contrast, XML uses the Web, immediate access, and flexible formatting. XML tags can be defined to handle the same functions as the EDI segment identifiers.

The EDI/XML foundation, indicated in Figure 7.5, includes templates to use rules for establishing process steps for the transaction. They can be incorporated with the DTDs to insure interoperability by providing the meta-data needed for corporations to understand each other's vocabularies.

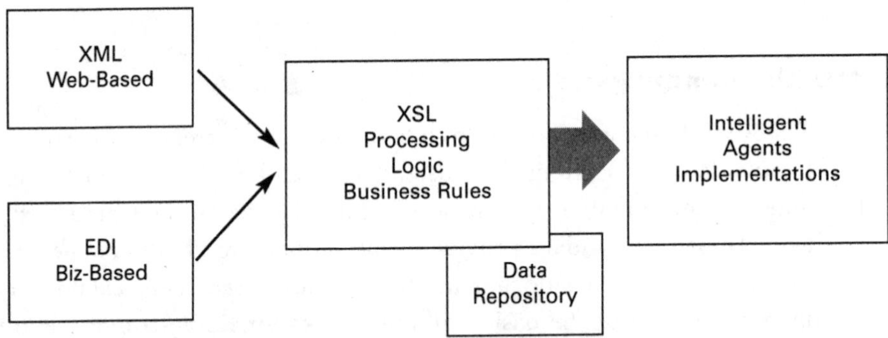

FIGURE 7.5 An EDI/XML foundation combines both technologies by using rules, repositories, and agents for implementation.

Intelligent agents use the templates to carry out the process steps, link the correct template to the appropriate task, and create new templates as needed. These agents can be created using XSLT, Java, ActiveX, or any other programming environment. The correct combination of these components results in a viable XML/EDI system.

XML/EDI Models

XML/EDI uses four models: star, ad hoc, hybrid, and Web. The *star model* is a standard EDI approach in which a central corporation defines the protocols for all the business partners. The *ad hoc model* is a Web-based approach that allows partners to modify their interactions on demand. The *hybrid model* combines the best of both worlds and employs a star model with ad hoc modifications. The *Web model* focuses on the information being transferred as opposed to the data transaction rules that are typical of a conventional EDI interaction.

By using these four models, XML/EDI developers can build an infrastructure for a wide variety of B2B systems. Rather than a limited EDI system, developers can use XML to build flexible and open systems that will scale-up to meet the needs of tomorrow's business opportunities. By adapting to the individual needs of the developer and the corporation for EDI solutions, XML applications allow for uniform systems and interoperable transactions.

Advantages of the XML/EDI Approach

The main advantage of the XML/EDI approach is the flexibility of XML to define the data and interactions more clearly and more robustly, with a greater depth than was possible with previous technologies. XML metadata: tags and DTDs allow the XML/EDI transaction to carry an "interpreter" with the interchange in order to let all parties understand the results. Another feature of the XML approach is that the XML/EDI foundation can be implemented as an entire system or as a partial solution that meets the individual needs of the developer.

The EDI of old was not exploited to its full capability because of its complexity. Typically, it was forced on trading partners as opposed to being embraced freely as a cost saving activity. EDI was used to send structured data to trading partners, but it was rarely used to send data to other corporations because of the high-dollar, proprietary software involved. In contrast, EDI/XML will be an enabling technology that saves money.

Using XML has many additional advantages and benefits. As stated, it uses open system standards that encourage broader use than the proprietary EDI standards. Therefore, more partners will participate than did previously in the EDI approach. The DTDs provide an additional layer of self-description to the interaction and transaction process. Because of its flexibility, XML will allow corporations to leverage their existing EDI capabilities and will allow vendors to provide new applications for existing systems. In addition to working with legacy systems, XML will provide a bridge from the past to the future, also working with emerging systems. Because it is built on open standards, XML applications tend to be less expensive than proprietary EDI systems. The Web approach encourages a real-time processing nature, in contrast to the EDI batch processing approach.

XML/EDI Document Management

XML is all about managing documents, as opposed to managing only the data. Many vendors are building document management systems that integrate with existing database systems and product data management systems. The advantage of a document management system is that the contained data have context and meaning, providing a richer capability than a simple database alone.

While traditional EDI systems were built for data transactions, the new XML/EDI systems will transfer documents, which can include more information such as catalogs, inventories, transaction histories, and audit trails. These capabilities can be developed initially as part of the transaction and maintained indefinitely as part of the normal process.

In addition, users will not need special EDI tools because they will be able to use their XML-enabled browsers to view and manipulate the XML/EDI transaction documents. For example, an XML/EDI document will contain the transaction data and the rules for handling the transaction. These rules may include routing, workflow, and event handling. The document may have sufficient embedded intelligence to automate its distribution list and the subsequent actions.

The XML specification was designed for the Web, but, just like HTML, an XML document can be used on the internal corporate intranet. So the XML/EDI process can be used internally as well as externally to facilitate the application-independent transfer of data and documents among organizations, whether or not they exist outside or inside the corporate firewalls.

Intelligent Agents

One of the powerful features of XML/EDI is the automation of various features by using templates, rules, and intelligent agents. Although the term *intelligent agent* sounds like something out of artificial intelligence research labs (in fact, it is!), these agents have been in use on the Web since 1995 or earlier. Many search engines use intelligent agents to index the millions of Web sites developed throughout the world. The familiar wizards used in the

MS Windows operating systems are based on intelligent agents. The Help function is also based on intelligent agent technology. For the purposes of EDI/XML, intelligent agent technology is fairly mature.

There is a wide diversity of intelligent agents from simple, repetitive 'bots to complex, rule-based workflow wizards. For example, a repetitive 'bot could be a simple script that counts the number of users who visit a Web page. It can include simple rules, such as sending out an e-mail message every time the number of users clicked over a new century mark. Although an agent is usually independent of the application, a complex macro for a spreadsheet or for a database could also function as an agent.

XML/EDI Connects to EDI

XML/EDI can transfer data between EDI applications by using rules and templates that provide complete backwards compatibility. The template maps the EDI messages into a usable format, which reduces the need for other transformations. However, XML/EDI files will be as much as 50 percent larger than normal EDI transactions. Of course, the EDI transaction contains much less information and works with fewer systems and applications. So, the size trade-off is clearly worth the benefit.

The use of XML can cut EDI data transaction costs by getting rid of the expensive transactions and proprietary VANs that EDI requires. However, companies where EDI is already a sunken cost and an entrenched technology are not about to switch to XML. Therefore, XML has to span both the legacy EDI world and the new XML B2B world. That's OK, it can do that. And at the same time, XML can enable use of EDI without a large, expensive IS staff to manage it. XML is a young technology, but, as it gradually replaces legacy systems such as EDI, it will grow up and mature into a well-rounded IT approach for data transfer. However, EDI-centric companies need not panic. XML probably won't completely phase out EDI for 5 to 10 years. Meanwhile, companies can use an EDI-to-XML translation capability to integrate the two technologies.

Risks

The situation with XML is like the environment for HTML in 1995 and for the relational database technology in the late 1970s. In the early days of relational databases, people did not fully understand how to exploit their capabilities. With XML, everything is still new and developers are just now learning how to use XML. However, most people have not yet had sufficient experience to leverage the full potential of XML. Let's look at the relational database model in comparison to the XML document model.

The relational database model does not put constraints on the way that developers store data. It provides the format, and the developer chooses how to define the tables, the columns, and the data. In the same way that relational databases revolutionized data storage, XML revolutionizes information transfer over the Web. Just like a relational database, XML does not put constraints on the content of the information or the way that it is structured. That is up to the developers who define tags to implement the vocabularies, structure, and content of the information. Both the relational database and XML models serve as scaffolding to support the structure of information in a more robust way than previously possible.

By exploring the lessons of history, we can understand the trends of XML. In the early 1980s, relational databases were superior to the next best technology, hierarchical databases. Vendors and developers created more and more new databases because the technology facilitated ease of development and use. In addition, vendors created a plethora of new database applications to support the development.

One of the first problems that arose from the development of relational databases was inconsistency. Corporations built hundreds of individual databases without integrating the results. Any set of databases might contain redundant data, but they could not exchange data because there were no design standards. Because of the patches and rework needed to exchange data among databases, other applications were delayed as 30-50 percent of the information system department budget was devoted to database integration and data transfer efforts.

For the most part, the problem arose from the lack of coordinated efforts to design a common format for all the databases. Design efforts were localized, if they even existed at all. Columns were not consistent across two databases, and integration links were difficult to maintain. The problems and complexities of database integration persist even today, decades later.

XML development has the same potential for overwhelming complexity due to a lack of integrated design and development efforts. There are efforts to standardize the use of DTDs within industries, such as the automotive industry, the retail industry, and the financial industry. Currently many of the B2B efforts attempt to standardize vocabularies within the B2B community, but that may not help an individual corporation or a company that belongs to multiple B2B concerns. However, the development of interfaces and data exchanges is facilitated by a limited number of vocabularies.

As the standards wars begin to heat up, corporations are hesitating to enter the XML domain, not sure which standard will win. However, this approach is poor because learning about the changes and then implementing them will be easier if the development team already has a little XML experience. Besides, there are many technologies that are emerging to help with the transformation from one standard to another. The battle for standards domination may go on for a few years, so avoidance may be a crippling business decision.

A much better approach is to jump into the middle of the activity to learn about XML, documents, and databases. Corporations can develop a collection of database applications and XML interfaces to work with the various standards until a few leaders emerge from the pack.

Being vigilant to complexity is important. The complexity of databases continues to taunt developers and integrators. XML's flexibility can multiply that complexity to swallow entire companies if they do not learn the lessons of the past. One way to wrest control from the spiraling standards is to develop a set of data and document models that represent how the company does business. The method for building these models comes under the general heading of *creating an architecture*, although this methodology appears to be lacking in these early days of XML.

Consider that most, if not all, XML programming books on the market discuss how to build and implement an XML system. These books describe the methods for defining a problem and for developing the DTDs for an XML solution. However, this author has not been able to find any books that detail how to create an enterprisewide XML document design architecture. A generalized design methodology for representing all corporate documents as a set of standardized XML documents would go a long way toward bypassing the pitfalls that befell relational databases. One approach for a stopgap XML document design architecture is outlined in the next section.

XML Document Design Architecture

One of the advantages of using an XML document architecture is that document components can be easily stored in a database or in other documents and then reused. Standardization of the document structure facilitates reuse. After data element types are defined, the structure of these data elements are guaranteed to be identical. Documents can be produced in quantity, can be automated, are immediately available, and have minimal production costs and predictable search fields. The challenge of standardizing XML documents lies not in the physical implementation, not in production, but in the initial design. XML document designers must define document components that are universally applicable and easily reusable across a variety of corporate documents. Although this task may seem insurmountable, there are well-defined steps for building an architecture, and the potential savings in production are immense.

An XML Document Design Architecture (XDA) consists of three layers: a conceptual layer, a logical layer, and a physical layer. This definition borrows aspects directly from database design, client/server design, and UML design.

The *conceptual layer* or model consists of the business requirements that are captured by all the various documents used throughout the corporation. Simply gathering all these documents into one location can be a Herculean task. But the payoff is significant in the longer term, and it is very much worth the effort.

The *logical layer* or model is a map from the business requirements and documents into a set of document templates that decompose into a standard set of document data element types. The Dublin Core standard (purl.oclc.org/metadata/dublin_core), which describes the components of a document and DocBook standard (www.oreilly.com/catalog/docbook/chapter/book/docbook.html), which describes documents from an SGML legacy viewpoint, may be good places to start for guidance.

The logical model assigns data element types to the specific document types to create an XML document type template that will be filled with data and text to satisfy some specific business function. For example, if you want to write a memo, you would choose the memo template from the collection of XML document types. Then you would fill in the various data elements and fields with specific data and text to satisfy your specific need.

The *physical layer* involves the creation of the document instance by filling in the data elements and fields. Because XML is so new, the editing tools are not yet mature, so development may be manual. This is the step that most XML books describe when they discuss the creation of DTDs and XML documents. However, by using the full architecture lifecycle, an XML document or database designer can create applications that can be easily integrated, transferred, and reused.

An important part of defining an architecture is to clearly define each layer: conceptual, logical, and physical. Relationships clearly map from conceptual to logical to physical. However, to define each layer, first collect data and inventory information about the business functions, the document types, and the document element types. At each layer, review this information inventory, analyze it for consistency and redundancy, combine items as appropriate, and build relationships within layers and across layers. This iterative process results in a well-defined traceability matrix that maps business elements to documents to XML functions. As functions change, documents may be changed or more documents may be added, and elements may be added. The process enables a robust implementation and a graceful, seamless process for extension.

XML promises to be a cathedral in the architecture of the Web and of information exchange. The vision is that it will provide a convergence of concrete data and abstract context in a format that is equal to man and machine. Ultimately, XML may be the key to unlocking the decades old barriers among data transfer, information interoperability, and the knowledge sharing. A disciplined document and database architecture is one step on that path to shared knowledge. And a clear corporate document architecture is a gateway toward exploiting the extensibility of XML.

CHAPTER 8

B2B Exchange

Introduction

Even though XML is the basis for most B2B sites, it is not the total answer. The goal of a B2B system is to link front-end individualized Web interfaces into the back-end enterprise system. A B2B system helps to deliver customer information to the marketing and sales departments and also opens up corporate databases to collaborative trading partners and vendors. XML provides the ability to carry out catalog development, change management, order fulfillment, inventory control, and the integration of these functions.

In addition to integrating the procurement value chain, XML can also provide access to the manufacturing floor. It is a great common communications interface for the various process-control devices found on the factory floor and in the enterprise in general.

Although XML documents are well-structured data and information repositories, developers cannot just code a few lines and pop out a full B2B enterprise system. A number of design steps must be taken to create a scalable integration solution that leverages the best XML standards to fit the job. In addition, like any program management activities, an XML project requires a situation assessment, needs analysis, alternative solution evaluation, and an implementation plan. The plan should include some instructions for converting legacy information into an XML-compatible format.

Even as the information exchange problems are addressed, developers need to explore how to integrate processes from different companies.

B2B provides many advantages: It greatly expands the market for a corporation, because the Web exposes the information to a worldwide community.

Strategic Advantages of E-Business

E-business has the following strategic advantages:

- Supports virtual enterprise initiatives
- Supports interoperability among suppliers, vendors, and partners for a virtual company
- Supports new business models
- Creates new procurement value chains
- Provides flexible customer personalization
- Offers higher value that increases the customer's cost to switch
- Integrates the design, development, and production cycles
- Decreases time to market
- Enables close partner integration, perhaps closer than previously possible in the single company
- Unifies interfaces to third party software through the use of XML

The potential payoff for B2B e-commerce is tremendous. Analysts predict that over the next few years B2B e-commerce revenues will grow into the trillions of dollars, as shown in Figure 8.1. Based on the growth in on-line access of U.S. children and teenagers shown in Figure 8.2, as well as the growth in business to consumers (B2C) in the United States shown in Figure 8.3, it is reasonable to expect the B2B market may increase in order to keep up with demand by worldwide consumers.

Dell is a well-quoted success story that allows consumers, both corporate and individual, to order customized PCs. In an industry where profit margins are slim, Dell has been able to squeeze a healthy profit because of B2B e-commerce. B2B e-commerce allows Dell to earn higher revenues per employee than most other companies. Corporations in all industries would do well to use Dell as a benchmark for B2B e-commerce.

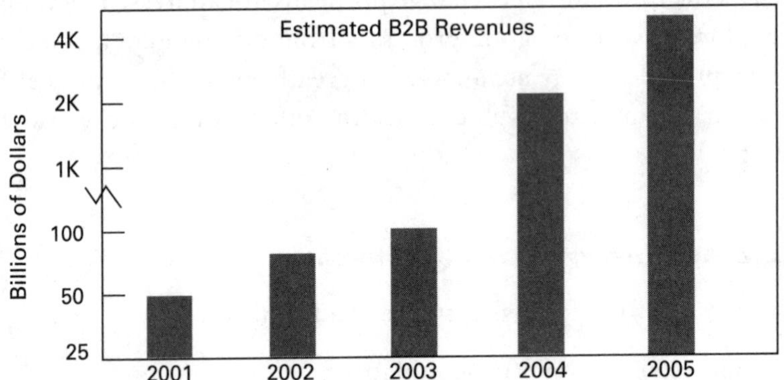

FIGURE 8.1 The estimated worldwide growth in B2B revenues over the next few years is expected to reach the trillion-dollar mark by 2004.

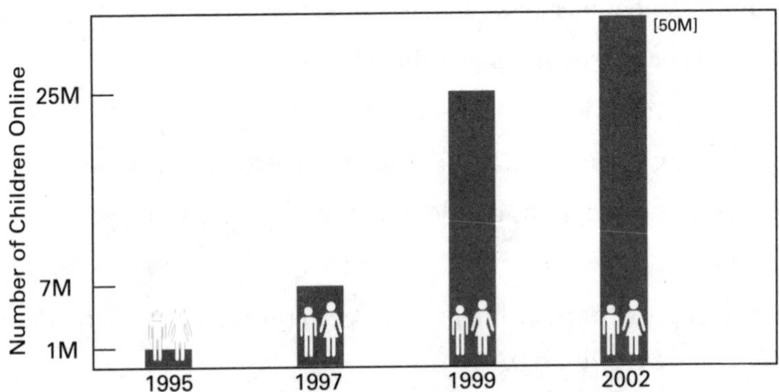

FIGURE 8.2 The growth in the number of U.S. children and teenagers who access the Internet is expected to break through the 50 million mark by 2002.

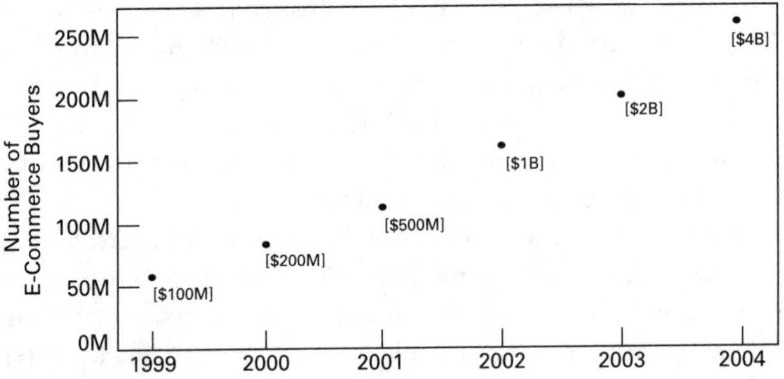

FIGURE 8.3 The growth in the U.S. B2C is a percentage of the worldwide market and may help drive the B2B revenues.

The Makings of a Successful B2B Implementation

A successful B2B implementation will have to manage a variety of factors such as the existing corporate culture, the corporate business model, the B2B business model, and the extent of the implementation. However, XML-based B2B e-commerce implementation is not an automatic, smooth as silk situation. First, the trading partners must come to some consensus about what XML standards and DTDs to use. Typically, the companies will have a general agreement with negotiations about the details. Next, the Web site cannot be a glamorous façade. It has to be functional and connected into the deep inner data sanctums of the corporation. Corporate data usually resides on a legacy database system. So, developers will build Web-enabled XML applications to access and retrieve this legacy data.

After the developers have integrated the back-end legacy databases into the B2B applications, they will have the potential to support a just-in-time supply chain. For this to happen, the developers will have to insure that database access is integrated to provide real time, on-demand response.

Corporations who want to cultivate B2B e-commerce developers can follow two paths. First, they can redirect their programming expertise to work on the e-commerce Web site. This can either be treated as a programming exercise or a business opportunity. As a programming exercise, the Web site will be cool, but it may not be compelling or good e-commerce. As a business opportunity, the Web site may be fairly boring from a technology special effects viewpoint, but it can still be compelling, useful, and a successful e-commerce site. Two good examples are Yahoo! and Dell.

Yahoo! is one of the oldest and busiest sites on the Web. You might think that a mature Web site would have accumulated the best graphics and the flashiest new technologies. But that is not the case with Yahoo!. The Yahoo! Web site has only a few tiny graphics and uses no flashy technology. It is also one of the fastest loading sites, one of the most visited, and one of the few profitable dot coms.

Dell is an example of B2B e-commerce. The Web site is clean, quick, and interactive. It uses a significant amount of new technology, which is all transparent to the user. The technology is on the back end, allowing the potential buyer to explore customized variations on PC configuration. One of the compelling points of the Dell Web site is that customers can play configuration what-if games all day long, without worrying about interference from commission-driven salespeople. A user can explore different configurations and immediately see the financial outcome from the exploration. The process is quick, responsive, and fairly intuitive. And it uses minimal whistles and bells up front.

However, the Dell Web site uses a significant range of new technologies that are hidden from the user. They are the mechanism for integrating with the back-end component databases, and enabling the what-if questions. In this case, the Web technology supports the business model.

Building XML documents that embody these business models will prove to be difficult for many users. Establishing a B2B relationship among a few companies can take an experienced programmer anywhere from a couple of hours to a couple of weeks, depending on the existing infrastructure. A carefully designed, scalable B2B exchange can take a few months. With this kind of IT experience at a premium, the complexities can overwhelm a development project.

Before any software is written, data analysts and business managers must define their requirements for B2B. They have to establish the trading agreements, channels, and connections long before the software engineers start writing code and integrating applications. Basically, the business people have to set up a conceptual architecture, or at least be guided in its definition as a representation for the B2B requirements. A set of graphics tools for visualizing the flow of information is useful. A simple flow diagram can depict the decisions and actions as a customer browses a catalog, explores a configuration of products and services, looks at the price list, makes a purchase, pays for the purchase, and receives the order. Eventually, graphical tools may be developed that will accelerate the steps from concept to implementation, making a B2B idea as easy to implement as a good presentation is.

A workable B2B system requires a business model that is different from the conventional model. Rather than automating paper-based systems, entirely new processes can be enabled. The majority of the procurement cycle can be automated. According to experts in the automotive field, this automation can eliminate the need for a large amount of paperwork, greatly speed up the process, and save as much as 90 percent of the procurement costs. Which brings up an interesting point . . .

Startup vs. Conventional

A reasonable assumption might be that startup companies would have a significant advantage over conventional established companies with regards to B2B. However, two fallacies occur in that kind of thinking. First, B2B requires a solid business model and good strategies. Large companies, such as IBM, Ford, GE, and GM are experts on building solid business strategies when they recognize an opportunity. Past failures were due to pride, not business planning. And the big companies recognize the profit potential of B2B. Once pride is overcome, these industry leaders can turn on a dime.

The other issue with B2B involves the new technologies, such as the Web and XML. Again, many companies have been involved with the Internet for much of its 30-year lifetime, longer than the lifetime of dot-com employees. Although they may not have superior XML skills, these traditional companies may be able to leverage their SGML expertise to rocket up the XML learning curve. Many of the humble SGML experts are proficient programmers who pick up new technologies as rapidly as a linguist picks up new languages. A good C programmer with SGML experience can pick up Java in a couple of weeks and XML in a couple of hours of training. The dot-com startups don't have the years of application experience stored at the conventional companies.

In fact, the biggest shot in the arm for XML came from the automotive industry with the announcement in February 2000 of the Covisint B2B collaboration among the Big Three automakers, Ford, GM, and DaimlerChrysler. Although many other B2B efforts were in progress, the $300 billion worth of products and services from the 30,000 automotive vendors really put B2B on the map.

Before that announcement, both Ford and GM were working on separate B2B activities. In fact, Ford has announced a plan to become e-Ford, a virtual company that leverages digital transactions and integrates (rather than manufactures) automobiles, products, and services. Ford will still make cars, but it will outsource as much of the work as practical. If it works, an apt comparison will be that Ford is the "Dell" for cars.

Established companies can take an exploratory approach to entering the B2B market, using a phased approach to learn quickly what works and what doesn't. Their advantage is that they do not put all of their products and services into one B2B basket, as the dot-com startups are forced to do. Established companies can fall back on their current business models if needed. And they can gradually transition more and more of their business from the conventional approach to an increasingly B2B approach.

The point is that corporations should be planning to do B2B e-commerce and e-business; this capability will soon be the cost of staying in the marketplace and staying competitive. Managers should not think that "even big companies can play." The business leaders should be thinking that B2B is growing because the big companies are building the business models at the forefront.

Cooperation is a *necessity*. B2B requires greater cooperation with partners and competitors. Again, consider the auto industry. Ford and GM are clearly competitors, yet they cooperate in their B2B venture. This is not really that difficult to understand. The Covisint B2B venture is not really a sharing of critical information and corporate secrets. It is a collaboration on procurement, vendors, and suppliers. Any company worth its salt already knows about the vendors used by its competitors. So there is no chance for loss of competitive advantage. What these companies are doing is sharing standards.

The auto industry shares many obvious standards. All major U.S. cars use the same fuel, the same oil, the same sizes of tires, the same batteries, etc. They also use a similar design for automatic transmission, for bumper heights, and for seatbelts. The look, feel, handling, and brand are the discriminators. So, the B2B collaboration merely creates another set of standards for the auto industry to agree upon.

These standards are XML-based descriptions of all parts and services and also of data transactions in the procurement supply chain. The standards make life easier and information transfer less expensive. XML enables the creation, collaboration, and extension of these standards. It is really a simple concept, somewhat as if all companies spoke a different language and then agreed to all speak English. That reduces costs involved in one level of translation. XML reduces costs related to shuffling paperwork among 30,000 different vendors and their supply chain applications. The single standard may help the vendors, because they won't have to keep a separate system for each automaker. In theory, the consumer should see some sort of cost reduction along down the line.

One of the potential outcomes of the B2B leveling of the playing field is that goods and services become commodities that are available from different vendors. In addition, a B2B exchange simplifies the process of comparison shopping for the best price. Therefore, companies will have to differentiate based on best value for the target customer. For example, if a vendor sells to the automotive industry, then the ability to delivery high volume goods may be an important factor. The automotive vendor may have an advantage over an aircraft vendor who sells similar goods, because aircraft tend to be low volume. Or a gadget seller may focus on packaging and service for individual customers, while a widget vendor may provide a favorable billing relationship for corporate sales.

Advertising Impact

Advertising will be even more important, not less, in the world of B2B e-commerce because vendors will have to clearly differentiate their products to the target group of customers. For example, Texas Instruments and Intel would not really want to compete with Radio Shack for the electronic hobbyist market. Although the margins are great and both companies can handle any levels of volume from hobbyists, neither company is set up to answer individual hobbyist questions. Both companies are happy to answer engineering design questions, but not questions like "I opened the back of my PC and now it doesn't work. What do I do?" No, those are questions better handled by Radio Shack, Gateway, or Dell.

In addition, advertising will help attract a whole new class of worldwide customers. Corporations throughout the world will be able to use B2B sites to negotiate deals that may be more favorable than terms from a local company. Through the use of delivery services, such as FedEx, a distant company may have better delivery times than a local company. Advertising will help build that reputation.

Benefits of B2B E-Commerce

So what are some of the benefits of B2B e-commerce for the corporations, trading partners, vendors, and suppliers? First, a B2B procurement effort can reduce costs by streamlining the entire procurement processes from initial order to fulfillment. It can provide the sellers with a more global marketplace exposure, allowing them greater leverage and visibility for their products and services without as much cost. On the flip side of the coin, buyers can use B2B exchanges to comparison shop more easily, exploring a wider base of suppliers that will have more competitive prices.

The financial benefits of e-business come not from increased revenues but from a new business model that increases profit margins and efficiencies. However, one big question is whether B2B is an overhyped or a viable new business model. One way to address this question is to benchmark some of the recent B2B efforts.

Some of the top B2B exchanges include CheMatch.com (www.chematch.com), which sells chemicals and plastics; PlasticNet.com (www.plasticnet.com), which sells material and news to the plastics industry; SciQuest.com (www.sciquest.com), which sells lab equipment, news, and supplies to laboratories and medical companies; Ventro Corp. (www.ventro.com), which builds vertical value chains; and Altra Energy Technologies (www.altranet.com), which sells to utility companies.

Another benefit that has emerged from B2B is the ability to purchase products, services, and information while on the go. As discussed previously in Chapter 6, wireless data communications, WAP (Wireless Application Protocol), and Bluetooth will enable m-commerce (mobile commerce), based on WML, a dialect of XML. So, as companies plan their B2B strategies, they will include options for wireless access to corporate applications, databases, catalogs, and inventories.

A B2B exchange is an example of a more efficient marketplace, because buyers and sellers gain insight into a more accurate picture of supply and demand. For example, sellers have immediate feedback on the demand and success of their products. They can get a better idea of customer desires and needs because they have closer contact with a wider population. Therefore, they can fine-tune their inventory needs, much the same as Dell Computers currently enjoys. Observing trends in product demands can result in better inventory control, which, in turn, can enable more accurate planning cycles and forecasting. With a closer feel for the pulse of the market, sellers can focus their time-to-market cycles and innovation schedules to match customer demand.

B2B Defined

In modern terms, B2B is nothing unusual, just one company selling to another across the Web. This type of transaction has been going on since around 1995 for the consumer. With B2B, other companies get into the act. However, sales and procurement across the Web is more than simply a method for selling at a distance. Telephone sales and 800 numbers have been doing that for decades. No, leveraging the Internet and the Web results in a revolutionary new business model that allows instant information, rapid financial transactions, and personalized service to millions of customers. In addition, B2B activities may be more business critical than customer interactions. For example, a bad network connection might inconvenience a single customer, but it might bring a company like Yahoo! to its knees, or it might bring many companies to a halt if the network belongs to a company like AT&T. With B2B, the stakes are much higher than they were in the 1990s.

Three Models

A B2B site is a virtual exchange unconstrained by location, size, distance, or time. In addition to the benefits of multiple selection and partners, a B2B site usually includes a variety of value-added services to encourage commerce. Consider three kinds of B2B models: individual, exchange, and intermediary. With an *individual* B2B, one company deals with another company, or many companies, one at a time. With a B2B *exchange*, multiple companies form partnerships, marketplaces, or auctions to elevate the efficiencies of scale by controlling millions to hundreds of billions of dollars worth of products and services. With an *intermediary* B2B, one portal company connects buyers and sellers. An anonymous auction site, where the buyer and seller are unknown to each other, is an excellent instance of an intermediary B2B.

The Payoff

One of the best-publicized applications of XML has been in B2B e-commerce. Companies and industry groups realized a few years ago that the Web and Internet presented an entirely new venue for B2C relationships and for B2B relationships. XML is the emerging format for describing business data because it is omnimorphic and can adapt to many different kinds of business data. Three of the primary arenas where XML is found include e-business, e-commerce, and B2B transactions and communications. These areas are addressed by B2B exchanges and by XML/EDI activities.

B2B Design Requirements

In today's business environment, there are a number of assumptions that follow B2B. For example, we assume that B2B means Web-based commerce activities of some type. Most B2B ventures are focused on one industry, although the vertical market exchanges are catching up. We assume that the exchange is fairly open to global customers. We assume that data and information exchange is platform and application independent, enabled by XML tools. And we assume that participants agree on and use a common DTD vocabulary for all transactions within the B2B exchange.

Defining the data is an important part of designing the B2B requirements. The first step is to define the B2B processes, such as ordering, database queries, data transactions, catalog entry, and financial transactions. From the processes, the next step is to define the needed documents, which can be modeled as XML documents. The designers use these documents to define the information that will be transferred.

From the information and data, the B2B developers can create a set of DTDs or schemas. The developers must consider whether industry-strength DTDs already exist or have to be created from scratch. Regardless of the source of the DTDs, developers can consider building DTDs with the idea that they will be transformed into schemas. Keeping this idea in mind may make the ultimate transformation process easier to plan and execute using tools like XSLT.

Developing the XML Documents

B2B exchange requirements are captured in the DTDs and schemas. The DTDs form the logic and define the tags of the XML documents. Using the tags defined by the DTDs, the developers can create the actual XML documents to represent the information needed in the B2B exchange. Once all the initial physical XML documents are created, the developers need to explore how to process these documents.

Processing XML

After completing the design and development phases of the XML documents, the developers can consider how to process these documents. An XML document can be processed in one of four general ways: Document Object Model (DOM), the Simple Application Protocol Interface for XML (SAX), the eXtensible Stylesheet Language (XSL), and eXtensible Stylesheet

Language Transformations (XSLT). All of these technologies have been discussed in earlier chapters. For quick review, DOM processes the XML document tree as a whole, while SAX processes the elements of the document as a data stream. XSL provides a powerful procedural language for manipulating and displaying the XML document. And XSLT provides a similar language for transforming the XML document from one format into another. The boundaries between these last two capabilities are blurred.

In a B2B application, the type of B2B processes will determine the best processing method. For a quick look at gathering some data, such as a mailing address for a delivery label, SAX may be used to extract the data elements, which are formatted using XSL. For transforming an incoming bill of materials into a format that is useful to the internal inventory system, the developer may use XSLT. To convert a catalog of products into a database-ready format, the developer might apply a DOM and then XSLT. EDI transactions might be handled using SAX and XSLT. Different combinations handle some of the standard B2B transactions. Many of the vendor B2B applications will handle much of this processing automatically.

Storing the XML Data

After designing, developing, and processing the XML documents, the developers have to determine how to store the XML document data. One way to store XML documents and data is to use a database. An object-oriented database reflects the organization of an XML document better than a relational database, but relational databases are far more commonplace. The tree structure and data elements can easily be represented in the table and columns of a relational database. Most major database vendors, such as Oracle, IBM, Microsoft, and Sybase, offer free tools and additions to make their products compatible with XML.

When the XML document data is stored in a relational database, it can be searched and retrieved as needed. A simple SQL command can retrieve the information as an XML document. In addition, the SQL command might retrieve subcomponents of the XML document to be used for other purposes or in other documents. Or the retrieved information can be parsed with an XML application, manipulated with an XSL style sheet, or transformed with an XSLT style sheet. For example, incoming data can be stored in the B2B repository. Then when a form such as an invoice, order, or shipping instruction is needed, XSLT can transform the data into the correct format.

Protect XML Documents from Manual Modifications

One of the issues to be aware of is the well-documented danger of text-based XML. XML is text-based to provide a common format and to make it easy for people to read. Sometimes, if people can read it, they assume that they can also change it. Bad move!

An XML document should always be processed with an XML parser, first. This step will always ensure that the document is well formed and that other XML applications will be able to manipulate it. Except for a few non-validating applications used for editing, XML applications will fail if the XML document is not well formed. Failure can occur due to unbalanced components, poor nesting, or even an out-of-place space. The trade-off for a tiny, compact XML parser is that the parser has a small brain and cannot venture outside the XML document rules. In the beginning, this rigidity will frustrate experienced HTML programmers who start developing XML documents. Hopefully, they will soon catch on to the advantages of developing well-structured documents.

For this reason, once an XML document has been validated, human hands should never modify the text directly, unless that human is ready to debug his work. In addition, users and partners should not modify an XML document using non-XML applications because these applications will not validate their work. They will change things, but they won't take responsibility for their own actions. Even for small modifications, use a valid XML application to be safe.

B2B E-Commerce Examples

At the end of February 2000, the three major U.S. automobile manufacturers, Ford, GM, and DaimlerChysler, announced the formation of Covisint, an unprecedented alliance to streamline their vast network of 30,000 suppliers for parts and services. This alliance represents the next step up the evolutionary ladder for improved use of information in the supply chain network. Covisint is built on XML because XML is a technology that makes e-commerce easier, business-to-business information exchange smoother, and everyday browsing better.

The Alliance

This centralized, common automotive-parts procurement exchange represents the largest e-business on the Internet. Capitalization estimates average in the neighborhood of $40 billion. Annual revenues from transaction fees, advertising, and other services will run about $3 billion per year. And the supply chain that flows through this venture will control nearly $300 billion annually.

An important aspect of this new venture is that just a few months ago Ford and GM were competitors in both real and virtual space. Both companies had their own separate e-businesses with no cooperation in sight. This situation had the promise of a billion-dollar shootout at the "OK Corral" with casualties of innocent vendor bystanders as they tried to figure which company to side with. Happily, the choice was cooperation, in a win–win–win situation. DaimlerChrysler joined rather than create its own exchange. This has an added benefit of forestalling a splintered European standard.

This unprecedented joint venture involving GM, Ford, and DaimlerChrysler is the world's largest, fastest exchange for transacting business—(e-commerce or otherwise) ever created. Naturally, there is some overlap of suppliers, but the entire supply chain accounts for about $300 billion worth of business each year.

Antitrust Red Flags

One of the downsides of talking about billions of dollars is that the government tends to want to get involved. However, this case has no exclusive monopoly. No information is shared, just data formats. The Covisint agreement is similar to agreeing to transfer money in leather bags. Everyone uses the same bag (data format), but people don't share the contents (the corporate data). An XML vocabulary is used to define the shared data formats. Auto companies have agreed on other standards, such as bumpers, safety equipment, and quality control. XML is just another standard. So, despite the amount of money involved, the government is expected to bless this venture, initially, then take a wait-and-see attitude.

The Federal Trade Commission (FTC) gave Covisint the go-ahead to establish the automotive B2B collaborative exchange in September 2000. Although it will continue to monitor the gargantuan exchange for anticompetitive practices, the FTC cannot rule on competitive concerns at this stage in Covisint's development. In addition to the FTC ruling, the Covisint venture needs the blessing of the German government's Bundeskartellamt (BKA) for its ruling on antitrust and anticompetitive practices. The regulatory agency, the European Union, has not planned to review the case. So Covisint plans to open its doors for business one month after a hopefully, favorable ruling from the BKA, expected in the first quarter of 2001.

Covisint plans to launch e-procurement, auctions, and an automated RFQ (Request for Quotes) service as its initial product offerings. After three to six months, the venture will offer collaborative design and conferencing applications. The goal is to get all tiers of the automotive supply chain involved with this B2B exchange. When the entire supply chain is on-line, the flow of parts and services should run close to $300 billion per year. Conservative estimates are that the exchange will save 5 percent in procurement costs within the first year. Visionary extrapolations (read: "marketing hype") predict cost savings on the order of 90 percent. Regardless of the percentages that are bandied about, the savings *are* expected to be in the billions of dollars, simply by making the process more efficient.

One concern from the vendors and suppliers is that the elimination of some of those inefficiencies may benefit the large automotive corporations and squeeze the smaller suppliers out of business. If one of the efficiencies is the ability to hold an on-line auction, then a larger supplier may be able to cut prices to squeeze out a smaller supplier.

In the traditional marketplace, the smaller supplier would simply go to another automotive manufacturer, but with the centralized, global auction all manufacturers may choose the best bid. The suppliers may have a concern that this kind of collaboration may lead to reverse price setting; all buyers (automotive manufacturers) will agree to pay only one price for their parts and services, making competition on other aspects, such as quality and service, more difficult. This is a valid concern. However, the government cannot rush in just because this might occur; it can only act after an antitrust action is taken.

For this reason, Covisint is expected to be very sensitive to these issues because it will be under public and government scrutiny on a global scale.

Linking Rivals

The astonishing magic of blending these powerful rivals was crafted by the Chicago consulting company, Diamond Technology Partners (DTP). DTP turned fierce foes into fast friends by focusing on the bottom line and ironing out the smaller technology problems. The elimination of procurement paperwork to the tune of tens of billions of dollars makes the cooperation a no-brainer. Let's emphasize that point. At no time are we talking about millions of dollars. All quantities are in billions of dollars, numbers that command respect in any industry.

In 1999, GM launched TradeXchange in collaboration with CommerceOne, an e-business company and XML repository. TradeXchange is best described as an Internet-based parts and components procurement system. On the other hand, Ford set up an e-business system called AutoXchange in collaboration with Oracle, to leverage the productivity of its $83 billion purchasing budget and 30,000 suppliers. Oracle and CommerceOne are both expected to provide services to the new venture. Cisco will provide networking products in a quick start kit for the more than 30,000 suppliers; Cisco's products will enable immediate for transacting business.

Other automobile manufacturers may eventually participate in the new alliance. For example, Isuzu Motor Co., Subaru, and Suzuki Motor Corp. (all GM's Japanese partners) and Mazda Motor Corp. (Ford's Japanese affiliate) are expected to join. France's Renault SA and its Japanese partner Nissan Motor Co. Ltd. will also participate.

With a flexible standard like XML, companies may tend to create their own proprietary standards for an advantage in a competitive war, so the emergence of two e-business systems raised a question. Would GM and Ford share their separate TradeXchange and AutoXchange XML formats? Or would all automobile manufacturers choose to splinter the efforts at unification and efficiency? The recent announcement is a wise decision and significant guidepost on the cooperative path to XML as a universal data exchange format. Standardization efforts are ongoing in other industries, but the automobile manufacturers' effort is the most dramatic to date.

The supply chain enterprise will be a separate company and will be open to other automobile manufacturers. It may eventually expand to include other industries. The use of XML as a standard will save money and time in the hundreds of thousands of procurement transactions in the typical supply chain. Some estimates suggest a 90 percent reduction in purchase order costs. By putting the three big automobile manufacturers on the same playing field *and* on the same team, XML has demonstrated that it is ready for the big leagues and is ready to score big.

This unprecedented cooperation by major representatives of the Industrial Age—the Automotive Industry—is a significant signpost on the path to e-business, worldwide. First, by choosing to cooperate rather than compete, the automobile manufacturers have demonstrated the power of building a common XML vocabulary and a single supply chain. This example provides a beacon to other industries to build a single e-business vocabulary, rather than splinter the efforts. Second, the immensity of the effort, $300 billion, puts high leverage on related industries to support the auto industry XML vocabulary as a global standard. If other industries team with the automobile manufacturers, companies like Microsoft will be pressured to join the consortium. We'll have an interesting irony. Members of the "Old Guard" may now pose a threat to a member of the "New," rather than the reverse.

How Can I Benefit?

Enlightened companies in the Information Age have realized that cooperation, even with competitors, improves efficiencies, costs, and customer service. Other industries, such as chemicals, food ingredients, and power utilities, have already set up exchanges. XML facilitates the ability to share information and data using a common format. For example, the data on invoices, bills of material, parts inventories, and other forms can be defined in a common format across all the vendors. Partners can then read any bill of materials, and information on the bill of materials can be seamlessly transferred to other forms, such as invoices and inventories.

It is clear that XML will affect every business, worldwide. If, by 2002, the number of Web users reaches 330 million and the e-business industry grows to $100 million, as some experts predict, then the potential and the opportunities will also grow proportionately. In the next three years, B2B e-commerce should account for roughly a trillion dollars worth of business. With a goal of cutting spending on parts procurement by 10 percent, when aggregated across all industries, the Internet-based XML model has the potential of saving trillions of dollars in productivity gains.

In fact, any company or industry can benefit by following the example of the carmakers. The aerospace industry is planning to start MyAircraft as a Web site for supply and inventory management.

The aerospace and defense industry group that includes Lockheed Martin, Boeing, Raytheon BAE Systems, and CommerceOne (a B2B e-commerce solutions leader) plan an independent Web exchange for the global aerospace and defense industry. This aerospace and defense exchange is separate from the MyAircraft exchange and will be based on the CommerceOne MarketSite Portal Solution. The four aerospace and defense companies will buy $71 billion in goods and services from 37,000 suppliers using CommerceOne. Aerospace companies are typically not on the cutting edge in technology, but then neither are the automobile manufacturers, typically.

The Financial Industries Markup Language is an initiative by J.P. Morgan and PriceWaterhouseCoopers. This is an effort to unify the data format for financial data transferred among large corporations.

The Steel Markup Language (SML) is being developed by WebMethods, Computer Sciences Corporation, and E-Steel Corporation. SML can be used to simplify data and information transfer across all partners in the steel industry. E-Steel does business with more than 1,500 companies, including USX and Dofasco. MetalSite includes Weirton, Bethlehem Steel, LTV, and Ryerson Tull. MetalSpectrum is an exchange for specialty metal products among Alcoa, Allegheny Technology, Kaiser Aluminum, North American Stainless, Olin, Reynolds Aluminum, Thyssen North America, and Vincent Metal Goods.

Johnson & Johnson, GE Medical System, Baxter International, Abbott Labs, and Medtronic plan to launch an e-business exchange. Health care providers could use an Internet exchange to reduce their procurement costs by 40 percent by reducing paperwork and automating processes.

Sears, Roebuck, & Co. and Carrefour SA have created a retail e-commerce venture called GlobalNetXchange, which is similar to the auto manufacturers' agreement. This exchange will represent $80 billion in supply chain business and link with 50,000 suppliers, partners, and distributors. In an activity separate from its support for the auto exchange, Oracle Corp. will also support this exchange. Wal-Mart, the world's largest retailer, has no plans to join; it will continue to use its own e-commerce system for supply chain activities. However, Sears, the second largest retailer in the United States, and Carrefour, the second largest retailer in the world, both plan to encourage other retailers to join the exchange. Perhaps as GlobalNetXchange gains more credibility and grows in number of members, Wal-Mart will also join the team. Buzzsaw.com is the exchange for the construction industry.

Novopoint.com is a food ingredient B2B site in collaboration with Ariba and Cargill. Novopoint.com competes with Inc2inc, which was also started by Ariba. Although these efforts provide greater experience, they can cut into the competitive advantage of the developer.

According to International Data Corp. (IDC), three types of B2B e-commerce exchanges exist. The first is the method of selling through a Web site, where there are few suppliers and lots of customers. The second is based on procurement, where there are a few dominant buyers, like with the automakers' exchange. An emerging third type will be digital marketplaces; which will be like farmer's markets across the Web, in which buyer and seller may come together in one of many marketplaces.

B2B Opportunities

If you work for a company that can exert some clout, consider collaborative efforts. If you are a small cog in a big machine, like the rest of us, explore various industry B2B e-commerce exchanges and compare what they offer. Also, look into some of the other exchanges. They are not fads and they are not going away. They are here to stay. You do not need to become an expert in XML, but reading a few articles to understand what it is all about will not hurt. The bottom line is that a little education can result in dramatic savings in procurement costs. You could be the champion for B2B e-commerce, the first on your block. More importantly, you could be the hero the next time your boss asks, "Do you know where we could buy some . . . ?" or "Budget is tight. Do you know how we could save a few bucks?" Then you could say, "yes" and save the day.

The implementation of a standardized Web-based B2B exchange for the supply chain is one of the most dramatic marketplace advances over the past 10 years. This B2B e-commerce convergence of industry verticals around a common XML vocabulary substantiates a trend toward improved procurement efficiencies and costs. Even if GM saves only 5 percent on procurement costs, consider that their costs are on the order of $138 billion, so 5 percent is more than the R&D budgets of most corporations.

With the wide variety of B2B and other alphabetic choices, what to do? If you haven't already joined the local industry B2B, explore it. There are trade-offs, similar to those of a standalone vs. a mall. If you are a large concern, like Wal-Mart, visibility is not a problem. But smaller companies may benefit significantly from working in a B2B. The downside is the immediate competition in the B2B; the upside is the visibility from all the vendors in one location. The downside is conforming to someone else's DTDs and XML vocabulary; the upside is avoiding the cost of development and maintenance. The downside is following rules of the B2B; the upside is global exposure.

In 1995, most companies, including Microsoft, were not interested in the Web. Five years later, in 2000, Microsoft is a major Web company and many companies strive to use e-commerce across the Internet. In 1999, few companies had heard of XML. Microsoft had learned from its previous experience and jumped on the bandwagon early. By 2005, most of business, bricks and clicks, will be based on XML and some form of Web-based e-commerce.

The next few years will result in the greatest changes in the business environment on a global scale. The realignment from conventional ways of doing business to streamlined B2B business models will redefine the concept that the customer comes first. Rather than demographics, businesses will look at individual characteristics at the B2B level and at the B2C level. While researchers explore the impacts, corporations will be running through different changes faster than scholars can analyze them.

To understand these changes, analysts will look to companies such as Cisco and Dell and to alliances like Covisint as examples of the evolving B2B business models. Many manufacturers, like Ford, will transform from traditional metal benders into B2B-enabled virtual integrators. Each industry has the opportunity to participate in this transformation in a unique way. The application of these new concepts and fundamental changes will be driven from above, by a B2B champion and visionary.

How can the existing business fit into an existing B2B exchange? What kinds of collaborations with partners, vendors, customers, or even competitors might make more economic sense? Is brand name more important than value added? And are those concepts as important as price or service? Does it make a difference whether these ideas are explored vertically or horizontally?

These are the kinds of strategic questions that the surviving leaders of tomorrow must ask. The executives who do not ask themselves and their staff these questions may not survive until tomorrow. Although change is inevitable, growth is only optional. Clearly, B2B and XML are effecting significant change throughout the corporate and e-business environments. The world is shrinking as the marketplace becomes more global, as it becomes a level playing field that is equally accessible to large corporations and small Mom-and-Pop stores.

Consider this scenario. A college freshman buys directly from the manufacturers and then builds computers in his dorm room and eventually scales up to become a billion-dollar company called Dell. Why couldn't a shrewd teenager use B2B concepts to become an integrator that builds customized cars (say, modified Mustangs) and competes indirectly with Ford? Although Linux does not have the unified business model that Microsoft has, it does show that a loose federation of programmers can create new operating systems across the Web. By using appropriate strategies, a coordinated B2B operation could slice market share from Microsoft. The field is level and it is wide open.

CHAPTER 9

XML Strategic Plan

Introduction

Aligning XML strategies with business goals is an absolute necessity. In fact, many successful companies are already committed to XML and embracing it with its associated tools. One of the better paths to successful implementation of XML follows an innovative, value-added, customer-centric XML strategy. XML is different from HTML format, intent, content, and presentation. The business perspective is more pertinent to building a successful XML business architecture than it is to developing a technical XML implementation.

A strategic plan must go beyond the current solutions in order to be successful with XML in developing new and imaginative opportunities that can be brought to market early as competitive advantages. The first step in implementing an XML strategy requires examining the predominant audience: the customer.

Customer Focused Strategy

Right up front, the focus of the strategy is *not* the competition. The goal of a company is not to beat the competition, but to enhance the customer and make a good profit. So the first focus of an XML implementation strategy is the customer—the customer's requirements, needs, wants, and desires.

From the customer's perspective, XML is like any business innovation. How will this innovation help the customer to improve his business and to make a profit? What problems will XML solve, what solutions and options will it provide, and what value does it add? An XML business strategy must address these questions for the customer from the beginning, because the next question is the most important one from the customer's viewpoint: "Who has the best strategy and the best value proposition to support an XML business implementation?" Addressing that question can make or break an opportunity to win new customers.

Business partners are the next group to focus on. As a new and complex technology, XML requires collaboration to implement successfully. The minimal collaboration involves use of industry standard DTDs, schemas, and document elements. Use of these standards improves capabilities for data transactions, information exchange, and interoperability. Successful collaborative business alliances will bring in new competencies and visibility from new customers, potentially resulting in new business opportunities.

The third area of concentration is the core competency. A core competency is not what the corporation believes it is best at. A *core competency* is a unique competitive advantage as perceived by the marketplace. Although Ford may believe that it makes the best cars, the marketplace may favor GM. Ford is one of the largest corporations in the world and one of the largest automobile manufacturers. But by the definition of a unique competitive advantage, building cars is not its core competency. Its core competency may be related to marketing, selling, or distributing cars, but the Ford cars, themselves, are not a business discriminator. In fact, Ford has created a new venture called FordDirect to address some of its other business areas, such as selling, as opposed to manufacturing, cars. This is the direction of the critical thinking required to determine a corporation's core competency.

A discussion of customer perceptions may be beneficial and prudent in order to define the corporate core competency because the corporate value proposition should be built on this definition. And the value proposition is what the customer is interested in. The customer wants to know: What value-added capability will an XML strategy provide? Who can best support or supply these capabilities to help me be more profitable? After these questions are answered, a company is ready to explore the building blocks for justifying and creating an XML implementation strategy.

Leveraging XML Features

After customer needs have been evaluated and the appropriate questions have been addressed, the next building block of the XML strategic foundation is to approach the features of XML not as a new technology but as a new business strategy. The technical approach involves a shallow method of converting a few Web pages from pure HTML to an XML hybrid without building a vision of the desired outcome and benefits. It demonstrates technical skill without business experience.

An XML strategy leverages the deeper business opportunities and value buried in the innovation. Leveraging XML may involve redefining core competencies, customer relationships, and business partnerships to mine the innovation for its mother lode. The most successful companies will uncover many opportunities and will polish a few facets to reveal the most profitable activities for providing the best solutions. They will align their XML business strategies and their business goals to achieve an early opportunity to stake their claims.

The best strategy builds on the business objectives. An XML implementation or migration plan is inserted into the existing business context. This method provides an existing vision with a direction for implementation and metrics for success. It is flexible because it starts from a solid foundation. The strategy should inherit and extend the value propositions and competitive advantages built into the corporate business strategy. XML is not a differentiator, but it is an enabler for building better market differentiation. With a business-based XML strategy in place, a corporation may be able to leapfrog the competition.

Creating Customer Satisfaction

A successful XML strategy supports the customer; it provides more satisfaction today than yesterday. It improves communications and offers better solutions and more convenience than the customer currently receives. The strategy may include partners, but it provides customer satisfaction and delight, and goes the extra mile to present a pleasant surprise.

One approach for creating new solutions for the customer is to think like a customer. XML improves information access. How will this help a specific customer? How do they use products and services in their day-to-day activities? How can XML enable superior solutions that result in return customers? Working with new business and marketing groups may facilitate answering these questions. This approach may yield a better definition of core competencies and value propositions in an XML context from the perspective of the customer desires.

As a corporation implements an XML strategy, new business assumptions, models, and opportunities emerge. The strategic planner recognizes these changes as opportunities and leverages them. Some general new outcomes from XML will include improved data exchange, better access to global information, and quicker ability to fuse facts from diverse databases. The strategist can extend these outcomes by exploring how the business will function with the increased interoperability afforded by XML. A customer-centric or business-focused conceptual model will guide exploration of future opportunities. There should be a conscious effort to develop and document these new assumptions.

Extending New Opportunities

In this context, new opportunities relate to how potential customers can benefit from an XML implementation. This critical task is supported by the business and marketing departments. One consideration is the selection of new products and services supplied to existing customers that would also draw in new customers. The Web, the Internet, and XML developments are so unpredictable that new opportunities may come and go like flashes of a lightning bug. However, the exploration is critical to discovering viable core competencies.

Discovering Viable Core Competencies

The Web, the Internet, and XML have changed many fundamental business assumptions. Core competencies gain value from the marketplace. If a competency is a commodity, then something else is needed to provide differentiation and value. In the Information Age, core competencies change as quickly as business and technology. A corporation's core competency, from the customer perspective—the only one of importance—may provide high value in yesterday's market place but may be diminished by tomorrow's new technology. A good example of this is the slide rule; as soon as calculators became cheaply available, they supplanted slide rules, which are now dinosaurs of a distant past. Technology changes competency.

A corporation builds core competencies based on changes in technology and in customer perception, resulting in a competitive differentiation. By leveraging existing products and services, while fostering XML-enhanced evolution through a profitable path, corporate managers can push for the creation of strategic advantages. The customer perspective provides the best way to understand, create, and exploit competitive advantages.

Rapidly changing external technology and business drivers create a need for new core competencies. The customer perspective is the foundation to start from. When the customer sees value in an XML implementation, then XML will become a new technology that has profit potential. The customer's values come first in coloring the viability of a redefined core competency.

Customer-Motivated Creativity

Customer-motivated creativity does not mean building and selling Texas-sized trucks just because that is what the customer likes. *Customer-motivated creativity* means exploring new ideas within existing corporate products and services that provide customer value or that were suggested by the customer. Improved interoperability provides customer value. Customers like to exchange information easily and seamlessly. The ability to transfer data and information more easily is a big selling point for an XML strategy. Each corporation has to translate that concept into the proper context.

XML will solve business challenges and create new opportunities. It can improve business transactions, data exchange, and information transfer. It can open up new, global markets. XML may initiate Internet and Web growth of a multiple language capability based on Unicode capabilities. Each corporation must explore its individual compromises among technology, business, and finance involved in potential business opportunities and customer-valued solutions.

Many of the e-businesses, like Dell and Cisco, represent a variety of Web-based business models that are worthwhile exploring and benchmarking. Successful business models have valuable lessons learned and best practices that can be enhanced by XML. Customers like new ways to address old problems.

Customers have problems and they want solutions. They want innovative solutions, because they have new problems or because the old solutions do not work as well as desired. With an active, XML strategy, a good innovator can locate the customer-focused, value-added capabilities of a corporate innovation, product, or service. A good solution will become a necessity to the customer.

Innovation can become profitable. The 3M model for Post-it Notes might just as well be, "a novel idea, once tasted, becomes a necessity." However, in most cases, novelty wears off. Using XML as a novelty to bring in customers is not a long-term strategy. Customers will expect something substantial, or they will quickly vote with their feet and abandon the product. The best XML strategy is to plan for an innovative product with a long-term vision, not a flash in the pan novelty.

Value-Added Response

The customer wants value. An XML implementation that does not provide value is a waste of resources. The value proposition provides a clear picture of the corporate plan for leveraging XML to provide value. Customer expectations, priorities, and needs support the development of the value proposition. XML issues to consider include cost effectiveness, risk, improved transaction capabilities, resource reuse, and cost avoidance.

XML-based products and services support multiple information capabilities from a single XML document repository. XML documents can be extended, by definition, and used by different legacy, current, and future applications. Standards are a crucial part of an XML strategy that enhance the cooperation vertically, with partners and vendors within an industry group, and horizontally across other industries.

The Business Model

From the business perspective, profit puts bread on the table. It is the bottom line. While the big question is how to use XML to provide value to the customer as part of his long-term objectives, the next question is what business model makes an XML strategy viable and provides a reasonable profit. Corporate profit models change over time as the relationship with the customer changes.

One advantage of XML is the ability to develop easily and modify quickly. XML applications and documents can be reused and repurposed. An XML implementation that provides value for one customer may provide value to another customer with minor modifications. A general solution can generate one level of profits, while a customized solution generates significantly more profits with minimal marginal costs. A classic example occurs in the airline industry.

A coach ticket on an airplane may cost only $300, while a first class ticket may run more than $1000 on the same aircraft. The difference is customer perceptions and customized service. Toyota had a different but related strategy. When the top of the line Toyota Lexus was introduced, it cost in the neighborhood of $50,000. The next level down, Toyota Camry, cost only $20,000. So what? A luxury car is higher quality and should cost more than a family car. This was not the case for the Lexus and the Camry. The Camry was already a proven, high-quality automobile. So, Toyota built the Lexus on the Camry chassis, and added a few dollars of luxuries to more than double the cost. The point is that customer perceptions can change the profit model. XML can help to fulfill these perceptions and expectations in order to improve the business model.

An XML implementation strategy can consider opportunities to leverage existing products and provide customized solutions with significant increases in profits. One opportunity that will emerge is the need to port legacy data to a more open, XML-based format. Initially, this activity will be very resource intensive. With time and experience, tools will simplify the process. However, the opportunity for varying service prices with correspondingly increased profits is clear. One rate covers a simple port, another rate covers a rapid port, and a third rate covers migration plans, with additional rates for training and maintenance. The window for this opportunity is open now, but it may close within the next five years as corporations update their legacy data.

The Internet provides a new economic environment with many new opportunities. Traditional profit models may not be the best. XML provides a significant new twist on a cutting edge technology and encourages experimenting with new profit models. The telephone profit model may serve as a useful example.

In the 1970s, a long distance telephone call could cost a few dollars per minute. With competition in the 1990s, service improved dramatically and cost plummeted to a few cents per minute. With wireless telephones, a service contract can be cheaper than a conventional telephone service.

In the 70s, few people made long distance calls. In 2000, the perception is that few people do not use their cell phones to make long distance calls.

This may be only perception, but the profit model suggests that the volume of cell phone calls competes with calls made by conventional telephones. XML and the Internet will provide similar opportunities for the innovative strategic leader.

Anticipating Change

In the very competitive environment of the Information Age, success is fleeting. Even Microsoft observed that few companies survive as leaders across technology discontinuities. This observation was near the time that the Web almost became its downfall. Times change and customers move on. However, companies can anticipate these changes and build contingencies.

One approach is to consider the customer desires during the process of creating an XML implementation strategy. The model of this approach includes customer strategies, goals, and desires. This model can be used to develop products and services that will delight the customer. Simultaneously, a feeling for future customer requirements can be extrapolated with a goal toward providing lifetime service. Also, consider if competitors can provide the same service more cheaply or more efficiently.

A traditional business strategy plans for contingencies and competition. An XML implementation strategy should also consider potential competition. Potential competition comes from offering new services. New services can be documented as features that are not cost effective at this time, customer desires that were not implemented, and the natural extension of technology and business trends. Two things that cannot be predicted are the potential customer who does not yet exist, and the potential competitor who does not yet exist.

Startups can provide a product or service that is not cost effective for the originator. The best defense against a startup is to leverage knowledge about the customer to provide the best relationship and the best service so that customers do not want to switch. In addition, discussing a migration strategy to provide new services will help retain customers.

Migration to New Services

An XML migration and implementation strategy begins before the availability of XML functionality and ends with full XML capability as well as a sustainment and maintenance plan. The gap between the current data and document architecture and the target XML architecture can be significant. A gap analysis will reveal different implementation phases for each corporation, and these phases each represent a migration stage. Three- to six-month phases, considering the speed of Internet development, are reasonable intervals for planning. Begin with the target and work backwards. The multiphase approach allows rapid adaptation and learning with minimal rework to repair mistakes.

A corporation with a new, innovative XML strategy gains the competitive advantage when it is first to market. The customer does not reward second place, and while other companies are waiting for clear standards, the innovator makes money, builds market shares, and learns from his mistakes. The sideliners miss the opportunity.

However, the reverse situation should be considered. Jumping in, headfirst, without a plan or a review of the surroundings can result in a broken neck. XML innovators know themselves, the customers, and the marketplace. They have mapped out potential pitfalls and possible strategies for when they slip up; they have built customer loyalty and worked on a long-term strategy to gain customer trust and partnerships; and they understand that the journey of one thousand relationships begins with the first customer.

Each step along this journey leads to the fulfillment of the final goal. At the end of each step, each stage of the strategy, is a measuring process to review assumptions and goals. Modifications are made as needed. And many changes will be needed during an XML implementation. All Internet technologies are changing, and XML is still in flux. While change is inevitable, aim for growth. With a carefully planned strategy, each stage grows closer to the goal. Checkpoints along the way allow for assessment and risk management. Small stages provide a flexible plan that parallels XML advances and allows for the desired growth.

An outline of business, marketing, and technology objectives for each phase must be created in order to design a multiphased XML implementation. Implementation stages should be aligned with business strategy such as assumptions, core competencies, and profit models. Define milestones, achievements, and lessons to be learned for each stage. Plan to document best practices, also.

These steps are fundamentally the same as the steps for creating a business strategy for any innovation. However, many businessmen, especially those who are technically minded, do not always take the time to put good business practices into place. Strategic planning is not a fun exercise, but a long-term strategy can save many sleepless nights and telephone calls about unexpected emergencies.

Reviewing and updating the strategic plan, maintaining contact with the customers, and communicating progress and goals is a continuous process. In most projects, better communications about the goals and progress result in a greater probability of a successful implementation.

The Plan

The plan for incorporating XML into your company includes three phases, which represent the standard design, development, and implementation lifecycle. These phases are also the steps used to define an IT architecture using a conceptual model, a logical model, and a physical model. Consultants tend to be so familiar with this textbook approach that they will try to get a head start by establishing the requirements and the scope in the first meeting with the client. They may even have a partial logical model developed before the initial meeting is complete. The hardest part is the discipline needed to gather the requirements, to stay on track, and to limit the scope.

Phase One

Determine the activity for which you want to build an XML solution. For example, do you want to improve some paperwork, make a business process more efficient, or participate in a B2B exchange? Focus on the specific process that you want to tackle, and then define the scope of the activity. If you want to improve a process in the finance department, don't get sidetracked by processes in the purchasing department. If you are interested in a B2B exchange for procurement, then you may not want to confuse things by building a Web site for marketing and selling your products.

Concentrating on one well-defined activity is critical for avoiding scope creep and for improving the chances of a successful implementation. Before even thinking about a technical solution, gather a well-bounded set of clearly defined requirements for the specific activity. This way, resources will not be spread out too thinly, and establishing crisp, achievable milestones is easier.

One method for approaching the first step is to look at the activities as a single business process. Define the initiation and fulfillment steps of the business process to ascertain an unclouded vision of the task at hand. Determine what you want to do to this process, build it, facilitate it, or automate it. As these concepts begin to jell, it is easier to define concrete goals and objectives to shoot for.

Draw a rough flow of the steps needed to go from the current situation to the target goal or solution. Gather as many requirements as feasible to portray the situation. Don't worry about being exhaustive, but fill in as many details and steps as possible.

Describe the problem, situation, or opportunity that you are trying to address by using a one-sentence description. This vision statement serves to crystallize the project both in your mind and in the minds of the team members. This sentence should state the problem as completely as possible without spilling over into the solution or technology. Many technology workers tend to think in terms of solutions, not in terms of problem statements; therefore, simply sticking with the problem takes considerable self-discipline. Addressing the solution first may work for small tasks that you can easily get your hands around; however, for more substantial projects, the problem statement is a good first step. The problem statement separates the technology from the solution and demonstrates an ability to think like a businessperson as well as like a technologist. While the problem statement presents the business case for the solution, the implementation is the technical method used for satisfying the business case. When creating the problem statement, consider how it can be linked to a corporate strategic objective or how it impacts the bottom line. Both of these are excellent business reasons for addressing any problem.

Phase Two

Building on what is already known, or already in place, use the conceptual model as a guide for writing down the steps needed to develop and implement the solution, based on the difference between the current state and the future solution. At this point, all you are doing is writing down the words that describe the flow of steps defined in step one. As you write it down, try to define known gaps. You can address some of the gaps, but you do not have to solve all of them at this step. But the more gaps that you identify at this step, the fewer surprises you will have at the implementation step. If you have made a solid effort to gather a complete requirements set, identifying the gaps will be much easier.

Describe the process flow that represents the problem with words in addition to the pictures. Document today's approach and situation by gathering process flow information from the people who do the actual work; do not just use the idealized procedures that may be documented as a corporate process. Although they may know the documented procedures, effective workers, including the CEO, usually find a more efficient process for doing their jobs, and then never get around to documenting their better approaches. So you can be the one who documents these better approaches. For each process, start with the initial requests or inputs and then follow the tasks in the process until the final outputs are generated.

At this stage, continue the focus on the business processes, not the underlying technology. Detailed models and data element types can come at the next stage. Only work on a narrative that indicates the flow of information and the various interfaces where information changes hands. An interface may be as sophisticated at a document management system or as simple as throwing a piece of paper over the wall to the next cubical.

Information is contained in some document. Identify the document as well as the responsible party for that document. Try to break the process down into unique steps. For each step in the process, explain what the inputs and outputs are, who processes the document information, and where its destination is. But stay at the general level rather than getting buried down in the details. Implementing an XML solution for a general process is much easier than doing so for a single specific activity.

Sequence the process tasks based on the original narrative. Identify specific tasks as events that depict the flow of information at any instant in time. The sequence of events should illustrate a logical flow of information that combines into a logical sequence of process tasks. At each event, an interface, either real or virtual, allows information to flow from one task to another task. Again, an interface may be as simple as a document or as complex as a transcoding system from one platform to another. However, defer technical details for physical or implementation phases.

At this stage, simply list all events in the right sequence. *When* they occur is important to the business. How they are implemented or any technical details are not yet pertinent. For example, in a B2B procurement exchange, the EDI transaction or the XML implementation is not yet important at this stage. What is important is that a department needs an item, it requests a purchase, a bid goes out to vendors, a winner is selected based on some criteria, the order is placed, the item received, and the department request is fulfilled. Those steps and the detailed events are what are recorded at this stage.

Although prototyping a solution may be possible, the results cannot be measured or managed with any fidelity. In addition, maintaining or extending a prototyped system is difficult if the complete set of requirements is missing from the very beginning. This process can be tedious, but it saves time and money in the long term by avoiding rework and inefficient restarts. When this step is completed, call this the logical model of the proposed solution.

Phase Three

Begin the implementation process.

Avoid any tendency to skip steps or go directly from design to implementation. Don't try to implement without detailed requirements and design phases! Implementation of an XML solution is sufficiently new that skipping steps could be disastrous. This lifecycle has been proven time and time again over many years to prove the structure needed for implementing a new technology. Skipping steps can eventually result in missing something or overlooking important gaps in the requirements.

Now is the time to build a model of the process flow. Start with a simple high-level view that can be presented to upper management. A high-level flow chart that fits on one slide is ideal. Crucial, business-critical details can be discussed on subsequent slides. Again, resist the impulse to jump to the solution, focus only on the current state and on the requirements of the situation. Include business partners, vendors, and customers, as germane to the situation.

The result of this step will be a picture of the target to shoot for, including all major roles, documents, information flows, and interfaces. Apply the narrative to this step to provide a sanity check that identifies any gaps and helps to streamline process and document flows.

After the events are documented, enlist the appropriate stakeholders to test and debug the entire process to identify gaps and to suggest additions. When the process model is complete, you are ready to implement the XML applications at the correct components in the process model. At this point, create a formal program management plan for implementation.

If you completed the phases 1 and 2 as described, then you have sketched out what is needed for an XML document architecture for the project. The events and interfaces can be represented by one or more XML documents. The information is represented as data element types within the document, with some negotiation as information is transferred from one stakeholder to another. The developer will define these types in the project DTDs or schemas. There are many good books coming out on the market that explain the programming details needed to create a good DTD. Or you may want to use some of the existing DTDs in your own industry. The latter approach will save time and trouble in the long run.

All milestones, activities, tasks, and events have been sequenced and can now be placed in a project schedule. The schedule should be reviewed for timelines and critical path to obtain reasonable durations. With minimal knowledge of the details of XML, a good program manager can build this plan.

XML Vocabulary Development

Building an XML document design architecture is a good start for any XML-based e-business solution. The basic steps are similar to those used in designing a database, since an XML document is a type of database. Like a database, an XML document can be used for a variety of data in a variety of industries. The auto industry, chemical industry, and steel industries all have their own brand of XML vocabularies.

Use an existing vocabulary if it will meet your needs, but, if you can't get a good fit, build your own customized vocabularies. Or, as with EDI, you may be able to use various tools and transformations to achieve the desired result.

Where does XML fit as a solution in your specific corporation? The simple answer is XML belongs wherever there are information transactions. But you may only want to convert a portion of your data to XML format. For example, some data may work just fine in the existing databases. And you can use XML and XSLT to convert data to present on other devices, such as cell phones and the wireless markup language, or speech processing and VoiceML.

For any application, the developer will have to determine the information flow process to determine if and where an XML solution is a best fit. For example, data might be extracted from a product data manager database and converted into XML documents to work with EDI, B2B, or multiple devices. After deciding on the tasks for XML, the developer can create the appropriate DTDs and style sheets.

The maturity of the project will be a driver in the XML development plan. A new project does not require transformations from legacy systems, but it does require a definition of the proposed applications. In contrast, an existing project will have some legacy baggage for XML to deal with. The more accommodation that XML development will require, the slower the implementation.

Data in a relational database is fairly straightforward to deal with. In fact, many database vendors provide tools to support XML. So, it is useful to consider XML support when reviewing databases and applications for use on a specific project. The difference between support and no support for XML, as well as the extent of the support, can mean the difference between hours and weeks for development of an information and data transfer solution.

An interesting paradox is legacy Web page conversion. The Web pages created in the early days of the Web do not conform to XML specifications. While tools are emerging to convert from HTML to XHTML, the process still requires a little manual tweaking. Each conversion will have to be decided on a case by case basis as to whether to devote the resources now or to wait.

E-Business Decisions

As you begin your journey into the e-business arena, you need to prepare a foundation for guiding the company through new territory. Although most Internet activities have profit potential, any new venture can fail when not managed. Therefore, make sure that any department or company that engages in e-business also has financial accountability for its efforts.

In addition, continue to assess and measure various e-business initiatives to learn from failures and to extract best practices from successes. The idea of failing quickly cannot be overemphasized. Assume success, but plan for failure, then learn, regroup, and try again.

The new paradigm for e-business is collaboration and relationships. Collaboration with partners, collaboration with vendors, collaboration with customers, and even collaboration with competitors. These collaborations should bring new opportunities to the relationship that are profitable or at least beneficial for all parties. Partnering and collaboration imply equal sharing of benefits. Determine if a collaboration, and what type of collaboration, would benefit your company.

There are different types of collaborations. *Procurement collaborations*, like Covisint, benefit the major partners, but do not detract from the competitive environment. Collaborators agree on certain standards in the supply chain, but how these standards are leveraged within the corporation is up to each company. Any way that companies can collaborate and make profits is possible.

Strategic collaborations allow a group of companies to gain a larger foothold in a marketplace. These alliances can lead to dominance in the marketplace, raising the red flag of monopoly to the government. The U.S. government was exploring Covisint because this B2B exchange had the potential to practice monopolistic practices among the suppliers. Without Covisint, suppliers have at least three automobile manufactures to sell to. With Covisint, there is only one marketplace, so vendors have no recourse if they do not like the conditions of the market.

In the mid-1990s, Texas Instruments (TI) used a term called *coconstruction of innovation*. This was a collaboration with customers to develop specific functions in a TI calculator, based on suggestions. When customers agreed on a set of functions, TI would implement them. This process helped both parties, because the customers got the functions that were important to them. Also, it was important to TI because the customized calculators had a ready market of consumers to purchase them. The calculators were general enough that a larger population was also interested in the new functions. But the point was that the collaboration benefited both parties.

Outline of an Example XML Document Implementation Plan

Figure 9.1 outlines an example of the 10 steps used to build an XML document; these steps are neither mandatory nor comprehensive. They provide a guide for requirements, analysis, and implementation needed for applying XML to a small, trade study type of activity.

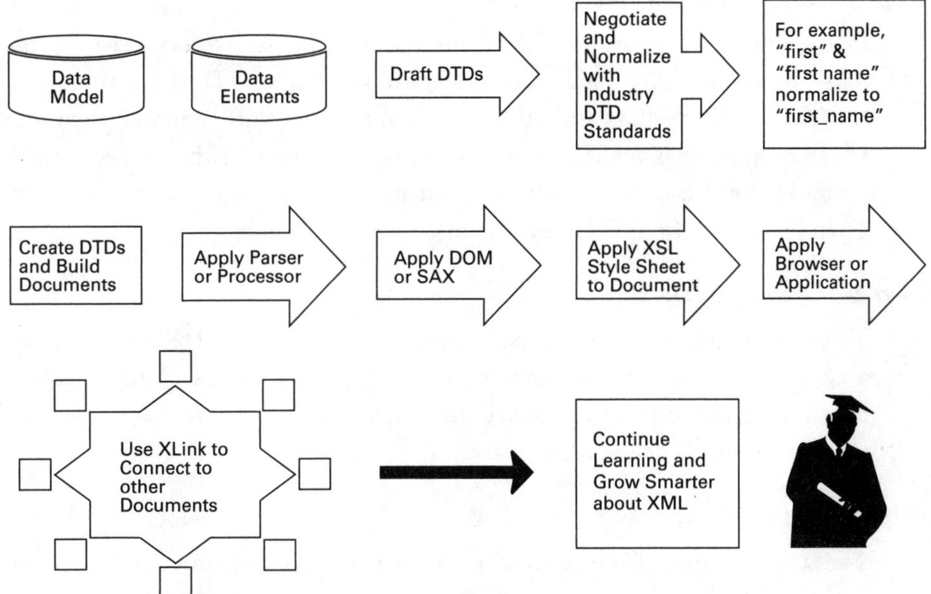

FIGURE 9.1 Outline of an example XML Document Implementation Plan.

Step 1: Data Model

XML is all about data, so the most logical first step is to construct a data model of the project. A process map of the data flow would also be handy. The data model provides the guidance needed to create the data elements that are used to define the tags in the XML documents.

Step 2: Data Elements

The data model provides a list of data types used in the project. The data types have interrelationships that can be represented as a hierarchy. Some data types may be combined with others to form a more general data type. Perform the analysis to address these issues. Then create a set of XML data element types that correspond to the project data types from the data model.

Step 3: Draft DTDs

Use the data element types to draft a set of DTDs or schemas. It is outside of the scope of this book to describe the details of programming DTDs or schemas, but there are plenty of excellent books for the interested developer. The draft DTD will be a model to use when investigating industry DTDs.

Step 4: Negotiate Industry DTDs

One of the major goals of XML is interoperability, so explore existing standards before building new ones. Compare the draft DTD to existing industry DTDs and schemas and attempt to modify the draft to match the industry standards. It is terrific if industry standards will fit the project, but be prepared for a combined solution that uses industry parts and draft parts. Then create the final DTD or schema.

Step 5: Create DTDs

This step is essentially the same as Step 3. This time, the DTD or schema is a combination of existing standards and generated DTDs. After they have been integrated, build a test XML document and validate it. For more information about DTDs, see Chapter 2.

Step 6: Apply Parser

The way to validate the XML document is to run it through a parser. The parser will either generate a hierarchy or an error. After all errors are debugged, the XML document will parse with no problems and will be validated in relation to the DTD. A valid XML document is ready for use.

Step 7: Apply DOM

Steps 7, 8, and 9 are closely woven details for using an XML document. It is not necessary to use all steps or even use them in order. However, each step provides useful experience. The output of a DOM is a hierarchy that is useful for other applications that locate data and relationships within the XML document.

Step 8: Apply XSL

XSL and XSLT can be used to modify the presentation or format of the document. Like writing DTDs, writing XSL scripts requires the talents of a developer. However, example scripts are always popping up all over the Web. The XML Web sites at Microsoft and IBM have a set of interesting samples that may be useful for this step. Review the information about XSL and XSLT in Chapter 4.

Step 9: Apply Application

This step is unique to the business. The application can be inventory tracking, database manipulation, or spreadsheet analysis, etc. This step is important for gaining experience with the capabilities of XML. Database access is a good candidate application to explore because databases are a core part of business data repositories and e-business capabilities.

Step 10: Distribute by Using XLink

This step is wishful thinking. At the time of this writing, XLink is about to be released as a standard. The general information is available, but specific implementations are hard to come by. If anyone has them, then Microsoft will have released a beta MSXML in order to incorporate the XLink standard into Internet Explorer 5.x. IBM and Intel may also have information when it is available. More information about XLink is available in Chapter 5.

A developer who has gone through all of these steps has accomplished a great deal. Congratulate that developer, or yourself, if that is the case, and have a celebratory lunch! Finally, relax for a few minutes and learn more about the new developments in XML that have been released since the beginning of your project.

CHAPTER 10

Concerns, Myths, and Hype

Introduction

An important part of an XML strategic implementation is an understanding of the hype and myths, as well as an analysis of the business concerns and risks. The first concern is the strategic business risk to implementation that may be specific to each corporation. The second concern relates to the unique aspects of XML, its myths, its hype, and its developments. The separation of these two concerns is artificial because they overlap, but this is the simplest method to present the ideas.

Many issues may block the success of an XML implementation strategy. If these issues are anticipated, managed, and addressed, the business opportunities and the chances for success will improve dramatically.

Move Quickly

Take steps to draft the XML strategy and to implement it quickly. Competitors following a similar approach may snatch up potential customers. A fast response to customer requests for innovation will capture market share. Inability to respond quickly can result in customers lost to competitors. A corporation that is structured to respond quickly to customer requests will be able to exploit the opportunities that XML presents. To be competitive, an executive needs to encourage a dynamic and innovative working environment, while discouraging bureaucracy and political posturing. The engineers must understand the business, the businessmen must understand the technology, and both groups must communicate freely.

Educate the Executives

Until they are educated about the benefits, executives pose a risk to the changes and new operating models introduced by an XML implementation. Change is scary. Executives like the status quo. But as the world accelerates to embrace XML technology, if a corporation does what it has always done, it could lose what it already has. The improved interoperability afforded by XML facilitates alliances. Alliances with partners to fill a gap, alliances with customers who value the complete picture, alliances with vendors who recognize prosperity, and even alliances with competitors who do not want to be left behind. XML will drive new ways of doing business and new operating models.

Conventional thinking leads to an inertial barrier that blocks innovation, agility, and versatility. The best approach for overcoming resistance is to embrace the goals of the corporation and wrap them in the new profit model based on the concrete potential of XML. XML is not a new fad; it will soon be the cost of doing business, just like the telephone, FAX, and Internet. A solid XML implementation strategy that addresses concerns and risks before they arise will go a long way toward allaying most fears and resistance.

Avoid the Wait-and-See Approach

The conventional business model is usually built on a conservative approach, which worked fine in the Industrial Age. But in the Information Age, a wait-and-see attitude can be fatal. Champions of the Industrial Age, Ford and GM recognize the potential and are moving forward to embrace the XML-based B2B opportunities. Champions of the Information Age must be pioneers who create new business models and anticipate new opportunities. Being the first company in an industry to offer XML-based services entails some risk, but it also strengthens the leadership position, when preceded with a strong XML implementation strategy. Another advantage of being first to market is that it puts the competition in the position of having to be reactive and play catch-up.

Best Foot Forward

The flip side of being first to market is the potential for making the first very public mistakes. Exhaustive testing in a separate staging area can reduce some of the problems that may arise with new XML applications. Customers may not return after a bad first impression, so quality is an important concern.

Changing Standards

As the business world accelerates, XML tools are released before the standards are finalized. The risk is that the tools will not be compatible with the final standard and will thus result in a dead end. The opportunity is that the tools will be adequate and adaptable to the standards and will thus provide a leap ahead of the more conservative competition. This situation, which changes every 12 to 18 months, is now considered the cost of doing business with technology. If change is expected and planned for, then this risk can be managed.

Despite good planning, corporations may be hesitant about accepting XML DTDs for a given industry or application because of changing standards. XSL comes to the rescue. XSL allows a company to map its internal standards to the industry standards at the time. As industry standards change, the company can remap its internal standards with minimal disruption. This is a significant change in the software industry, where reports of vaporware would have a major impact on a company's IT strategies. XSL allows a company to include change as a normal part of its strategic plan.

Security Concerns

Information security is always a concern when sharing information outside the company. The risk can come from intentional corporate espionage and competitive intelligence, or it can come from unintentional laxness on the part of the partners. Security risks are part of doing business and the risks can never be fully mitigated. However, the risks can be managed and reduced. Although XML documents are meant to use open standards, XML processors can be designed to provide some level of security. Security consultants can provide suggestions or create an entire security architecture. Although security is a growing issue, corporations do pay sufficient heed.

However, if customers do not trust the level of security, they will hesitate to do business.

Security is still a big question mark with XML. While LDAP and PKI may help with these issues, resource sharing and document management provide a new wrinkle to "eyes only." Today, if I have a Web page and I don't want someone to see information on the page, then I can comment it out and the browser will ignore it. However, many users can look at the source if they want to see all of the information.

The same issue is being explored with XML. Although the browser and XSL will segment control, a clever user can still look at the original XML document data. In other words, don't send the entire set of department salaries in one XML and expect the employee to look at only his with the accompanying XSL style sheet. A little curiosity can go a long way. But these issues are being explored.

Legal Issues

The Web opened up many legal issues regarding copyright laws and freedom of speech. XML promises to raise these issues to new heights because the definition of a document will change drastically. If the user downloads a document that is composed of components from four other documents that reside in globally dispersed databases, which laws govern the legalities? Questions of international law come to the forefront. Strict legal issues in one country are nonissues in another country. Customers or foreign governments may object (or worse) to the potentials for XML content. Legal issues will remain a significant risk as governments and businesses negotiate on the laws.

Financial Planning

Initial XML development efforts will depend on the size of the application or the number of documents to convert. As a general rule of thumb, the first project will take at least two and a half times longer than originally estimated. XML development is most like building a data model. However, today's data models are built by systems analysts or systems engineers who do not have enterprise data modeling expertise. What is needed is a dying breed called data analysts. Data analysts used to be responsible for coordinating the data needs for an entire corporation. That is the type of expertise required for the first few corporate XML conversions. Otherwise, manage the risk by multiplying estimates by 2.5.

Adequate Infrastructure

XML documents will require significant bandwidth to fulfill much of their capability. As quickly as the Internet is growing, the demand for bandwidth is outpacing it. When modems provided 300 baud, users were happy with a line at a time. Today, with T1 lines running 1 Mbps, users want even more bandwidth. The risk is that a corporation will not have sufficient bandwidth to keep up with customer demands on XML resources. One approach for managing this risk is to build a technical architecture migration strategy, which grows as the business demands increase.

Interoperability Concerns

There is a significant desire among information technology workers to have standard file formats for sharing data and documents across applications. Most people who have used a computer have run into the problem of transferring information from one application to another. In the early 1980s, people had problems sharing data between IBM mainframe computers and other computers because of IBM incompatibilities with ASCII characters. In the early 1990s, people had problems sharing information between Apple Macintosh computers and IBM-compatible PCs because of different file formats. WordPerfect and Microsoft Word had incompatibilities. And even Microsoft Office 97 was not completely compatible with Microsoft Office 95 because of file format inconsistencies.

Unfortunately, XML may not solve the problem. Although XML is an open standard for creating interchangeable file formats and documents, the DTDs also have to be open standards. Just as Microsoft created its own version of HTML and extensions for Web pages, other companies could create similar proprietary DTDs that are optimized for their applications. In fact, optimization from proprietary DTDs is a possible strategy for a competitive advantage in the B2B market. Use of proprietary objects and standard tags will add functionality available only to members of a specific B2B exchange. This defeats the idea of open standards. Why is this bad?

In a pure capitalist society, proprietary standards provide a corporation or an industry with a competitive advantage. On a limited scale, this results in a healthy market and competitive business practices. However, a large B2B exchange may be in a different category. If it holds a monopoly position over their industry, it can set standards for the worldwide market. That would not be bad, if it publishes the standards so that all documents and file formats could be interchanged. Everyone wants a single common standard. The risk is that large B2B efforts, as well as smaller companies, will splinter the XML standards. Splintering the XML standards will effectively defeat the purpose of XML. That is the risk.

However, the problem will not likely get out of hand. Considerable global pressure exists to create a set of open standards based on XML. The momentum is significant. If any B2B effort attempts to corner and close the open standards, peer pressure from the corporate and user communities or legal action from government agencies will block these attempts. Although B2B e-commerce is big and growing quickly, the Internet is bigger and growing even more quickly. Although this issue may be overreacting, it does address a real risk.

Transforming HTML

HTML developers can quickly develop a Web page, and Web browsers are forgiving of sloppy or unplanned development. However, XML requires careful planning. HTML programmers may not like the initial analysis required to generate a DTD. Creating a corporate data model is tedious and time consuming. Poor planning will result in miscommunication and loss of data through incompatible applications. Isolated DTD development, in relation to industry standards, can result in lost time and opportunities. The migration to XML can thus result in dramatic growing pains for a corporation.

Designers and developers must analyze corporate needs and build models of the data element to map to a set of XML DTDs. These corporate DTDs are compared to industry standards and normalized to enhance information sharing. Omission of any step can undermine a carefully conceived XML implementation strategy.

By making DTD development compatible with other companies, vendors, and partners, a corporation will benefit through smooth data transfer. Negotiations and work arounds will have to be made to accommodate the greater good, but the improvements in electronic data exchange will provide long-term benefits.

Unstable DTD Standards

Because industry acceptance of XML has been so rapid, standards have not yet been solidified. The definitions of DTDs and schemas remain in flux. Many different standards groups have created their own sets of DTDs but with no clear effort to create a single global core set of DTDs for all developers to draw upon. This crack in the flexible armor of XML presents a risk to future development efforts.

Corporations may take a “not invented here” approach to develop their own sets of DTDs, without regard for the resulting fragmented standards and lost interoperability. Uncoordinated efforts to design DTDs and schemas, with no intent for collaboration, will produce incompatible results. Even with collaboration within an industry, different industries may develop DTDs that are incompatible with other industries. For example, the chemical industry may create a set of useful DTDs that are not compatible with DTDs from the automobile industry. However, clearly the two industries will want to communicate and share data. XML development portends a risk of communication bottlenecks, the exact reverse of its original intent.

Even One Can Make a Difference

A risk is posed from even one industry trying to set up DTD standards in isolation, because suppliers and vendors will use the same DTDs. Without collaboration and forethought, a clear solution is not obvious. Collaboration among the powerhouses from industry such as IBM, Microsoft, General Motors, AT&T, and Wal-Mart may be a possible way to address this risk.

As XML standards evolve, proprietary DTDs will provide a competitive advantage. One company, like Microsoft, would need a significant incentive to continue to play fair. There is a risk that immediate profit and market pressure could outweigh long-term interoperability and peer pressure. Is it more important to facilitate the general exchange of information or to promote a competitive advantage? Each company will have to make that decision and live with the consequences.

Sloppy HTML Coders

One of the advantages of HTML was that it was forgiving of sloppy or unplanned development. XML does not forgive sloppy planning. This can be seen as an advantage or a disadvantage. A well-planned corporate data model implemented in a set of XML DTDs will provide dramatic increases in interoperability, communications, and data sharing. Poor planning can result in miscommunications and loss of data through incompatible applications. Someone once said, "Computers are powerful tools for making more errors, more quickly, and more precisely." That statement refers just as easily to XML.

Designers and developers must carefully analyze their needs so that XML is applied appropriately. A developer can build models of the legacy data structures and map data models to a set of XML data elements. The XML data elements are collected into a set of DTDs that can be used to build a well-defined tree structure for each document.

However, DTD development should not occur in a vacuum. If a corporation tries to develop its own applications and DTDs, it may find that its development is incompatible with other companies, vendors, and partners. Developers can avoid incompatibilities and "standards wars" by learning about the various industry standard DTDs.

The main advantage of XML will be for sharing data, so all companies will benefit by using the same standards. Compromises can be made to ensure widespread and future interoperability. These compromises may make XML documents larger or less fine-tuned than other solutions, but the increase in data sharing will be more than worth the trade-off.

Industry Standards

Companies and industry leaders are collaborating to develop standardized DTDs to share information and to automate business processes. For example, if Ford, GM, and DaimlerChrysler agree on a standard B2B e-commerce DTD with a set of rules for their procurement needs, then they could ensure that their partners, vendors, and customers could write compatible applications. The interoperability that XML promises will become a reality as more and more companies develop industry-specific DTDs.

The focus across vertical industries such as electronics has been to define specific DTDs so businesses can exchange data. Business-to-business e-commerce and document management are among the areas that will benefit from the adoption of standardized sets of XML tags. Once interested parties collaborate on a set of XML tags and a corresponding DTD for a given industry and application, they can seamlessly exchange data encoded with those tags. As each company or industry decides on a level of detail for its DTD and document structure, other companies can build on top of the standards and ignore details as appropriate.

Companies should keep watch of the many industry standards efforts to help define consistent XML DTDs and data elements. Some of these standards groups can be found at www.accord.com, www.xmledi.com, and www.openapplicationsgroup.com. Commerce XML Resources at www.cXML.org is one such registry for order processing and catalogs, and it is growing in support.

Bowstreet Software at www.bowstreet.com has deals with IBM, Microsoft, and Novell to store XML meta-data by using a Lightweight Directory Access Protocol (LDAP) technology. Microsoft, IBM, and Sun Microsystems are all working on strategies for leveraging XML to improve the portability and interoperability of data and information.

Splintering

Industry acceptance of XML has been faster than HTML and even faster than Java because everyone has data—too much data—and no one knows what to do with it. So business people are trying to discover what XML means for their data. Executives, managers, and developers attend XML conferences trying to learn what it is, and, more importantly, what it is not.

The strength of XML, its flexibility, is also its weakness. Because any group can create its own standard DTDs, there is the tendency to take the "not invented here" approach, which results in many fragmented standards that decrease, rather than enhance, information sharing and interoperability. Two uncoordinated efforts to design DTDs and schemas will produce incompatible results. Also, different industries may develop industry-specific DTDs that are not compatible with other industries. For example, the auto industry may create a set of useful DTDs that are not compatible with DTDs from the retail industry.

However, if industries set up and follow common standards, a dramatic step in the right direction will be made. But even one industry cannot set up a standard in isolation because suppliers and vendors will also use the standard. Some universal standard will be needed as a foundation for industry-strength development.

Parallel development of XML may provide a strong evolutionary environment. Standards will facilitate the general exchange of information, while proprietary DTDs will provide a competitive advantage. And all companies would like to create their own set of standards. So, trade-offs will occur as XML standards evolve. In fact, entire nations may be involved.

International Trade Agreements

Nations may negotiate new trade agreements to support XML-based international commerce. The same functionality that facilitates sharing of data may encourage exchanging personal data about consumers. While the release of personal buying habits may be considered only an annoyance in the United States, European government privacy laws are less provincial and more strongly enforced. Rather than violate these laws, European corporations might not participate in some of the XML standards and opportunities. Without an international agreement that protects consumer privacy, a clear solution is not apparent.

Overreaction?

XML will change the face of the Web; the Web of tomorrow may not resemble the Web of today. Just as the Internet of 1990 is nothing like the Internet of 2000, the XML-based Web of 2004 will have a richer array of functions than the Web of 2001. Why is this a risk?

Most Web sites are based on the static technology of HTML. However, with XML, users may shun a static site in the same way that they avoid a slowly downloading site today. This implies that the millions of HTML Web sites will have to be converted to the more dynamic XHTML in some way. Those sites that are not converted will either contain useful, standalone text that remains in some dead-end Web alley, or will simply be deleted from existence.

The impact of this transition is that corporations will prepare new Web pages using well-structured content, written in XHTML, or some other

XML dialect. A smooth transition strategy will be the least disruptive to most corporate plans. This strategy should include an XML document design architecture that anticipates reuse and repurposing of information and content by segmenting text into useful components. Information that is presliced into bite-sized components will be the easiest to digest and to incorporate into the overall XML-based Web infrastructure over the long haul.

XML's omnimorphic capability can be a curse to developers who try to force fit it into less flexible technologies. For example, many of the current Internet protocols and applications cannot handle scalable and device independent graphics files that are written in text. How does a server handle information that is portable across speech processing, Braille, and graphics? XML can handle some of these technologies today, but the Web infrastructure cannot yet keep up. To fully exploit XML's potential, changes to the infrastructure will have to occur.

With a full-blown peer-to-peer communications protocol, such as proposed by Intel, what does a company do with its servers? How does it redirect its WAN/LAN bandwidth? Although the infrastructure for XML is there already, the new capabilities may require a new mindset, just like starting out with the first corporate intranet.

Semantic Web

For the past few years, Tim Berners-Lee, the inventor of HTML and the World Wide Web, has been describing the Semantic Web that leverages the capabilities of HTML. XML may have blindsided some of those development efforts. In fact, any intensive development efforts, such as the new efforts to build corporate or personal portals, may have to be redirected to implement these ideas using XML. In the long run, XML is an enabling technology. But any changes in plans can make those plans slip to the right, extending the apparent schedule.

As XML becomes more widely accepted and adopted, an XML project should be faster than the equivalent HTML/Java development. But if a project is making progress, do you change horses in midstream with the potential for slipping, even if the horse is faster in the long run? XML presents that dilemma.

Start Over?

One thing is clear. We are not going to scrap the Internet and the Web and create an entirely new infrastructure for XML. When gopher arrived, nothing changed on the original Internet. Gopher was added on top. The same was true with HTML and the Web. And the same is true with XML and its various vocabularies. The existing standards and protocols are proven, they are debugged, and they work. WAP will not replace HTML, XHTML, and XML; it will sit on top or on the side. We do not want to take the risk of fixing something that is not broken.

What about all the different vocabularies and dialects that B2B is propagating? The last count was quickly approaching 600 different DTDs and schemas. Capitalism may come to save the day. One of the nice things about capitalism is that it is politically blind. It works on simple economic contingencies. It does not care about political dogma. Therefore, any industry that wants to participate in B2B e-business will have to conform to an open XML vocabulary to exchange data. In fact, as B2B gains more global influence, participating countries will have to fit in, too. A closed or proprietary XML vocabulary will tend to isolate the owner, rather than provide a significant competitive advantage. Today, communications is the cost of doing business on the Web. With XML, communications will be even more open tomorrow.

Fighting Apathy and Ignorance

One of the problems with explaining XML is its simplicity. People ask why it is important to separate the data from its presentation. Consider the corporation that has plenty of data that is not in a database or transferred using an interface. Most of the corporate intellectual capital is tied up in its documents. Two tremendous benefits come from managing the data, the structure, and the presentation separately.

The first benefit is that the data can be reused and repurposed. For example, the CAD drawings for an airplane are used to create the technical manuals. These drawings go through significant processing before they are ready for the manuals. These same drawings go through a completely different kind of processing to produce training manuals to teach technicians how to repair the airplane. What if we could put the drawings into an XML format that both technical manual software and CBT (Computer-Based

Training) software could both use without any processing? We could use the same data and the same structure, but change the presentation to fit the task. This method would save millions of dollars in translations costs alone.

The second benefit is improved processing capabilities. If we tag the documents, the drawings, the manuals, or the CBT with some forethought, then we may be able to migrate to new technologies, such as wireless and voice processing, more effectively. In addition, these tags could facilitate changes in the drawings and propagation of these changes throughout the entire process. With a disciplined methodology for writing the tags, we can reduce the size and the processing needed to parse the tags. The structure of the document helps to accomplish this goal.

When we don't worry much about the parser, we worry less about the browser, reducing or eliminating the repeat of Browser Wars. XML supports these benefits and many more, but this is the basic backbone. By separating data, processing, and presentation, we can modify any component without touching the other two. By imposing disciplined tag markup and a clear structure, we can easily manage the data and focus less on the parsing. And by agreeing on standards, we gain interoperability and improve profits.

Summary of XML Standards Issues

One of the great challenges that hinders the global adoption of XML by the corporate community is the potential fragmentation and splintering of XML standards. Corporations are concerned about three standards.

First, corporations are concerned that companies, such as Microsoft, will not adhere to the W3C recommendations and specifications. This concern is probably not valid because all of Microsoft's actions to this moment have implied full support of emerging XML standards. The only deviation is when the standard is not yet well defined, so Microsoft produces software that is based on an interim standard. Then when the true standard is finalized, Microsoft reissues its software. For the most part, these software applications are free, with no major financial impact.

Second, corporations are concerned with the variety of possible XML vocabularies and dialects that a department, corporation, or industry may produce. One of the major goals for XML is interoperability; however, its main strength, extensibility, results in a conflict. On the one hand, interoperability implies a single, stable standard. But on the other hand, extensibility implies the ability to change easily and quickly as the need or desire dictates. Clearly the solution to this dilemma is to balance the two issues by negotiation, compromise, and consensus. A lack of consensus and agreement will inhibit the acceptance of XML by industry and will impede the progress toward interoperability. For this reason, striving for some common standards is in everyone's best interest.

Based on the number of B2B implementations, more than 100 different business vocabularies of XML are being used for e-commerce and procurement exchanges. If smaller efforts are included, that number may rocket as high as 10,000 different DTDs. This number grows astronomically, if carried to a natural extrapolation, but a more rationale eye sees a logical convergence.

There is simply no business case for an irrational growth in the number of XML DTDs and vocabularies in the corporate world, especially B2B. In the case of B2B e-commerce, intercommunications will slow the propagation of DTDs. If a company from one industry wants to deal with a company from a different industry, it will have to agree on a common DTD for data transactions and information exchange. Just as the automotive companies have observed, cooperating on a uniform XML standard is more efficient than choosing to compete in that arena and possibly alienate vendors and partners.

For reasons of efficiency and cost effectiveness, corporations within industries will increasingly agree to use a common XML vocabulary. As the number of industry DTDs shrinks to a manageable number, vertical consortia will agree on standards that follow supply chains across industry boundaries. These boundary spanning vocabularies will combine the best of each separate XML dialect following a Darwinian evolution of DTDs, keeping the best and the fittest choices for the most global solutions. The term *global solutions* refers to the best approaches across both industry and country boundaries.

In 2001, nearly 400 of the Fortune 500 companies will be exploring XML with varying levels of prototype projects from internal markup languages to data transactions and information exchange. In addition, nearly 100 of the Fortune 500 will be using XML in production-level applications. There is an overlap between the companies building prototype and the companies who are building production-quality XML applications.

Industry analysts speculate that the 100 or so DTDs in 2001 will merge into fewer than 20 major DTDs by 2003 and then fewer than 5 DTDs before 2006. There will still be more than five total DTDs, but the major, broadly used DTDs will number less than five, possibly only one baseline vocabulary.

One way that this convergence will come about is through a number of standards groups that provide for both cross-industry and international collaboration. These standards groups, consortia, and other organizations will be the most efficient way to shepherd the XML flock into a single direction.

The third XML standards issue that corporations are concerned about is the split between DTDs and schemas. Currently, the large majority of XML vocabularies are defined by using a DTD. However, the number of schemas will grow quickly in 2001, and in 2002 the number of schema-based XML vocabularies will exceed the number of DTD-based XML vocabularies.

This gradual migration from DTDs to schemas will allow developers and vendors to program better applications for transforming from one metadata representation to another. As a result, this standards issue should be only a minor concern that is already being addressed by organizations such as IBM, Apache, and the W3C, in the form of transcoding, Cocoon, and XSLT, respectively.

CHAPTER 11

Summary of Industry XML Projects

Introduction

It has been a learning experience to watch the avalanche of collaborative B2B deals among the world's largest Industrial Age companies—the "Big Three" automobile manufacturers, Sears and Carrefour, Dow Chemical and DuPont, Boeing and Lockheed—all using the state-of-the-art, bleeding-edge technology to become e-companies. Ford and GM had the chance to compete in the B2B environment or cooperate and happily they chose to cooperate. If they had competed, they could have splintered the automotive XML vocabularies. Instead, when Covisint takes off, it may be a catalyst for converging, common XML vocabularies across industries.

From a media perspective, the announcements of B2B ventures continue. Other cooperative deals among competitors will be announced over the next few months. Scratch the surface a little bit and you find Oracle enabling the technology with its XML dialect. Dig a little deeper and you find the potential for a global XML vocabulary standard, backed by a $300 billion per year flow of parts and services from the auto industry. Irony #1 is that the "Old Guard" may accomplish what the "New Guard" could not—XML vocabulary standards, rather than splintering. Irony #2 is that Oracle created its XML dialect by working behind the scenes and keeping quiet about it, rather than hyping too much.

If these multibillion-dollar efforts result in (XML-based information transfer) bridges among the various industries, the promise of information anywhere, anytime, to anyone, about anything, may become a reality within 18 months or faster. The irony (Irony #3) is that now if we could get Oracle and Microsoft to cooperate, without increasing the hype decibels or the vaporware promises . . .

Regardless, many vendors are working with XML. Each company has its own expertise and offering. Rather than fail to make an exhaustive list, this chapter provides a broad assortment of some activities in XML. This list should be sufficient to show the reader that XML development is ongoing in almost every industry.

Automotive

Covisint (www.covisint.com) is the B2B e-commerce site that started it all. It was not the first B2B, but it was the largest one announced in the early part of 2000. Even though this $300 billion supply chain covers much of the automotive industry, its major focus is procurement of parts and services. The "Big Three" automobile manufacturers retain a strong interest in developing their own competitive B2B sites for other purposes.

DaimlerChrysler (Stuttgart, Germany, and Auburn Hills, Michigan, USA; www.DaimlerChrysler.com) has created an industry-specific DTD with the intent of defining a standard where none exists yet. The DTD is based on an SGML DTD that was developed for the automotive industry. The company is developing internal XML applications to gather information from different sources and combine it into a graphical format for engineers. DaimlerChrysler's eventual goal is to release the XML applications and DTDs, externally, as a common standard within the automotive industry.

Ford (Detroit, Michigan; www.forddirect.com) sells cars over the Web, allowing customers to add features, compare costs, apply for loans, and ultimately purchase their vehicles. FordDirect is an independently managed, combined venture among Ford and its dealers to fulfill the customer demand for car purchasing over the Web and to provide a point of contact for subsequent support. Although competition exists from sites such as Carpoint and Autobytel, the FordDirect site has the advantage of backing from Ford, with the potential for special promotions and individualized deals.

GM (Detroit, Michigan; www.gm.com) plans to use XML to develop an enterprise portal linking its 8,500 information systems and 110 terabytes of storage. The company will use DataChannel's RIO, an XML-based solution for building dynamic two-way corporate portals with publishing and retrieval capabilities. Besides making information more available to employees, the system will also improve the customer buying experience. One GM pilot involves bridging engineering systems to the Web through a browser with virtual reality support, enabling engineers to view components and then access legacy systems with relevant information, such as who engineered a part and what defects have been reported. GM is developing other custom XML portals for quality e-commerce and manufacturing. GM uses XML because it enables total portability and access to information, and DataChannel had the most robust implementation of XML. GM's existing legacy data can be XML enabled so that it can be accessed from any application. GM is also teaming with dealers to build a Web site for car comparisons.

Volkswagen (Germany, www.vw.com) is working with ArborText to use the power of XML to provide service information to dealerships and service repair centers. It uses the Web to deliver the most up-to-the-minute information. Technical information for Volkswagens can total more than 70,000 pages of data, including service repair manuals, owner's manuals, videos, technical bulletins, and wiring diagrams. By using XML, Volkswagen can reuse this massive amount of information both for the dealers and for the public. Before the XML solution was implemented, technical information was delivered on CD-ROM from the manufacturing facilities in Germany and Mexico. Now the information is available across the Web on the same day that it is created. The information can be provided quickly and accurately, allowing Volkswagen to be more responsive to dealerships and to customers. Customers demand current, comprehensive, and accurate information. Volkswagen can fulfill these demands through the use of XML to deliver information in a format that will ultimately support different devices (such as vehicle computer systems, desktop systems, electronic books, and wireless devices) and provide customers with more options to choose from.

Chemical

DuPont, Dow Chemical—and, indeed, most of the chemical industry—is working on a chemical XML vocabulary for B2B e-commerce. As described in Chapter 8, the chemical B2B market is one of the most successful. This market includes the standard chemicals and lab equipment, but, depending on the products and services, can also overlap with the petrochemical industry and the metals industry.

A big advantage of a chemical B2B marketplace is the ability to tap into a global marketplace, which allows the smaller houses to compete on a more level playing field with the giants of the industry. Despite a growing number of different chemical B2Bs, consolidation is expected in the near term. It would also be productive if these B2Bs were to collaborate with some of the other industry B2Bs to develop a common baseline vocabulary.

Bayer AG is a global chemical and pharmaceutical corporation that is moving its procurement processes to the B2B world. The transfer to B2B e-commerce is expected to reduce its $5 billion annual procurement costs by $250 million, for a savings of roughly 5 percent simply by going digital. By streamlining procurement processes, Bayer hopes to participant in the new e-business global supply and demand to increase profitability.

Sequencia Corp. in Phoenix, Arizona, is a major player in chemical batch processing software. It has launched some new XML-based software products that enable companies to share manufacturing and formulation information over the Web. The new products are designed to help companies collaborate, as well as buy and sell chemical process manufacturing capability through chemical B2B exchanges. By simplifying collaboration, chemical-related companies can reformulate products more rapidly, speed new products to market, and extend existing capacity.

Sequencia's new XML-based gRecipe software enables companies to create and manage product-manufacturing definitions in the form of general recipes throughout the supply chain. The software can adapt its generalized recipes into specific manufacturing instructions for the chemical batch-processing task at hand. XML facilitates the ability to provide a standardized way to define and describe a process product. In addition, it supports a complete start-to-finish B2B solution by providing a comprehensive process product definition including formula, recipe, equipment, work instruction, and bill of material information. By using international standards, gRecipe will shorten the production update cycle from months to only hours.

The company shares its two XML schemas, allowing customers to share processing information even though they use different software programs and operating systems. The schemas can be used to adapt existing data models, solutions, and applications for B2B e-commerce. The XML approach allows companies from specialty chemical, pharmaceutical, as well as food and beverage, to share site capabilities, recipes, and formulations. The efficiencies yielded by the XML solution will allow process companies to approach the benefits enjoyed by semiconductor and electronics fabrication houses.

Computer

IBM (Armonk, New York; www.ibm.com) is throwing significant resources behind XML. They are partnering with a number of companies, including Microsoft, Sun Microsystems, Oracle, and Adobe to bring XML applications to fruition. IBM has released a number of free XML/Java developer tools, as well as XML information at its Web site. The tools include editors, parsers, and markup language applications.

Microsoft is a huge supporter of XML and its open standards. Most, if not all, Microsoft products are becoming XML compliant to some degree. In addition, Microsoft has developed BizTalk, Microsoft.Net, and SOAP. These activities are detailed in separate "Microsoft" and "Microsoft.NET" sections later in this chapter.

Microsoft's Office 2000 uses XML to give the user control of the layout of Office documents. Everything is transparent, and nothing about Office 2000 tells the user that documents can be saved as XML. Office 2000 can export files to XML quite easily through the File/Save As... or the File/Save As Web Page . . . dialogs. But, Office does not say anything about XML at all. To the user, XML is a Web page or advanced HTML format.

Sun Microsystems (Palo Alto, California; www.sun.com) was an early backer of the Web, although it has not kept up with the powerhouses in e-business. It has developed the in-house support needed to offer these new services in the form of supply chain e-business, auctions, and a centralized infrastructure for e-commerce. Auctions, through Web sites like eBay, provide Sun with additional exposure to new businesses that have never purchased Sun products. B2B auctions can bring in as much as $1 billion. Most of Sun's on-line purchases have been EDI transactions. XML-based B2B procurement should simplify the process, resulting in millions of dollars in savings.

Sun is working with i2 to provide B2B customers with system, purchase, and delivery transaction information. These B2B processes can shrink manufacturing turnaround times from three weeks to three days. Improved communications and collaboration with suppliers can yield more than $100 million per year.

Sun has also devoted significant resources to developing many Java tools that support XML development. These tools are improving daily, and the Sun Web site is worth exploring to learn what new tools, applications, parsers, editors, etc. are being offered.

Cisco Systems, Inc. (San Jose, California; www.cisco.com) is leading an effort to apply XML to management data. The Service Level Management Suite uses an open XML interface to support service providers with the ability to monitor their Virtual Private Networks (VPNs). A browserlike interface will integrate with Cisco's network hardware and will measure service levels for VPNs, e-business, etc.

Lernout & Hauspie (Burlington, Massachusetts; www.lhs.com) developed a powerful intranet portal application called L&H Clinical Reporter on top of Sequoia Software's Interchange2000 system. Doctors use the application to automate the entry of spoken data into patient records as part of their data entry process. This significantly speeds the process of data entry. Researchers or physicians can analyze data immediately rather than waiting hours or weeks for a data transcription.

Oracle Corporation (Redwood Shores, California; www.oracle.com) expects XML to improve B2B communications by supporting a common set of tags to describe structured data and information. It has created a pair of free XML parsers in C and C++ languages to facilitate the use of legacy data. The parsers work with existing parsers for Java and for Oracle's PL/SQL language, and they support the transfer of legacy information between applications using the features of XML. These parsers are intended for use with the Oracle Applications Server in Oracle8 and Oracle8i, and they support Document Object Model and Simple API for XML.

Oracle has also released an XML parser for Java that includes an eXtensible Stylesheet Language Transformation processor (XSLT), XML SQL utilities, and XSQL servlet so that users can retrieve database information and deliver it in XML.

PeopleSoft (Pleasanton, California; www.peoplesoft.com) uses XML as a communications link to help customers with B2B e-commerce initiatives and with back-office application integration. The XML capability will allow users to deliver their activities across the Web. It will exploit the power of the Internet and give the application a Web browser look and feel. In addition, PeopleSoft 8 has wireless support and Unicode integration, anticipating WAP and multilingual requirements.

SAS Institute, Inc. (Cary, North Carolina; www.sas.com) builds products to support interoperability with other repositories via an import/export facility, either through its support of MDIS or possibly, a more direct interchange. SAS products, such as SAS/Warehouse Administrator software, SAS/EIS software, SAS/MDDB software and the MDDB procedure, all create or use OLAP-related meta-data. SAS/Warehouse Administrator software could define MDDBs (multidimensional databases).

TekInsight.com Inc. (New York, NY; www.tekinsight.com) uses XML as the foundation of its BugSolver technology. It uses XML not to carry out data transactions but to provide massive amounts of failure and monitoring data to IT departments. It uses streaming XML to break data into sequenced, self-contained packets that provide a more efficient way to transmit, store, and retrieve large XML documents and data. Rather than using once-a-night batch processing, customers can get real-time data on demand by using the XML tools. The tidal wave of batch data is now subdivided by XML into a format that can be analyzed more easily. TekInsight has been so successful that they have applied for a patent on their streaming XML capability.

Education

Education is another area that XML and e-commerce affects. For example, e-books are available for both desktop and wireless access. XML provides an excellent opportunity for turning adult education into a billion dollar growth business. Most corporations, the government, and the military spend multibillions of dollars per year on education. The Web provides the necessary infrastructure to accommodate the schedule of today's busy adult.

Two vehicles for adult education are "edutainment" and "webucation." "Edutainment" is the concept of delivering information in an entertaining gamelike format. "Webucation" is the idea of delivering Computer-Based Training (CBT) in an interactive format across the Web.

After an initial startup cost, once the curricula and lessons are in place, delivery costs are the same whether there is one student, one hundred students, or one million students. In addition, training can go on anytime and anywhere to anyone. For example, while traveling across the country, a busy executive might learn about new technologies, such as XML and WAP, by viewing an interactive CBT on a cell phone. Upon arrival, that executive is just a little more knowledgeable about new technology.

At the moment, education developers take advantage of advances in the entertainment field for new CBT software. This means that many of the computer games developed by professional computer engineers eventually make their way into the foundation of CBT software. Also, many of these same engineers may be called on to develop the CBTs with a limited timeline and budget. However, for effective instructional design, well-established research and methods from educational psychology and technology should still be used. But first someone has to pay for the development before such educational software can be deployed on the Web. So far, the software companies are footing the bill and paying professional computer engineers to create education software in the same way that they create game software. Eventually, big companies and the military will probably use the expertise of educators to develop in-house CBTs. As that trend develops, XML-based adult education will become a growth industry in its own right.

Financial

Just as the conservative automotive industry is embracing XML, so is the traditional banking industry.

Wells Fargo & Company (San Francisco, California; www.wellsfargo.com) is exploiting the capabilities of XML to leverage its legacy data for reuse and repurposing. The IT division is using Java and XML to collect data from distributed back-end databases to build new ways and profiles for analyzing customer data, information, and trends.

While many companies have been taking a wait-and-see attitude, Wells Fargo has been a leader in the use of XML technologies. Rather than sit back and let competitors make all the mistakes... and learn all the lessons, Wells Fargo has jumped in with both feet, gotten a little dirty, but also found that XML can improve access to legacy data.

The Java-based XML system is built on a multitier architecture that is compatible with a variety of existing platforms. This example shows how XML will be applied to current and proprietary data systems to squeeze new knowledge from old information. The system allows Wells Fargo to understand customer trends and to take advantage of these trends by targeting the appropriate customers with new products, services, and loans. For example, if a young couple bought a mortgage about 15–20 years ago, they might now be interested in a college loan.

This analysis benefits both parties. First, the couple will not need to go through the trouble, anxiety, and cost needed to locate the best terms and the paperwork hassle of establishing credit for the loan. Second, because Wells Fargo has much of the information already on file, it has a detailed history of mortgage payments, and it has a motivated client with excellent credit and collateral. None of these are guesses based on a simple loan application. These clear trends are known by using XML to pull this information from the legacy databases. A little information may need to be updated, but nothing like the background data that must be collected for a new loan approval. XML enables the potential for a good deal for both parties: a win–win situation in a painless, timely manner.

Another way that Wells Fargo has planned ahead is to design in special attributes for security and privacy that allow for expansion and modification for new regulations and privacy laws. These attributes are simply carried along in the XML documents and add minimal value and require little overhead. But when the regulations change, as they do on a continual basis, a couple of keystrokes, or a search and replace, and all the data will be in conformance. With legacy systems, that kind of modification might take an entire rebuild of the database with significant costs as the system is checked and double-checked. Because the infrastructure is already in place, waiting for the changes, implementation and testing should be straightforward.

With the special attributes in place, Wells Fargo can also exchange data with other companies while solving two problems with one application. First, XML documents can easily be modified to be compatible with the data formats needed by the receiving company. In addition, XSLT can be used to transform imported data into formats that are compatible with the Wells Fargo systems. And second, the existing privacy attributes allow Wells Fargo to transfer data without sending carefully regulated personal information or closely guarded proprietary data. A little forethought goes along way.

The company has significant experience with XML. In 1999, Wells Fargo paid Micro Modeling Associates, a consulting firm, the fee of $200,000 to develop its intranet. Developers performed the initial XML conversions manually, and then the system automatically creates subsequent XML as needed. Employees can convert Microsoft Office Tools applications, such as Word and Excel documents, into an XML format. These XML documents provide a simple data warehouse capability that allows all managers and employees to search through the information. The cleaner formats enable easier access to corporate knowledge, providing significant timesavings and efficiencies over the previous HTML-based systems.

Dow Jones & Company (New York, New York; www.dowjones.com) collects data feeds from 6,000 periodicals, converts it to XML, and sends it out to business customers. Customers can parse and manipulate the XML-based data in a way that can be combined compatibly with in-house data to create decisionable information.

Dun & Bradstreet (Murray Hill, New Jersey; www.dnb.com) uses XML applications to build a common interface among its worldwide offices. XML automates data exchange between legacy data sources, even when the data sources have different access protocols. Reporting systems are also easier to use and maintain because database queries and answers are consistent across legacy databases and there is only one DTD for all the legacy interfaces.

First Union (Charlotte, North Carolina; www.firstunion.com) has developed an industry-specific DTD to define the standard, rather than waiting for independent standards. The company plans to use XML for authentication and, after the bugs are worked out, to release the DTD to internal business units across the company and also to clients. First Union uses IBM's e-commerce framework to share data among applications.

Merrill Lynch & Company (New York, New York; www.ml.com) has developed XML applications to transfer data processing from the server to the desktop. Although HTML data is primarily text, XML data is true information that can be manipulated without returning to the server. This functionality allows a user to sort financial data on the desktop to improve both resource use and response time.

Insurance Firms

XML is acting as the catalyst to help the insurance industry migrate from its legacy data and manual processes. Several insurance companies have implemented a new XML specification developed by the Acord consortium.

Acord is an insurance consortium that is working on implementing the XML specifications, called Acord XML, to help bring insurance business processes on-line. Acord is the same consortium that developed and implemented the EDI specifications for the insurance companies years ago. New XML transitions are expected to help keep the agents competitive as more services are offered across the Web. The current XML specifications only cover complex business policies, because each type of policy offered will require a different XML specification.

When the XML specifications for the complex business policies are fully implemented, insurance companies and agents will be able to interoperate more effectively. In addition, the systems should be able to connect with the agency management software used by independent agents.

Some of the insurance carriers that are already using this new XML insurance vocabulary include Hartford Financial Services Group, Travelers Property Casualty, Safeco, and Manulife Financial. Other insurers are in the planning phase.

The Acord XML insurance vocabulary serves as the foundation for building interfaces among the various incompatible insurance systems that are used by insurance carriers, agents, rating services, and on-line brokers. This new XML standard and the new interfaces will enable these insurance groups to exchange policy and customer information. The benefits of lower operating costs and more efficient customer service are expected to be the positive outcome of the expected automation and improved response times.

In addition, the new software will enable agencies to use browser-based systems to communicate with back-end systems and databases. Because of the improvement in response and turnaround times, information exchange will occur in seconds rather than hours, resulting in the ability to close a sale to customers right on the spot. These improvements will help put agents on a level playing field with Web-based services such as InsWeb and Quotesmith.

The leading agency management software and application vendors are working directly with Acord and the insurance companies to develop the XML-based interfaces. As the number of insurance companies that use these interfaces, grows, the independent agents will grow in proportion. The agents will be able to exploit the common interfaces and XML data standards to compare policies and quotes from within their agency management interface software.

The process is similar to what is happening in the automotive industry with the Covisint B2B exchange. Because all 30,000 vendors use the same XML standards, automotive manufacturers can compare parts, services, and prices from a single interface. This encourages the vendors to differentiate on something rather than prices, and it allows the automakers to compare offerings more easily.

With the Acord XML standards, independent agents will be able to compare insurance offerings in order to provide their customers with the best value for their individual needs. This method will be much smoother and easier than the old fashioned method of learning each individual proprietary interface and then rekeying data multiple times in order to make simple comparisons.

Although getting total buy-in from all insurance carriers will take a little while, competitive pressure will eventually win out. And then the full benefits of XML in the insurance industry will become apparent to the corporations, the agents, and the customers.

News Media

While XML has established its reputation in B2B e-commerce, industries and corporations are also exploiting its ability to stream massive amounts of content and data. For example, the Wavo Corporation, www.wavo.com, uses XML to enable its MediaXpress service, which streams news, sports, and entertainment to various Web sites wanting to boost their content with real-time news stories and on-demand information. The system works on MS Windows platforms as well as Linux and other Unix operating systems. Content comes from 1,800 media sources.

MediaXpress leverages its XML applications to send information to customers in a format that is completely compatible with their requirements. In fact, the use of XML makes it possible to tailor the information to the appropriate format for any target system or device, such as wireless, by normalizing and transforming the content.

The MediaXpress XML application automatically marks up the content, indexes it for location and keywords, and then pushes the information to the customer Web site. The application is a full-blown markup engine and it allows MediaXpress to classify information for its customers. XML provides the general interface capabilities, which allow MediaXpress to both receive and send information in the needed format.

Telecommunications

More than 300 telecommunications corporations, including Motorola, Nokia, Ericsson, are developing the Wireless Application Protocol (WAP). Chapter 6 discussed the Wireless Application Protocol and Bluetooth, which are the major XML drivers in the wireless industry.

Another application that is becoming famous is VoiceML, which will be used for speech processing and various kinds of standardized voice input.

Covad Communications, Inc. (Santa Clara, California, www.covad.com) is a Digital Subscriber Line (DSL) service provider that provides the XLink API capability for Internet service providers to build and maintain DSL services. This XLink API is XML based and it supplies uniform data fields for customer and vendor interactions, resulting in more reliable and cost effective data exchange.

USENET

Usenet (User's Network) is an important component of the Internet, as well as the Web and XML revolutions, that has been mostly ignored by the general media. A 20-year old bulletin board just does not seem to have the same allure as a two-month old startup. However, the 30,000 individual newsgroups within the Usenet bulletin functionality have more diversity and more information than the Web and most intranets. Usenet information may grow at the rate of millions of postings per day.

Many newsgroups are devoted to XML developments, and companies such as Microsoft and IBM have their own newsgroups for XML news. In fact, as the W3C releases information about new trends in XML technology, it posts the information on Usenet.

Usenet is an untapped resource for e-commerce. It is the penultimate place for networking with people, learning about new topics, and discussing new ideas or products. One of the reasons that it is unused as a resource for e-commerce is because it is bad netiquette to use Usenet for a hard sell. Marketeers don't like the soft sell, on the order of "here's a bunch of free information, and by the way, we sell a product that might solve your problem." They operate more like here is the free information, let us come give a presentation, and we'll call back until you buy. That kind of attitude does not play well on Usenet.

Usually people visit newsgroups in much the same way that they would gather around the water cooler. The discussions may be organized and fairly regular, but they are always informal.

Few companies have been able to profit from Usenet, and most of those were search engines that, like most search engines, get revenues from Web-based advertising. However, one company, ClariNet Comunications (San Jose, California; www.clarinet.com) has found a way to make profits on Usenet. ClariNet sells "pay for view" or subscriber news articles across Usenet, on the order of 2,500 articles per day.

When B2B e-commerce companies explore Usenet, they will find that they can leverage this community for a new value proposition by tapping into its diversity and providing focused information to individual subscribers. Usenet is a vast resource. If e-commerce on Usenet is approached with taste and netiquette, then the profit potentials should be dramatic.

Microsoft

Microsoft Corporation (Redmond, Washington, www.microsoft.com) is involved with XML standards, as well as XSL, DOM, and Namespaces. Microsoft is supporting e-commerce standards at its www.biztalk.org, which is used as a repository for XML schemas. One of the advantages of Microsoft's BizTalk is that it has many of the functions needed to take over for EDI using XML technologies. Many companies will be able to use BizTalk directly in order to pass data between different platforms, without needing to develop new EDI capabilities.

The Microsoft BizTalk Toolkit, available at www.Microsoft.com/biztalk, is a free download that provides developers with a set of XML tools needed for building XML applications that are compatible with the BizTalk standard. BizTalk applications use XML-based transaction models and XML documents to reproduce and exceed much of the functionality provided previously by EDI. All XML documents and applications that are developed using the BizTalk tools should be easy to make interoperable with other BizTalk applications.

The BizTalk thrust is one of Microsoft's strategies for supporting and promoting the use of XML throughout and across the enterprise. One of Microsoft's business strategies for BizTalk is to support the BizTalk server. That idea makes good business sense. However, Microsoft has remained faithful to the XML standards and continues to support the W3C in general, the XML committee, and each specification as it is accepted.

Early adopters of BizTalk have been able to develop transaction applications that can integrate customers with backend legacy database systems. Rather than laboring over complex programming of new APIs, developers can pull together a system with relative ease. Most of the components for an end-to-end system already exist in the BizTalk toolkit, so all a developer has to do is define the requirements and link the pieces needed to satisfy them.

BizTalk also facilitates data and information exchange among business partners over the Web. Integration and interoperability merely require an agreement on the XML tags available in the BizTalk suite. The diversity of companies from different industries on the BizTalk steering committee has assured that the BizTalk schemas and tags could conform to the needs of most corporations. In addition, if adequate schemas do not exist in the BizTalk repository for some application, then companies can agree to register their own definitions with BizTalk. This way the repository works both ways—for storage and for extension.

As an EDI capability, BizTalk serves as the foundation of Microsoft's B2B e-commerce offerings. The BizTalk schemas are customized to support business transactions, much the same as EDI applications. In fact, BizTalk Server 2000 includes tools for transforming EDI content into XML and for maintaining it. Companies such as Dell, Boeing, Andersen Consulting, SAP, and CommerceOne support the BizTalk technology, using it for e-commerce and for integration. However, despite this support and Microsoft's backing, general corporate acceptance of BizTalk has been slow. BizTalk Server 2000 is part of the .NET tool set used to develop e-business solutions.

Microsoft.NET

Microsoft is betting $2 billion on the Internet and on XML with a dramatic new strategic thrust called Microsoft.NET. Based on a potential market that approaches a trillion dollars and on the established need to develop individualized information and interfaces, Microsoft's vision is to use Microsoft.Net to leverage XML technologies to enable developers to blend interfaces, computers, and communications. In addition, developers will be able to develop on the PC and deliver to all other XML-enabled platforms. Microsoft.NET echoes the capabilities of XML and the motto of Sun Microsystems in the 1980s: "The Network is the Computer."

Microsoft proposes a number of components to build the Microsoft.NET capability, including a .NET platform of development tools for distributed services, a Windows.NET system with associated desktop .NET tools, and the promise of third-party developers to support the effort to create an interoperable, interactive environment for an integrated information experience.

The promise for consumers is networked, integrated services that are available anywhere, from any devices, at anytime. The potential for corporate users is a uniform development environment that works transparently with wireless, desktop, intranet, Internet, and e-commerce activities. The opportunity for developers is to build reusable and repurposed applications, fulfilling the "write once, reuse everywhere" vision. Microsoft.NET development tools are specifically designed for building interactive Web-based systems deliverable on any XML-ready platform. The tools automatically generate XML statements and should integrate well with Microsoft's BizTalk tools. In fact, Microsoft intends to offer a set of core Microsoft.NET functions that developers can use as building blocks for more efficient deployment of resources.

Some of these tools include security applications with levels of authentication, messaging applications with e-mail and messaging, profile applications with rules and preferences for individualization, XML repository applications with SOAP, calendar applications with scheduling, directory applications with search capabilities, and automated application update capabilities with upgrades on demand.

Microsoft's objective is to weave the PC environment and the Web environment together. This integrated capability will adapt to the needs of the user, according to Microsoft, rather than the user adapting to the computer, as has been the case in the past. In addition, with the use of Microsoft.NET, each environment (e.g., desktop publishing, accounting, browsing) will offer seamless interfaces to improve the productivity of the user. These environments will be device independent and will adapt to the needs of the user.

Some of the technologies that will enable this vision are available as a set of capabilities, architectures, and tools. These include a Natural Interface with multiple capabilities such as speech, handwriting, and natural language understanding; a collaborative Universal Canvas based on XML to enable seamless information availability from distributed sources; and a preferences manager called the Intelligent Agent that gives the user greater control over personal information and histories.

Microsoft is pulling out all stops to exploit the Internet and XML. It would appear that the "embrace, extend, extinguish" model has been abandoned for the collaboration model. The improved user interface environment is interesting. If Microsoft has 90 percent of the PC operating system market, then it seems that user interface issues or difficulties would probably originate in Microsoft's backyard. And the same is true for users needing to adapt to the computer rather than the reverse.

From a good business perspective, Microsoft.NET offers tools to enable collaboration. Users can build or buy, and Microsoft will benefit if they buy. This approach works well for everyone if the tools add value and there is competition in the marketplace so that the tools can evolve.

With an open source policy, Microsoft might lose market share to many of the same developers who have created the Linux tools and some of the Macintosh tools. Many XML development tools are already freely available through any search engine. From one viewpoint, Microsoft.NET adds another set of options.

There is one significant advantage to the Microsoft.NET approach. The biggest concern about XML is the standards and the splintering of vocabularies. Microsoft has the size and clout to guide the convergence of DTD and schema vocabularies and transformation tools needed for XML to realize complete integration and interoperability. The XML market has diverged a little, but it has not yet splintered. BizTalk has not appeared to affect this divergence one way or the other. Microsoft.NET or another incarnation may be the guiding force for unification.

Microsoft.NET is the latest step in the Microsoft evolution from "a PC on every desk" to "Information at your fingertips" resulting in "Information on any platform, anywhere anytime." The .NET strategy counts on XML and SOAP to allow applications to interoperate in a more user-transparent way. This means that any platform, such as a cell phone or a Coke machine, that provides data access, may also provide Microsoft.NET compatibility. Although the device may not use a Microsoft operating system, Microsoft does want to ensure that some part of the information chain will depend on a Microsoft product such as Microsoft.NET.

Microsoft.NET Changes for Applications

Upgrades, operating system changes, and application modifications are disrupting and frequently frustrating. In the move to Windows 2000, some companies also moved from MS Exchange to MS Outlook. Although the operating system upgrade was minor, the mail change caused many little annoyances with profiles, preferences, and personal mail lists. These little issues tended to wash out the smooth transitions.

One of Microsoft's goals is to use Microsoft.NET to make changes, upgrades, and modifications simple or even transparent. It intends to exploit the flexibility of XML to allow users to ease into modifications by using the schema meta-data to effect the change.

The single Microsoft.NET schema is the key to the entire process. All applications share this schema. Any changes in the Microsoft.NET schema will ripple consistently through the entire platform, uniformly. In an ideal Microsoft.NET implementation, having version 2.3 of one application and version 3.1 of another will not be possible, so resulting version incompatibilities will not occur. All Microsoft.NET applications use the same schema, can understand the same data, and therefore maintain smooth interoperability.

In theory, application installation and removal will be as simple as copy or delete. Microsoft.NET should eliminate complex installation commands that leave ghost files throughout the file system. As discussed throughout this book, XML does have the capability to support these kinds of features, if designed correctly. So, if .NET is installed correctly, it should work as reliably as any other Microsoft product.

The Risks of .NET

With the new Microsoft.NET platform, Microsoft promises a more stable environment than even on their NT boxes. This means no more downtime, no more reboots, no more blue screen of death indicating that all work has disappeared into hyperspace. However, SOAP, one of the foundation components of Microsoft.NET, is neither secure nor reliable, so Microsoft still has a long way to go before the corporate world will fully embrace its vision. In addition, a fault-free system requires fine-tuning and a fault-free installation, with fault-free support.

Training and support have not big strengths with Microsoft. However, Microsoft is also training vendors and partners in focused classes and workshops, augmenting the standard on-line tutorials and information. Historically, the best support for Microsoft products seems to come not from Redmond, but from the local bookstore. The lack of clear help has resulted in a lucrative business for "third-party" self-help authors, who write about Microsoft products.

Most companies, therefore, will probably wait a few months, perhaps for version 2.2, before buying into this new full service business model. In the case of new Microsoft operating systems, a wait-and-see attitude has never been a poor choice.

Another approach is to send your developers and implementers from the IT operations department to Microsoft for all of the Microsoft.NET training. Although this approach is expensive and risky, a simple one-year training contract will slow the leak of knowledge from walking out the door. In addition, a stipulation of the training can be that the developers will also train people to replace them, distributing the wealth of knowledge. Microsoft's .NET platform is sufficiently complex; it won't hurt to have a team of experts in-house. The savings in productivity may be worth the cost of training.

Simple Object Access Protocol (SOAP)

Simple Object Access Protocol (SOAP) is a W3C specification to allow applications to communicate across different platforms and through a firewall. SOAP requires special protocols, security, and authentication in order to be successful as a method of cross-systems communications.

SOAP is an XML-based open standards-based, protocol used to provide a common messaging format for interoperability, independent of application technology. It will link business applications in the same way that XML will link data exchange. It is supported by companies like Microsoft, Sun,

Compaq Computer, Hewlett-Packard, IBM, and SAP. Their goal is to agree on a single SOAP standard and to avoid the incompatibility problems experienced with XML.

SOAP will allow companies to leverage XML and share, not only data, but also application technology. For example, a computer manufacturer can download a parts inventory from a vendor's Web site. In this way, Dell might explore and compare parts from Intel, AMD, and Texas Instruments to establish the best deal for that week. An accounting firm might browse a client's books as the numbers come in, so Ernst & Young might have caught the problems with Proctor and Gamble's books and prevented the 26-point slide in stock price in early 2000.

The SOAP specification will allow developers to create applications and services that can be more easily integrated, independent of operating system, programming model, or programming language.

CHAPTER 12

The Outlook for XML

Introduction

XML provides a foundation for information interoperability. It can serve as the central point for exchanging data among different databases and systems by providing a universal data format. Because the major software and database vendors have embraced the XML standard, in an ideal world, data integration across different systems is guaranteed.

The ability of an XML document to be self-describing through the use of a DTD elevates the importance of meta-data. By designing data elements defined in the DTD to be used as meta-data, XML developers will enhance the ability of data warehouses, modeling tools, and enterprise portals to exchange meta-data. Once meta-data can be exchanged, information can be more easily shared, blended, and united into a virtual document that addresses an immediate requirement. A reason for creating data element meta-data stored in DTDs or schemas is to provide more efficient document information searches.

Universal Data Format

XML is the major enabler for Web-based, interoperable applications that share information in a universal data format. By functioning more like a database than a word processor, XML blazes the path for more effective document management, electronic data interchange, and e-business functionalities.

The use of XML as a universal data format will improve corporate communications and data transfer across the Web and intranets. It will enhance the capability of working with systems from yesterday, today, and tomorrow. A universal data format alone is not sufficient to guarantee interoperable access of information to everyone, everywhere, every time. Client and server applications, as well as any two XML applications, need a common set of protocols and standards in order to communicate. These standards include the types of data, a common definition of the types, and the representation of these types during data transfer. The XML DTD provides a common method for negotiating these definitions and standards between applications.

XML-Based Data Warehouses

It is not that big of a conceptual leap from a set of standardized, tagged documents to a corporate repository of all documents. If a centralized, industry-strength DTD ties these documents together with a common set of markup tags, then these documents can be searched for information. A data warehouse is a large data repository with consistent, time-independent data. That sounds very similar to the definition of an XML document repository. Corporations will build more of these XML-based data warehouses as they realize the cost saving and the efficiencies involved. A startup company has an excellent opportunity to develop a niche market, converting legacy information into an XML document repository with data mining capabilities.

Semantic Web

The idea of the data warehouse can be taken a step further. If a set of standard DTDs are developed and used, then teaching the computer about meaning may be possible. If the browser has been taught that a "car" has "tires," and that a "tire" is "whitewalled," then in the future, the browser may be able to understand that a "car" with "whitewalled" "tires" is the same concept, but with different syntax. Now, the browser will understand not only the concepts of "car," "whitewalled," and "tire" but also the relationship in meanings between "whitewalled" and "tire." As this Semantic

Web (as Tim Berners-Lee calls it) of meaning extends to other domains from e-business to education, the Web evolves into a massive data warehouse of human knowledge, consistently organized and machine readable.

Corporate Backing: IBM, Oracle, Microsoft

Many companies support XML. However, the support of these three major corporations indicates the importance of this new technology. All three companies offer many free XML tools over the Web, as described in other chapters. Clearly each company has efforts to support its business model. IBM intends to encourage interoperability with its larger computers. Oracle wants to ensure that its databases are compatible with future development. Microsoft does not want to be caught off guard as it was with the Web, and it would like to nudge the XML evolution toward standards that benefit Microsoft products.

IBM supports XML by developing a significant offering of XML technology that is available for platforms including AIX, Windows NT, OS/390, HP-UX, and Solaris.

Oracle has developed XML components to facilitate the smooth exchange of data between XML documents and Oracle databases. These components include XML parsers that also support XSL, DOM, and SAX for XML interfaces. XML is a natural match for Oracle relational databases, which include a good data dictionary and referential integrity, facilitating the extraction of data into an XML document.

Microsoft is spending big bucks to make people aware of XML and to lay the framework for XML development over the next six to eight months. One of the interesting developments is in data mining. The Microsoft research team is working on a set of standards to leverage existing products such as the SQL Server database. If these standards were integrated into SQL Server as an XML-based data-mining engine, then Microsoft might corner the document management market on a platform-independent, system-independent, and application-independent content management system.

Microsoft is developing a new architecture called DNA 2000, which uses XML to enable a complete transaction server package. In addition, Microsoft plans that the next generation of Windows platforms will be strongly based on XML technology, will be customizable, and will interoperate better with non-Windows platforms.

Forecast for the Next Decade

Extrapolating forward from the previous 10 years yields many promising and astounding innovations and developments. XML will help to drive many of these developments, just as the Web has resulted in greater global communications.

Faster Connections

The first improvement is broadband connections to the consumer for permitting multicast video and real-time global interconnects at megabit or faster speeds. Current cable modem technology exceeds megabit transfer rates. Increased demand will result in increased bandwidth.

B2B E-Business

The Web has an amazing tendency to level the playing field for small companies and large corporations. The agility and versatility of the small company has been catching up and passing the conservative infrastructure and bureaucracy of the large corporations. One significant change in the business environment is improving information sharing among business partners. While the major corporations may hesitate, the smaller companies embrace partnering to create virtual companies with complementary skills. Partnering to share strengths synergistically is efficient, and XML enables this type of collaborative environment.

International Trade

XML will elevate international trade laws, issues, and differences into the public spotlight as new trade agreements are negotiated among the nations. Taken to extreme, dramatic changes may occur in international commerce, resulting in a new set of unified world trade agreements.

Convergence

Convergence has been a buzzword for many years, and is reminiscent of picture phones of years past. These are a reality today and the integration among computers, telephone, and video is growing more efficient every day. As the Internet Protocols enable convergence, XML will extend it and elevate it to a higher plane. Today finding and using a data snippet or a quotation requires search time and expertise for even a hope of success. Tomorrow, XML tags will enable rapid picture, audio, and video searching in ways that require millions of dollars today. In their time, the *Star Wars* and *Jurassic Park* movies were considered break throughs in computer animation. Today, students create similar effects for computer games. Tomorrow, corporations will pay license fees and use XML-based technology to create advertisements and movies by manipulating archives of deceased celebrities, even animated nonmovie stars like Abraham Lincoln. The technology exists today, but costs are prohibitive. It will be a desktop function. XML will enable access to the correct pictures and videos.

Peer-to-Peer Computing

With the millions of computers and information repositories available across the Internet and the Web, access and use is still limited. XML and XLink will drive advancements in these areas. With the power to build distributed data warehouses and corporate portals based on XML, customers will demand greater access. With the complex linking afforded by XLink, increased access to "self-aware" knowledge bases and powerful computing resources will appear just as quickly as the appearance of Web-driven modem increases, which leads us to the next technology.

Wireless Internet

Nokia already offers a wireless Internet capability through its cell phones, and Sprint PCS is spending $750 million to build wireless Internet access. Sprint advertises that Sprint PCS wireless phone owners can use the Sprint PCS wireless Web Browser to view text versions of selected Web sites. It also has plans to spend the $750 million on Samsung and Motorola telephone divisions. The plan includes having Samsung's American division sell $500 million in wireless phones and Motorola sell $250 million, both efforts to help support the Sprint digital wireless network and Internet access.

Just as cell phones have become ubiquitous, wireless computing will also be the norm. Although it is a natural progression to go wireless, XML, and especially XLink will facilitate the evolution. Today, wireless access and computing is a convenience (although many business people will argue that it is a necessity). With the ability to synthesize information, anywhere and anytime, people will want their intelligent computer assistants available 24 hours a day to address both common everyday problems and challenging, strategic business opportunities.

Ubiquitous Web Servers

Ubiquitous Web servers, which will be XML-enabled, are a natural and predicted consequence of the coming new Internet Protocol standards. These Web servers are strongly coupled with wireless resources. If the computing resources for the house, toaster, and sprinkler do not have to be physically connected, and if the connections are wireless, then anything that can have an Internet address *will* have an Internet address. All of these possibilities can be speculated on, but the focus here is on automobiles. With the use of the Web, XML, and Global Positioning intelligent highways, then cars that drive themselves may become a reality. These three technologies can be linked today to address that opportunity, but a few more years are needed for the logistics and engineering bugs to be worked out to public satisfaction.

XML promises to increase the value of data, the value of information, and the value of communications. The potential is just as bright as the Internet in the 1980s and the Web in the 1990s. The best way to summarize and predict the value of XML is by a similar question, "What is the value of a newborn baby?" XML technology has recently been conceived and given birth. What is its value, indeed?

Emerging Specifications

XML, even though it is omnimorphic, cannot deliver application integration by itself. Application integration involves much more than self-describing, extensible message formats. The applications must be adapted to learn to communicate using XML. Additional integration services are also required to route requests, manage tasks, and translate between different DTDs. A complete solution also includes services to ensure acceptable performance levels and to maintain security.

Many new applications and tools are being developed as this book is being compiled and published. For example, a new specification for XSLT was released just before this document was completed. This section addresses some of the emerging tools. Many very recent tools, by necessity, are omitted in order to stay within time limitations and scope.

Channel Definition Format (CDF) is a Microsoft sponsored specification that provides a standard set of tags for building push channels to automate the active flow of information from the server to the browser. CDF uses a DTD that defines the content, the descriptive information, and the download schedule.

Document Content Description (DCD) is a specification used to build structural schemas or document content format descriptions. It will provide one standard for defining different types of document formats based on content, meaning, and purpose.

Meta Content Framework (MCF) is a Netscape sponsored meta-data model that reflects a network of XML and HTML information nodes that describe Web sites and pages. The MCF model facilitates the ability to visualize and navigate through an interconnected Web space of documents.

Open Software Description (OSD) was developed to deliver software updates over the Internet to target locations that include both Web sites and client platforms. OSD has the capability to automatically download and install software programs.

Resource Description Framework (RDF) is a specification that governs meta-data and applications interoperability. RDF will use the XML syntax to leverage tools built around XML. The collaborative RDF effort is based upon several other meta-data initiatives. RDF meta-data can be used to provide better search engine capabilities, to catalog the content at a Web site, to facilitate knowledge exchange via intelligent agents, to describe multiple physical documents that represent a single logical document, and to describe the intellectual property rights of Web pages.

Web Interface Definition Language (WIDL) is a method of defining interfaces among Web applications. It enables automated Web-based processes by providing client systems with information about Web services. WIDL applications do not require a browser.

Meta Object Facility (MOF) is the Object Management Group (OMG) standard for distributed data repositories and for meta-data definitions. The XML Meta-data Interchange (XMI) is the combination of MOF, XML, and Unified Modeling Language (UML) supported by the OMG. XMI will support the use of object-oriented methodologies for meta-data and XML development.

XML Software Autoupdate (XSA) is a simple XML application designed to extract information from Web documents and use it intelligently. The information can be reused in different ways, and information suppliers can use different DTDs for their pertinent applications.

XSLT is a new specification that defines how style sheets can be applied to process XML documents. It may be a simple conditional language or it may be based on Scheme, a dialect of LISP. If XSLT is Scheme-based, it opens up tremendous possibilities for smart XML documents using well-proven artificial intelligence techniques developed over the past 30 years. The XSLT definition is still emerging.

Opportunities

XML enhances the Web just as dramatically as HTML enabled the Internet. Many of the concepts of automation that were initiated years ago, such as the paperless office and globally distributed information access, will be realized with XML. With careful planning, XML will yield new applications for increased productivity of information and knowledge on a worldwide scale.

Data Processing

Corporations will share data by using XML documents, so applications and data formats can be separate issues. The interapplication communication will be XML based. And the data in the documents will be processed as if the data resided in a relational database. In the early stages of XML development, XML consultants might come in and translate legacy data and document to an XML format.

Transaction Processing

The current necessity for middleware applications will be supplanted by the use of XML on the Web. XML makes middleware unnecessary. Rather than using special middleware applications, transaction processing and requests for data will use XML technology. With XML, the format of a database and the protocols for dealing with it are irrelevant. The retrieved data will return in the form of an XML document. XML provides a system-neutral interface that is also format neutral and data neutral. With all of this surrounding intelligence, an API can be very simple—Send_Document, Receive_Document—and the requesting application automatically figures out the document type based on the request or transmission.

Semantic Web: Machine-Understandable Information

The Web is an information space that is useful for human-to-human communication, with some computer-to-computer interaction. However, most Web pages are designed to be human readable. Even database information is converted to a structure that is optimized for people rather than for intelligent agents and Web robots. The XML-based Semantic Web approach will develop information in a machine-readable format.

Simple XML documents do not have great power, and the reason to use XML is not immediately evident. The answer is that the XML documents can be combined with documents and data from other applications on the Web. Applications, which run on the Web, will use a common framework for combining information from all documents and applications. For example, XLink will allow multiple, distributed documents to be combined in many clever, unpredictable methods. In addition, new query languages may exploit the flexibility of powerful logical expressions emerging from XSLT to provide unforeseen capabilities based on combining information from simple XML documents. XML will enable the smooth progression of the Web into a Semantic Web, a web of data, with features of a global data warehouse.

Just Logic, Not Intelligence

The concept of machine-understandable documents does not imply artificial intelligence, which will allow machines to think like people. It only indicates the ability to solve a problem by performing well-defined operations on well-structured data. For example, a spelling checker does not understand how to spell; it simply uses some simple rules and a large dictionary. In analogy, the Semantic Web will use rules for connecting meaning and data. Instead of asking machines to understand people's language, it still involves asking people to conform to the machine by structuring the document and the data.

One advantage of XML over initial artificial intelligence efforts relates to combining knowledge. Many knowledge representation systems had a problem connecting separate knowledge bases. They did not scale and could not create new, independent concepts. However, XML will facilitate documentation of relationships between originally independent concepts by providing meta-tags that assign meaning and can be used in associating new concepts.

Data Models

An Entity-Relationship Diagram (ERD) maps a set of relationships. The Web allows a relationship between two documents or data elements to be stored separately from other information about these documents or data elements. This approach is different from object-oriented systems used to implement Entity-Relationship models, in which information about an object is stored in the object.

For example, one person may define a dog as having a number of legs and a tail but does not mention a color. Another person may define that a specific dog is white with black spots. In an object-oriented approach, the lack of color in the original definition might cause a problem. In XML, color is added by simply adding another data element tag. Apart from this simple but significant change, many concepts involved in the Entity-Relationship modeling transfer directly onto the Semantic Web model.

Relational Databases

The Semantic Web data model relates directly to the model of relational databases. A relational database consists of tables, which consist of rows and columns. Each row consists of a set of data. The row and data are similar to an XML data element node with the data values. The mapping is direct: a row is an XML node; the data element name is a logical data element; and the data is a physical value.

The Semantic Web facilitates linking the data to many different models. It enables the addition of information from different databases on the Web and thus allows sophisticated operations to be performed across them.

XML Logical Architecture: DTDs and Schemas

The basic XML model allows applications to map the data in any new format. The DTD and schema layer of the XML model declares the existence of data elements and new properties. While the DTD declares existence, schemas can also define more complex relationships. The relationships can constrain the types of objects and elements to which definitions apply. For example, the schema allows a relationship such as "the color of the tires is white," and prevents a nonsense relationship such as "the tires of a white wall is a car." These constraints can be propagated to the next layer of the XML model, the logical layer.

The logical layer provides the method for defining rules for relationships; for deducing one type of document, such as a memo, from another type, such as a letter; and for resolving queries by disambiguating terms. The schema layer and the logical layer will enable automated knowledge extraction.

Intelligent Information Retrieval

The XML committee has developed tool specifications (such as DTDs, schemas, XSLT, and RDF) that have the power to express inference rules at the logical level. For example, it will be possible to encode the following: "If the color of the tire is white, then the tire color of the tire is white."

Two fundamental requirements are needed to build a processor for automated knowledge extraction. First, the processor needs the ability to read a set of XML documents and deduce how to interpret new similar documents. The DTDs and schemas will help with this requirement. Second, the processor needs the ability to extrapolate from one type of document to another type of document, such as using the format of a memo to understand the information in a letter.

The logic level defined by XSLT, DTDs, and schemas can be used to define inference rules for knowledge extraction. The concept of reasoning is not addressed. XSLT and RDF can be used to write rules, but cannot be used to specify how to apply them in the same way as an expert system. For all intents and purposes, a rule application at this stage is sequential and mechanical. Meta-rules with expert systemlike functions will be a new development.

Intelligent Search Engines

Search engines cover a huge number of Web sites and index millions of HTML pages. However, these same search engines will frustrate users because they find too many inappropriate answers to the searches. Then the user must search through the answers and manually filter the desired responses.

XML will enable development of an intelligent search engine that combines a reasoning system with the search engine. The tools and technology are available. And the intelligent retrieval community and the expert systems community have the expertise. When the tools and expertise are combined, the result will be more than just a Semantic Web, it will be another evolutionary leap to the Knowledge Navigator.

In the late 1980s, John Sculley of Apple Computers, Inc. (Cupertino, California, www.apple.com) described a concept called the Knowledge Navigator. The Knowledge Navigator was a futuristic, intelligent assistant that could search the global network to collect and combine information from across the world. With XML, tools can be created to allow one Web site to automatically collect information from many other Web sites and then combine the results into a coherent presentation for the user. Although this is a sophisticated application, it is simply not that difficult to design, considering the flexibility and power already built into XML. The promise of XML is that the Knowledge Navigator, and more, is right around the corner.

CHAPTER 13

Summary and Conclusion

Introduction

According to Tim Bray, a coeditor of the XML specification, a massive amount of static, intellectual capital is locked up in legacy, proprietary, and inaccessible document formats. Business opportunities will emerge from unlocking that intellectual capital, leveraging it, and exploiting it for new profitable ventures. XML can be the catalyst for these opportunities.

In the early part of 1999, acceptance of XML was slow because of questions about standards and specifications. As specifications were defined, acceptance of XML accelerated. On the whole, corporations have been enthusiastic about the power and utility of XML applications. With so much support behind XML, the technology may exceed its hype. With the growth of the Internet and the support of major corporations, the potential may exceed the hype.

XML will be everywhere, and it will be transparent to the user. XML standards will be firmly embedded within applications in the same way that TCP/IP is a firmly established but unobtrusive standard of Internet communications. When XML is ubiquitous, even more so than HTML, it will be just like any other standard, and it will no longer be news. Just like TCP/IP, HTML, and CD-ROMs, XML will be accepted as just another technology to be exploited, until the next killer app comes along.

XML will change the Web landscape just as significantly as HTML cultivated the open fields of the Internet. Many of the seeds of automation that were planted years ago, such as the paperless office and globally distributed information access, may grow and flourish in the fertile XML fields. With careful cultivation, XML will yield a new crop of applications for increased productivity of information and knowledge on a worldwide scale.

How to Apply XML

Ralph Oliva of Texas Instruments emphasizes the need to be decisive and take action. Corporations that take a chance learn faster than others who wait. Making a mistake and recovering is frequently faster than sitting and waiting by the sidelines for more information. Hesitating to make a decision is effectively the same as making the decision.

Clearly B2B e-commerce is the hot new topic. Also WAP is growing in popularity. But simply implementing a way to exchange data and information more easily can reap significant benefits. Dun & Bradstreet gained a huge benefit from building just a small XML application. And that is the secret. Build a number of small XML applications to create a chain of successes and early wins. Get early wins to build implementation momentum quickly. The key to building momentum to successfully exploit XML comes from prudently selecting a problem that can be tackled in a reasonably short period of time, say six to nine months. Make sure that the XML solution will have some visibility and will have a demonstrable impact on corporate operations and on financial improvements.

One method for finding the low-hanging fruit that can be easily picked as a successful XML implementation is to collect and rank a list of ongoing corporate problems and challenges. Every corporation has a set of problems that no one has the expertise, resources, or time to address. Solving that one juicy problem will build momentum for XML.

Consider the benefits of XML for transferring data among applications, and exploit that capability to the best corporate interest. For example, a standardized memo format can use XML to define and insert tags that identify date, people, subject, and key topics in the memo. Then the memo can be presented as simple text, or a parser could select out the date, people, subject, or key topics from the memo for other applications. After selection, this information could be presented to another application, like a database, for further manipulation. In addition, all memos could be stored in a document repository. As the repository grows, it would become like a data warehouse, with much less overhead than a conventional data warehouse. The warehouse effort can be leveraged to a full corporate knowledge management strategy. These efforts begin with a simple memo DTD. XML can be implemented for many other projects like this that are specific to each corporation.

XML will provide dramatic functionality to data warehouse and data mining applications. Not only does it allow for modeling, XML also uses built-in meta-data in identifying data content, context, and meaning. Taken the next step, an XML document repository can serve double duty as a data warehouse with no additional development. This capability can easily be extended to the Web. More and more documents will be published in XML format, and these documents can be used as part of a worldwide distributed data warehouse for intelligent data mining using XML-enabled search engines and tools.

Planning an XML Implementation

Planning an XML implementation is much like any program management activity. Designing a standard XML format for documents and other corporate information is similar to designing a data architecture or a database. XML will be a core technology in the Information Age and will affect the local desktop computer and the global information exchange. It can provide standard formats for the Web, for documents, for databases, and for any application that exchanges information.

Taking the risk to embrace a technology early is driven by the desire to gain a competitive business advantage. Before attempting to implement change, the prudent executive will gather knowledge and then plan a strategy. An outline for an XML implementation strategy is provided in Chapter 9. The key to good planning is *not* gathering as much information as possible for making a good decision; by the time enough information exists, competitors will have leapfrogged ahead. So the key to good strategic planning is to gather enough information to develop a flexible plan that can adapt as the environment changes.

Because of differing XML standards, many companies have taken a wait-and-see attitude, while their competitors have explored the technology. The competitors learn about the standards and conflicts, they learn from the errors, and they gain valuable experience that rockets them up the learning curve. From this experience, smart competitors can build a flexible XML strategy that will adapt to any emerging standard.

To build an XML strategy, an executive can look at current corporate applications and documents; review business-to-business transactions, electronic data interchange, and e-business opportunities; and explore how the corporation can leverage XML's ability to organize data into a well-defined structure for manipulation or transfer across the Internet. There is an important difference between a researcher and an executive. The researcher wants to test the outer limits of innovation and worry about implementation later. The executive is more focused on exploiting the state of the practice and leveraging it for a competitive advantage that provides a growing return on investment.

Leveraging Collaboration

One way to focus on the easy, low-risk opportunities is to collaborate with other corporations that are already building XML applications. The list of standards and repositories for XML DTD standards is a good place to begin. These standards are frequently segmented by industry, so location of a colleague should not be difficult.

XML, itself, can be the basis of corporate collaborations. With XML, tools can be created to allow one corporation to share information from many other corporations and then combine the results into a coherent presentation. This sophisticated application is not difficult to design, considering the flexibility and power already built into XML.

Corporations that embrace XML from a high level will improve their information flow and open new opportunities. They will also leave the slower technology laggards behind in the dust.

While exploring XML, do not abandon existing SGML or HTML applications, yet. The infrastructure, ease of use, and cost of switching will probably outweigh the perceived technology advantage of attempts to convert everything to XML. Adapt to the changing directions of an emerging technology.

Business Potential

XML offers many advantages to organizations, software developers, Web sites, and end users. As an industry standard for expressing structured data,

XML will open key markets such as advanced database searching, on-line banking, e-business, and other fields. Extraordinary opportunities result from sharing actual data rather than simply presenting the data.

XML revolutionizes end-user functionalities on the Internet by implementing a rich array of business applications. XML DTDs can be used to markup existing information on Web sites. These DTDs will help corporations exchange information between customers and suppliers.

Development tools are being developed, but there is a growing need for more tools that support collaborative Web sites. Legacy data is another area of opportunity. Tools for generating XML data from legacy database information and from existing user interfaces will fill a significant need. As a corporation collects lessons learned during an XML implementation, the tools and experience developed during the effort might be shared with other corporations for considerable profit.

Polylingual Potential

XML provides the ability to read internationalized XML documents, for example in Japanese. The use of Unicode will open up XML and the Web to most of the world's character sets and languages. With the addition of enabling tools, even SGML products will be able to read valid XML documents. To read internationalized XML documents, SGML software will need modifications to handle the Unicode ISO 10646 character set.

The advantage of XML and Unicode is that tags and documents can be written in a variety of native languages or even mixed languages. HTML-based Web pages could use other character sets, but the HTML tags still had to be written in English.

Using XML and Unicode, then, means that English no longer needs to be the predominant language of the Web. However, it may also create a Tower of Babel as countries choose to use their native tongues for building the DTDs, tags, and the documents. Probably a common ground will eventually merge, especially for e-business.

Information Reuse

One area to focus on is document, information, and data reuse. XML makes it easy to reuse information. Rather than rewriting a document, someone can simply modify an existing XML document. Carefully constructed DTDs will enable the creation of XML-based information elements that can be easily reused across multiple media.

A standards-based XML document with additions, changes, or conversions can be used as a template for creating other documents for specific applications, specific media, or specific customers.

For example, by using an XML format, a corporation can automatically publish information to the Web, to print media, to CD-ROM, or to HTML-based pages, without wasting time and effort developing separate versions for each different type of media. This also eliminates the need to juggle multiple vendors to accommodate proprietary technologies for the various media.

In addition, XML documents can be easily customized to provide one-to-one marketing by tailoring information for targeted customers. XML enhances a corporation's ability to provide customers with the information they want, when they want it, and in the format they want it.

In fact, XML provides the framework for creating a unique corporate set of documents that can be tailored to specific business processes and corporate standards. The rigidly defined structure of XML provides an almost chameleon foundation to build corporate standards that can provide the versatility needed to differentiate between the competition in the marketplace.

Moving to XML

Planning an XML implementation strategy is one thing. Implementing it and migrating corporate information to an XML format is a completely different mountain to climb. A corporation should build a migration plan to take strategic advantage of the XML promise for flexible documents and improved information flow. The migration plan should have three general steps: (1) building a XML data element model; (2) evaluating tools to develop, deliver, and manage XML documents; and (3) managing the documents.

The Data Model

Converting information and data from a display format such as HTML to a structured format like XML requires determining the information meaning and content by analyzing how the corporation uses it. The result of the analysis is a corporate information model. Established industry-standard information models may be used instead of starting from scratch.

Once the relevant information models have been constructed, the effort to convert existing information into the XML format can proceed. If the model is complete, with sufficient detail to the data element level, conversion to a set of XML documents and DTDs will proceed smoothly. These efforts can be done in house, through collaborative efforts, or they can be completed with the help of qualified consultants.

Content Model

XML provides a method for creating standards for document content and for modeling the content. *Content modeling* is the process of showing the relationships and flows of data content within a corporation, application, or database from the conceptual model to the logical model to the physical implementation. The best reason for modeling is for planning purposes. A content model maps data elements to business needs; this mapping reveals gaps and facilitates built-in adaptability to changing needs.

For example, the Dublin Core document model organizes the number of possible data elements for a document into three categories with a total of 15 element types. These element types can be used to define new document types to fulfill various business functions. Indeed, any business function can be represented by a finite set of data elements. The full set of business functions, data elements, and their interrelationships makes up a corporate model. If a new business function is required, the defined data elements can be used to satisfy the requirement, illustrating the adaptability of a corporate data model. A week of modeling can save a month of new, unplanned implementation. In other words, correcting a problem during conceptual or logical design is more cost effective than debugging an error during implementation.

XML adds another tool to the modeler's application toolbox. Developers can use XML DTDs to model data inputs and outputs. Because of expected XML tool standardization, model development and the transition to implementation should be much simpler than with many existing tools. The momentum behind XML is growing because XML will be the new standard for meta-data, modeling information, and data content. Software companies such as Microsoft, IBM, and Sun are focusing on XML applications and products. Developers can create application-specific DTDs and vocabularies using XML. Although XML is hyped as a document processing language, its greater value will come from database applications. In addition, XML can be used to create middle-tier servers that enable smooth communications across databases with different formats.

XML facilitates modeling data, documents, and even e-business transactions. By using tags to define elements, entities, and attributes, a developer can apply XML to create models. The logical structure of a document is represented by its elements and the physical structure is composed of its entities. The attributes can be used to specify element-level meta-data.

Document Components

Most business applications have some form of inherent structure. Documents have well-defined structures that match the type and purpose of the document. For example, e-mail usually consists of a sender, a recipient, a subject, a message, and a closing. A memo includes similar information with a date and a little longer message. An invoice includes a sender, a recipient, and a message. A letter includes addresses of the recipient and sender, as well as a more formal closing with a signature. From a purely functional approach, the format for e-mail could be seen as a subset of an XML DTD for a formal letter. The e-mail would not use some components of the letter. The invoice components may be similar to those used for e-mail.

A useful document structure is easier to define than a good data structure. The corporate document structure has evolved, either formally or informally, through years of use. By comparing and analyzing the structure of corporate documents, a developer will find common patterns of usage. The developer can then use XML to encode these common patterns and structures, helping to standardize the document and make it more interoperable. More importantly, the standards, as defined by XML DTDs, will support better document management and better information exchange.

Data Structure

In fact, the ability to transform data structures for different applications is the true strength, the killer app of XML. XML structures, identifies, and tags the data content—the information—of a memo, a letter, or a job offer. For example, in a job offer, the date, applicant, job title, and salary are identified. Much later, an XML parser or browser could be used to search a repository of job offers, to sort them by job title, and to build a virtual database table of salary offers. Then, by including the date information, a spreadsheet or graphic can be built to show how salary offers have grown over time. These types of functions could help to keep a corporation more competitive in the hiring market. Office automation with this kind of flexibility will dramatically change data-driven workflow.

Creating the infrastructure for an XML document management system is not a trivial task. Developing the DTDs to match the data structures is a significant effort. Careful data analysis is required in order to build an architectural model that maps business functions to data structures and elements. The same rules that apply to building a normalized relational database provide a good starting point for developing DTDs. A data element should be the simplest item of data field that can be used distinctly.

Technology and Tools

Moving legacy data into XML is a data conversion task and a reformatting task. It is also a strategic operation to add new business value to the data. XML and SGML tools will help to map the value to the data and to support conversion tasks. Lists of tools have been provided in various sections in this book. In addition, new tools are being developed every day. Many tools are free, and price is not necessarily proportional to quality, but perhaps to options.

A Controlled Approach

Once the repository of XML information has been created, it must be treated differently from the legacy information. The older applications, file systems, and other software may not work well with XML. These traditional tools will not exploit the new flexibility and value in the XML information. Again, many tools are available to support XML document management; some of these have already been discussed in previous chapters.

While managing the XML document repository, consider three ongoing activities. First, manage the XML documents that result from the migration in order to fully exploit their value and leverage their reusability. Second, continue to convert legacy information into XML documents and structured formats to reflect business usage. Third, as new, external information arrives from partners, vendors, suppliers, and marketing define a process for converting the information to XML before it is propagated corporatewide. Users will resist this process, but if the process is automatic and facilitates dissemination, it will reduce the resistance and pain.

Implementing the XML repository will help to improve content design, process engineering, and workflow automation. The use of standard DTDs and XML formats will raise information and document management to another level of functionality.

Concerns and Contingencies

Despite the extensibility of XML, there are trade-offs. The advantages are not free; they come with very real costs. For example, one of the advantages of nonreadable object files is that no one can read them or modify them without another application. A novice could not easily do damage without learning something about the application. With XML, a novice may be able to modify a set of database commands as easily as running a text editor.

Many companies have documents written in different formats. Historically, it has been easier to transfer and translate raw text to different formats and across platforms. One vendor advantage and user disadvantage was the switching cost related to the transfer and translation. For example, some corporations simply did not want to deal with the trouble of switching between Macintoshes and PCs, or WordPerfect and MS Word. This avoidance helped Microsoft capture the PC software market. However, XML will open information transfer, leading to reduced switching costs. Microsoft is aware of this and has put an XML strategy in place to guarantee customers that they will be able to exchange information with other customers, corporations, or entities.

Microsoft is a very visible supporter of the XML standard. If Microsoft sets the standards for DTDs and schemas, that may provide control and a competitive advantage that inhibits interoperability.

The simplicity of XML encourages developers to create their own elements and tags. XSL and cascading style sheets will combine with XML to define a custom formatting language. XML is like a locomotive. With a good plan, XML is like a train on a straight track and can carry a great deal of information cargo with many long distance benefits. But with no direction or in isolation, corporate XML efforts can be dangerous, inflicting unpredictable damage, much like a train that jumps the tracks and crushes everything in its path.

A custom DTD can separate a company from the rest of the industry, and one of the goals of XML is improved rather than separate communications. Indiscriminately combining tags from different industries without planning is like trying to mix oil and water.

With its flexibility and inherent power, XML also has the potential to be the worst maintenance and incompatibility nightmare since the Year 2000 problem. It is said, with tongue in cheek, that a month of implementation, maintenance, and repairs will always save an hour's worth of careful planning. In other words, collaboration, coordination, and careful planning across companies will greatly improve the benefits that XML promises to deliver and will prevent thousands of dollars of wasted effort.

In addition, XML-based interoperability assumes the use of fast computers. The cost of interoperability is computer cycles. In some cases, for the immediate future, legacy documents will be translated from one application format to XML and then back to a different application format. This computer-intensive translation process among three data formats, for the sake of interoperability, may result in slower, initial processing times.

Another important design issue is for the developers and users to collaborate on the structures and elements. The creation of corporate standards will probably require trade-offs. For example, people like to create their e-mail quickly and they like to make their memos unique to match their personal styles. Attempts at building standardized formats will fail if latitude for personal style is not taken into account. In a pre-Web development activity to automate corporate standards for document formats, the author asked for user suggestions and added a few extra options for style changes in the paragraph arrangement, the fonts, and the closings. These minor changes had no effect on the information content or structure. The automation of standard formats improved the speed of generating memos, improved their readability, and greatly improved response time to memos and information requests. The author learned an important lesson. Although automation and standardization are meant to support and improve corporate processes, ultimately these activities involve people. Any changes can fail if they do not ultimately involve and improve the working environment of these people.

Omnimorphic Possibilities

What can a potter do with a piece of clay? What direction does a sculptor take with a block of marble? What could Picasso do with a pen and a napkin? What profit potential can a clever manager find in a technology that adapts and conforms to the structure of his corporate data and information?

At the first level, an IT manager can explore simple XML projects that deal with data transfer between applications or between departments. Plenty of software is freely available on the Web, such as at the Microsoft, IBM, Oracle, and Sun Web sites. In fact, Microsoft's Windows 2000 and Office Tools 2000 use native XML in the data formats. Exploring those paths is a fairly safe way to learn about the technology.

At the second level, an IT department can look into the various XML markup languages and vocabularies from different sources, such as the repositories, the B2B efforts, the WAP activities, XHTML, or VoiceML. Many of these technologies are well proven and have millions or even billions of dollars of support behind them. From here, the step to the third level is easy.

At the third level, an IT developer can build an XML vocabulary that is customized to address the specific challenges and problems of the corporation. So a company might roll its own XML interfaces, inventory system, reporting system, or XML document warehouse. With experiences like these under its belt, a corporation is ready for some insanely great killer apps.

XML enables the ability to transfer information among a variety of devices. So information on a desktop can be shared with a wireless device. With a fast wireless connection, a wireless device can use XML and peer-to-peer technology to share the disk space and processing on remote desktop computers. What this means is the ability to tap into the computing power of the Internet from a handheld device at any location.

XML enables the convergence of technologies needed to do more than interoperate—to share distributed sources as if they were one. As shown in Figure 13.1, XML pushes through the complexity barrier that stopped conventional technologies; it allows developers to transfer data and information in ways that were previously difficult, if not impossible. Because XML is omnimorphic and can serve as a universal translator across all platforms, it provides the appropriate data format. High bandwidth wireless provides the communications, and peer-to-peer computing provides the needed protocols.

What would a corporation do if it could tap into computing power as easily as pulling in a radio signal? What would consumers do if computing power were free, and how could companies make a profit off of it?

Currently, information is virtually free over the Web. Companies leverage this by selling advertising, providing search engines, and filtering the infor-

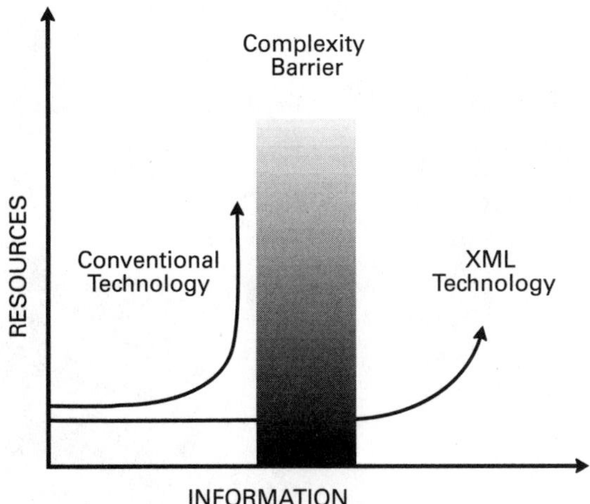

FIGURE 13.1 XML punches through the complexity barrier by allowing information and data to go where conventional technologies were unable.

mation. Free computing power brings additional complexities to the equation and multiple possibilities. When the technology grows this pervasive, XML will be as ubiquitous as transistors or electricity is today. Both quantities are all around us and both are taken for granted. Extrapolating from the example of Web technology, ubiquitous computing will be possible by 2005. If Nokia and other wireless communications companies make some breakthroughs with WAP, and if Intel does the same with peer to peer, then these capabilities could appear even faster.

But for all of this to come together, companies must embrace XML, as the trends have indicated. XML will do for business in this decade what the Web did in the late 1990s. In fact, XML will do much more. It will help to level the playing field and allow small companies to compete with large companies on a global scale. By improving access to information, XML will improve corporate efficiencies. It is a significant Internet technology, worthy of exploration for its many potential applications.

APPENDIX

W3C Addresses

The World Wide Web Consortium (W3C) keeps a Web page for each XML technology specification. Some of these are well written and easy to read, and others are technical:

www.w3c.org/TR/xslt—XML Stylesheet Language Transformations (XSLT)

www.w3c.org/TR/xml-stylesheet—XML Stylesheet Language (XSL)

www.w3c.org/Note-xml-stylesheet—XML Stylesheet Language (XSL)

www.w3c.org/TR/xlink—XML Linking Language (XLink)

www.w3c.org/TR/xpath—XML Path (XPath)

www.w3c.org/TR/1998/WD-xptr—XML Pointers (XPointer)

www.w3c.org/TR/REC-xml-names—XML Namespaces (Namespaces)

www.w3c.org/TR/xml-schema-1—XML Schemas (Schemas)

www.w3c.org/TR/REC-xml—eXtensible Markup Language (XML)

Glossary

A

A2A (Application to Application)—Communications data transfer from one application to another.

Acronyms—Abbreviations for common phrases that help simplify the transmission of ideas. Unfortunately, acronyms can also inadvertently exclude novices and people who are not experts in the field, or in the know.

AIML—Astronomical Markup Language, used for instrument control.

AMPS (Advanced Mobile Phone Service)—An analog network protocol used by cellular operators in the United States. In other parts of the world, cellular service is based on digital, not analog protocols.

Analog—The use of continuous frequencies and signals as opposed to digital signals. Voice telephone calls used to be analog. Grand pianos are still analog devices.

API (Application Programming Interface)—A collection of subroutines that provide the software connection or interface between the operating system and another program. For example, an application program might call an API subroutine to get mouse information.

Artificial Intelligence (AI)—The study and development of software and associated hardware that performs tasks, which if performed by a living thing would indicate a level of intelligence.

ASCII (American Standard Code for Information Interchange)—Seven-bit Latin character set.

ASP (Application Service Providers)—Companies that lease or rent applications and services to support them. In general, an ASP vendor provides a system at its own location with installed applications (e.g., SAP R/3, Notes, Peoplesoft, Oracle Financials) that are sold to customers on a "per seat" basis. This concept is similar to Web sites that provide stock portfolio support. The user logs in, enters his stock information, and uses applications on the Web site to analyze his portfolio. An ASP is, effectively, a source for application outsourcing.

ASP (Active Server Pages)—ASP refers to ActiveX scripted pages, when *asp* is used as a file type, such as *server.asp*. Active Server Pages are similar to other scripted Web pages such as those using Java Script, CGI, or Perl.

Attribute—A modifier of a data element tag. Meta-data about a specific element.

B

B2B (Business to business)—Implies communications or data transfer.

Back Door—A hidden method of access, such as a secret password or account that a hacker can use to gain access to a computer without permission. A back door can be installed during development by the original programmer, or it can be created by a Trojan Horse.

Bit—The smallest unit of data in a computer. However, computers usually store data and execute instructions in multiples of bits, called bytes. A bit is abbreviated with a small *b*.

Blob—Binary large object.

BML (Bean Markup Language)—IBM's markup language for accessing and configuring JavaBeans.

Bricks and Mortar—Slang term used to indicate non-e-commerce, physical stores.

BSML–(Biosequence Markup Language)—A graphical language for genetics.

Byte—There are eight bits in a byte. A byte is abbreviated with a capital *B*. In communications and data transmission, a byte may be composed of 10 bits because of overhead, compression, and error checking.

C

CBL (Common Business Library)—A set of business schema developed by CommerceOne, Inc.

CBT—Computer-Based Training.

CDATA—Character Data used to represent a string of alphanumeric text data.

Clicks and Mortar—Slang phrase used to describe retailers that have both an e-commerce presence and a physical store. (See also "Bricks and Mortar.")

Client—A computer or software program that requests services from another computer, called a server.

Client/Server—Combination of client software and server software. Typically, a client/server system has multiple layers of functions, such as a presentation layer, a processing layer, and a data layer.

CML (Chemical Markup Language)—Used for chemical information.

Content Model—Range of content that is allowable for an element.

Crawler—See Spider.

CSS (Cascading Style Sheets)—Used to define a page layout for HTML-based Web pages.

D

DataCraft—IBM product that provides an XML view of databases.

DCD (Document Content Definition)—A schema facility for specifying rules for the structure and content of XML documents. An alternative to DTDs.

DDML (Data Definition Markup Language)—Used for making data models.

DFD (Data Flow Diagrams)—Provides schematics of data pathways through a system.

DHTML- (Dynamic HTML)—Animated and nonstatic version of HTML that allows developers to create Web pages that are more responsive to user interaction than previous versions of HTML. Netscape Navigator 4.0 and Internet Explorer 4.0 use different methods to implement DHTML.

Document—In XML, document is a general construct that includes data and markup.

Document Element—Highest level element in an XML document.

DOM (Document Object Model)—An API-defining standard for developing interactions with XML tree structured elements. The DOM supplies a uniform method for applications to interact with XML. SAX is an alternative API standard to DOM.

DoS (Denial of Service)—A term used to describe an attack on a Web site by flooding the URL with data or requests, with the intent of crashing the server or clogging it so that other visitors cannot get service.

DSL (Digital Subscriber Line)—A method of transmitting up to 1 Mbps over copper wire.

DSSSL (Document Style Semantics and Specification Language)—The style sheet language defined under SGML.

DTD (Document Type Definition)—DTD defines the XML document, structures, rules, and elements. Used to define the tags in an XML document.

E

ECMAScript—Combined Java Script and JScript standard that is used as a scripting language for XSL.

ECML (Electronic Commerce Markup Language)—Supports e-commerce.

Element Type—Components of an XML document as defined in the DTD. Element type is usually indicated by tags.

Entity—Component of an XML document. May be the physical structure defined by the element or may be a variable used to present user-specific information.

Extended Link—XLink link that has multiple target locations.

F

Firewall—Software (or a dedicated computer) that keeps unauthorized users from accessing a Web server. Prevents malicious programs from gaining access to valuable information.

Freeware—Copyrighted software that is distributed free over the Web, but can't be sold by a third party because it is still owned by the original developer. Some XML parsers are freeware. The developer, who controls distribution and future releases, may charge for the second release of the software. Freeware may be used, but not resold.

FTP (File Transfer Protocol)—Used for transferring files between two computers across the Internet.

G

GML (Generalized Markup Language)—The first of the markup languages.

H

Hacker—Someone who deliberately gains access to other computers without the knowledge of the owner. Malicious hackers do this to cause damage or steal information.

HTML (HyperText Markup Language)—The standard of tags defined by the World Wide Web Consortium (W3C) to define how a Web page is presented in a browser. HTML is a subset of SGML.

HTML Writers Guild (http://www.HWG.org)—International organization of Web developers with members throughout the world in more than 130 nations. HWG promotes standards, practices, and techniques for Web authoring. In addition, HWG provides help on all aspects of Web development, including XML.

HTTP (HyperText Transfer Protocol)—The standard used for transferring information between two computers across the Web.

I

Intelligent Agent—An intelligent agent is a small artificial intelligent software program that can carry out a number of different kinds of functions without further direction. Agents may use technologies such as expert systems, neural networks, fuzzy logic, and genetic algorithms.

Internet—Collection of networks connected by the Internet Protocol.

IP (Internet Protocol) Address—The identifying number of a computer or Web server. Static IP addresses always use the same number. Dynamic IP addresses are assigned a new number every time the computer is logged onto the Internet.

ISO (International Organization for Standardization)—A collective, worldwide standards group for computing, communications, manufacturing, and engineering processes.

K

Killer App—A popular and useful application that is so compelling that it builds the interest in a new development, such as XML or the Web. Mosaic was the killer app for the Web.

L

LDAP—(Lightweight Directory Access Protocol)—A method for storing and retrieving connection information to directory and database servers. LDAP is an industry standard for storing access information in a centralized global directory for easy administration and easy access by all users.

M

m-Commerce—Mobile commerce.

MathML (Mathematics Markup Language)—A language for representing complex mathematical formulae. As MathML evolves, it may also provide a capability for processing math.

MCF (Meta Content Framework)—An effort of Netscape to standardize meta-data. The intent of MCF is to create a common meta-data vocabulary and a data model to facilitate global interoperability.

Meta-data—Information or meaning about data. Typically, a general categorization about a collection of similar data. For example, a library card catalog, *TV Guide* magazine, and the index in the back of a book are meta-data about their sources at various levels of detail.

MOF (Meta Object Facility)—A standard created by the Object Management Group for managing common meta-information and distributed repositories.

MP3—Stands for MPEG 1, Layer 3 (or Motion Picture Experts Group, Audio Layer 3), which is used for compression of Internet music or audio.

MPEG 1, Layer 3—Moving Picture Experts Group (MPEG) is a set of standards for encoding multimedia data. Also known as MP3. MPEG-1 and MPEG-2 are the previous standards.

MSXML (Microsoft XML)—Microsoft's version of XML before the final standard was defined.

MusicML (Music Markup Language)—Provides a language for representing musical notes.

N

Namespace—The specific pathname or segment used to define a specific location or URL.

Namespaces—Collections of universal resource identifier names. Namespaces provide a way to collect data from multiple sources into one document and to tag the information with its respective source.

O

OFX (Open Financial Exchange)—The format that Quicken and Microsoft Money, etc. use to exchange information with banks. This text format simplifies interchange of financial information.

OMG (Object Management Group)—The standards organization for technologies involved with object-oriented methodology.

Omnimorphic—Serving as a universal foundation on which to construct any form, structure, character, or style.

OOAD (Object-Oriented Analysis and Design)—The steps used in object-oriented methodology.

Open Source—The source code of a program that is available to the software development community for free. This idea was resurrected by Linux and the assumption that a broader group of developers across the world will evolve superior software and distribute their results to others. Another example is Netscape Communicator, which is open source, although there is no proof that programmers are distributing improvements.

ORB (Object Request Brokering)—An integrating layer of software or middleware that encapsulates the intelligence needed to recognize actors and hide the details of their internal representation from other actors. ORBs serve as proxies to represent objects to a larger system.

ORM (Object Role Modeling)—A powerful method of designing and querying an information system (such as a database or an XML document) at the conceptual level and mapping between conceptual and logical (for example, relational) levels where the application is described in terms that are readily understood by the users. Because developers discuss applications with subject matter experts at the conceptual level by using natural language, more reliable and effective communication occurs, permitting the analysis of knowledge in simple information units. Compared with models created by using other methodologies, data models designed with ORM are richly expressive and semantically stable.

P

P2P—Peer-to-peer computing.

Parser—Software application that processes text, validates its syntax, determines its logical content, and builds structures to represent data content and relationships.

PatML—IBM's pattern match and replacement system for translating XML documents to XML or non-XML documents.

PDF (Portable Document Format)—Invented by Adobe Systems to represent documents in a platform-independent format.

PGML (Precision Graphics Markup Language)—Language used for rendering vector graphics.

Port—Electronic connection that allows data to travel from the client PC to the server over a network.

PPC—Peer-to-peer computing.

PPN—Peer-to-peer networking.

Prolog—First statement in an XML document containing processing and DTD information.

PtP—Peer-to-peer computing.

R

RDF (Resource Description Framework)—A method of processing metadata. It provides machine-readable interoperability and enables automated processing of Web-based documents.

RDBMS–(Relational Database Management System)—The middle-tier software used to access and manage data stored in a relational database.

RTF (Rich Text Format)—A Microsoft format used for exchanging information between different applications.

S

SANs (Storage Area Networks)—The combination of data storage systems and networking technology. Storage is not linked to any single server, but is deployed separately and managed independently.

SAX—Simple API for XML elements. Alternative for DOM.

Schema—An alternative to a DTD that is more suitable for data-intensive XML applications. Schemas (or schemata) provide the formal expression of an XML document structure by representing the defining elements (or objects) of a data model, their attributes (or properties), and the relationships between the different elements.

SDMI (Secure Digital Music Initiative)—Digital music standard intended to provide the functionality of MP3 along with a security layer to protect the copyright and to encourage a pay-for-use business model.

Servlet—A small server application, as opposed to a client-side applet application.

SGML (Standardized General Markup Language)—The "mother of all markup languages." SGML is a meta-language from which HTML and XML were derived.

Shareware—"Try-before-you-buy" software that is distributed free on a trial basis. If the user likes it, he or she pays for it later. The software may have a built-in expiration date to prod the user to purchase it. Sometimes shareware authors do not require monetary payment, but request items of local interest, such as colorful stamps, unique coins, or postcards.

SMIL (Synchronized Multimedia Integration Language)—Used to provide multimedia presentations distributed over the Web. SMIL is intended to provide multimedia functionality in analogy to what HTML did for hypertext.

SOX (Schemas for Object-oriented XML)—A methodology for defining the structure and content of XML objects.

Spider (Web Spider or Web Crawler)—Spider is a program that searches the World Wide Web automatically by retrieving a document and all documents linked to it. Web crawler is a program that retrieves on-line documents and all the documents linked to it, downloads their contents, and indexes them. This enables the user to go to a search engine to retrieve information needed with minimal effort. Web crawlers are used to organize the numerous Web sites, and their contents, that are found in the World Wide Web.

SQL (Structured Query Language)—A standard query language used for database information retrieval.

T

TCP/IP (Transmission Control Protocol/Internet Protocol)—The international standard used for sending information over the Internet.

TEI (Text Encoding Initiative)—An academic organization that has created standards for document structures.

Terabyte (TB)—Usually means 1 trillion bytes, 1,000 gigabytes, 1 million megabytes, or 2^{40} bytes.

TeXML—An XML-document formatting tool created by IBM.

Trojan Horse—A malicious program that masquerades as a harmless program, but opens up a backdoor, so that hackers can gain access to someone else's computer. Trojan Horse works just like a virus, but does not propagate the way a virus would.

U

UDDI (Universal Description, Discovery, and Integration) project—Seeks to build a directory that allows companies to look up other businesses and to get information about their products and services, much the same way that a telephone book's yellow pages work. UDDI also provides the ability to look up what XML DTDs, schemas, and other data formats that businesses use for information transfer.

UML (Unified Modeling Language)—Used for object-oriented methodology.

Unicode—A 16-bit character set, similar in concept to an extended ASCII character set. It includes Latin, Greek, non-Latin characters, ideographic characters, mathematical characters, etc. within a 65,000-character set.

URL (Uniform Resource Locator)—The address of a Web page.

UTF (Unicode Transformation Format)—Abbreviation for the various unicode standards, including UTF-8, UTF-16, and UTF-32.

V

Valid—Term used for an XML document that is well formed and conforms to a DTD.

Virus—A malicious program that penetrates a computer system and then replicates to tie up valuable resources or to damage valuable data. A virus may hide in an executable program that is transferred from computer to computer.

VPN (Virtual Private Network)—A network that uses security protocols to allow proprietary corporate transactions over a public network, such as the Internet.

VRML (Virtual Reality Modeling Language)—Used to define three-dimensional graphics on the Web. The standard is not popular because it is slow to download.

W

W3C (World Wide Web Consortium)—The international standards group for the Web.

WAP (Wireless Application Protocol)—The protocol used to send information, specifically text-based Web pages, to a cellular phone or wireless system.

WDDX (Web Distributed Data eXchange)—Describes complex data structures, such as arrays and records, so that they can be moved among applications.

WIDL (Web Interface Definition Language)—Enables application-to-application communication. WIDL uses a meta-data syntax to define APIs. A DOM maps application or document data elements to program variables.

WML (Wireless Markup Language)—Uses WAP to convert HTML Web pages or XML data into a format that cell phones, digital assistants, or other wireless systems can display on the small screen.

Worm—A malicious program that penetrates a computer system and progressively travels throughout the system damaging data along its path. A worm may hide in an executable program that is transferred from computer to computer.

WYSIWIG—Stands for "what you see is what you get," which implies that the text on the computer screen will look the same when it is printed on a page. The term is usually associated with word processing.

XFA (Extensible Forms Architecture)—An open-standards-based forms architecture created by JetForm Corp., in Ottawa, [www.jetform.com] and submitted to the W3C to help define XML requirements for business forms. The W3C standards that support on-line forms will include a combination of XFA and XFDL.

XFDL (eXtensible Forms Description Language)—An open-standards-based forms architecture created by Uwi.com, in Concord, California, [www.uwi.com] and submitted to the W3C to help define XML requirements for business forms. The W3C standards that support on-line forms will include a combination of XFA and XFDL.

XHTML (XML-based HTML)—HTML 4.0 is based on SGML; XHTML is the result of rewriting HTML functionality as an XML-application language.

XLink (XML Linking Language)—Specification that provides a functional approach to document linking by using XML. XLink provides new functionalities for Web linking.

XLL (XML Linking Language)—The same as XLink.

XMI (XML Meta-data Interchange) Format—A standard that combines XML and object-oriented advantages using UML and OMG's MOF standards.

XML (eXtensible Markup Language)—A meta-language subset of SGML used to create markup languages that can identify the meaning or the semantics of a document.

XML Bean Maker—An IBM application that automatically generates JavaBean classes for any DTD.

XML-Data—An alternative to DTDs that uses XML syntax and includes data typing.

XML Editor Maker—An IBM application that automatically builds visual editors.

XML Parser—Parser that reads XML data, builds a tree structure, and validates the data using DTD or schema.

XML Productivity Kit—IBM application that is a companion to the XML Parser for Java.

XML-RPC (eXtensible Markup Language–Remote Procedure Call) Protocol—The method used for interapplication service requests.

XML TreeDiff—IBM package of Beans for differentiating and updating document object model trees.

XPointer—eXtensible Pointer for a location within an XML document.

XQL (eXtensible Query Language)—A query language similar to SQL that is used to query XML documents and then return well-formed XML documents containing the retrieved information.

XSL (eXtensible Stylesheet Language)—Refers to formatting objects that are similar to CSS. XSL is used to extract data from the document and convert it to another format.

XSLT (eXtensible Stylesheet Language Transformations)—Includes a set of features and processing capabilities such as templates, patterns, scripting, and tree processing.

Index

Y

About the Author

Solomon H. Simon (Arlington, TX) has more than 20 years of senior management experience in advanced IT. He holds a doctorate in Information Technology and a master's degree in Nuclear Physics, both from Texas A&M University. The author of over 90 articles on science and technology, he is a contributing writer on XML and wireless technologies to *Intelligent Enterprise*.

